W9-CHL-392

ADVANCES IN INVESTMENT ANALYSIS AND PORTFOLIO MANAGEMENT

Volume 7

EDITORIAL BOARD

James S. Ang
The Florida State University

Christopher B. Barry
Texas Christian University

Stephen J. Brown
New York University

Edwin Burmeister
Duke University

Carl R. Chen
The University of Dayton

Ren-Raw Chen
Rutgers University

Son N. Chen
National Chengchi University
Taiwan

C. W. Sealy
University of North Carolina-Charlotte

Choel S. Eun
Georgia Institute of Technology

Jack C. Francis
Baruch College

Dong Cheol Kim
Rutgers University

Stanley J. Kon
Smith-Breedan Associate, Inc.

Yun Lin
National Taiwan University

William T. Moore
University of South Carolina

R. Richardson Petti
University of Houston

Scott C. Linn
University of Oklahoma

ADVANCES IN
INVESTMENT ANALYSIS
AND PORTFOLIO MANAGEMENT

Edited by CHENG-FEW LEE
Department of Finance
Rutgers University

VOLUME 7

JAI PRESS INC.
Stamford, Connecticut

Copyright © 2000 by JAI PRESS INC.
100 Prospect Street
Stamford, Connecticut 06904-0811

All rights reserved. No part of this publication may be reproduced, stored on a retrieval
system, or transmitted in any form or by any means, electronic, mechanical, photocopying,
filming, recording, or otherwise without prior permission in writing from the publisher.

ISBN: 0-7623-0658-0

Manufactured in the United States of America

Printed and bound by Antony Rowe Ltd, Eastbourne

Transferred to digital printing, 2005

CONTENTS

LIST OF CONTRIBUTORS

Gurdip S. Bakshi

Department of Finance
University of Maryland
College Park, Maryland

Michael Gendron

Departement de Finance et d'Assurance
Universite Laval
Sainte-Foy, Quebec, Canada

Christian Genest

Departement de Mathematiques ed de
Statistique
Universite Laval
Sainte-Foy, Quebec, Canada

Michael J. Hartley

Department of Economics and Finance
University of New Orleans
New Orleans, Louisiana

Karen M. Hogan

Department of Finance
St. Joseph's University
Philadelphia, Pennsylvania

Kin Lam

Department of Finance and Decision Sciences
Hong Kong Baptist University
Hong Kong

Wei Li

Department of Finance and Decision Sciences
Hong Kong Baptist University
Hong Kong, and
College of Economics
Jinan University
Guangzhou, China

Donald Lien

Department of Economics
University of Kansas
Lawrence, Kansas

William T. Lin

Department of Finance and Applications
Tamkang University
Taipei, Taiwan

Michael S. McCorry

Barclays Global Investors
Sydney, Australia

Gerald T. Olson

Department of Finance
Villanova University
Villanova, Pennsylvania

Elizabeth A. Sheedy

Centre for Studies in Money, Banking, and
Finance
Macquarie University
Sydney, Australia

Gordon Y.N. Tang

Department of Finance and Decision Sciences
Hong Kong Baptist University
Hong Kong

Robert G. Trevor

Centre for Studies in Money, Banking and
Finance
Macquarie University
Sydney, Australia

Li-Ju Tsai

Department of International Trade and
Finance
Fu-jen University
Taipei, Taiwan

Yiu Kuen Tse

Department of Economics
National University of Singapore
Singapore

R. Douglas Van Eaton

Department of Finance
University of North Texas
Denton, Texas

Bonnie Van Ness

Division of Finance and Economics
Marshall University
Huntington, West Virginia

Robert A. Van Ness

Division of Finance and Economics
Marshall University
Huntington, West Virginia

Robert A. Wood

Department of Finance
University of Memphis
Memphis, Tennessee

Yin-Hua Yeh

Department of International Trade and
Finance
Fu-jen University
Taipei, Taiwan

EVALUATING THE RISK OF PORTFOLIOS WITH OPTIONS

Elizabeth A. Sheedy and Robert G. Trevor

ABSTRACT

Many portfolio managers use options in their investment strategy, yet the issue of performance measurement for such portfolios remains unresolved. This study examines the nature of risk for option-affected portfolios and identifies appropriate risk measures for them. We find that the main issue is not skewness (as is commonly supposed), but the fact that risk is changing. The implication is that option affected (and other) portfolios can be meaningfully examined in a mean-variance framework, provided that appropriate risk measures (identified in this study) are applied.

I. INTRODUCTION

Many portfolio managers now use options as part of their investment strategy, yet the funds management industry still grapples with the problem of evaluating the performance of option-affected portfolios. The purpose of this study is to examine the nature of risk for option-affected portfolios and identify suitable risk measures for them.

Advances in Investment Analysis and Portfolio Management, Volume 7, pages 1–18.
Copyright © 2000 by JAI Press Inc.
All rights of reproduction in any form reserved.
ISBN: 0-7623-0658-0

A typical scenario might involve a diversified portfolio where growth assets are protected with, say, rolling quarterly put options. There are at least three potential problems in measuring the performance of such a portfolio, namely:

1. *Departures from normality.* Returns of such a portfolio may be characterized by skewness (for example, see Bookstaber and Clarke, 1985; Lewis, 1990; Balzer, 1994);
2. *Changing variance.* The variance of the portfolio will change over time, depending primarily on the "moneyness" of the option. In addition, volatility clustering in the underlying assets may further exaggerate heteroscedasticity;[1] and
3. *Discontinuities.* At the expiry of the option, or if the option is sold prior to expiry, the variance of the portfolio will jump to a new level.

These issues are not, however, unique to option-protected portfolios. Many portfolios with active asset allocation strategies have similar characteristics. Active asset allocators may introduce skewness, changes in variance, and discontinuities in variance without the use of derivatives. Thus the results of this study can be broadly applied to a range of investment portfolios where risk is known to change over time and where discontinuities occur.

Various risk measurement alternatives have been proposed for option-affected portfolios. Lewis (1990), for example, proposes the use of lower partial moments such as semivariance. Some of these proposals, however, are confusing to investors and may not address the underlying problems associated with the evaluation of option-affected portfolios.

This study differs from others by applying techniques from the generalized autoregressive conditional heteroscedasticity (GARCH) literature to portfolios with options. The study also considers *exponential smoothing* which is related to GARCH but simpler to implement. These techniques have been proposed to accommodate changing risk (heteroscedasticity) in asset returns but have not previously been used to measure the risk of option-affected portfolios.

While not attempting to be exhaustive, options are used in the funds management industry to: automatically adjust asset allocations (Millman, 1995); diversify investment portfolios with managed futures and options portfolios (Peters, 1994; Schneeweis, Spurgin, and Potter 1996); create investment vehicles with upside potential but low risk of capital loss (Cerulli and Casey, 1995); hedge against adverse market movements (Gastineau, 1995); enhance returns (Bensman, 1994; Schwimmer, 1994; Simon, 1994); and exploit investment specialties through the use of "overlay" services (Layard-Leisching, 1994; Sy, 1996).

The wide variety of option strategies employed in the funds management industry creates obvious challenges for those wishing to evaluate performance. In many cases, investors and/or consultants have only scant knowledge regarding the use of options in a particular fund at any point in time; therefore it is useful to identify risk measures that are effective in a wide variety of situations. The study assumes that the researcher does not have detailed knowledge concerning the use of option strategies in a given fund.

Later sections will show that risk measurement is most difficult where the principal of embedded options is large relative to the value of the portfolio, gamma is high (meaning that option deltas can vary considerably), or where options are held to maturity. In these circumstances the portfolio risk is most likely to change significantly and suffer discontinuities. Clearly, practice varies enormously with respect to all of these issues, so we initially consider a portfolio whose characteristics magnify potential risk measurement issues: a stock portfolio fully protected with at-the-money put options. Once having understood the risk measurement issues in relatively difficult circumstances, other portfolios are also considered, including those devoid of options.

II. EXAMINING THE RISK OF OPTION-AFFECTED PORTFOLIOS

We first examine option-affected portfolios under the simplifying assumption that the risk of the underlying asset is constant. Since this assumption underlies the Black–Scholes option-pricing model, it allows the true risk of an option-affected portfolio to be determined at any point in time. The simplifying assumption of constant risk of the underlying asset is relaxed in later sections.

In a continuous time Black–Scholes environment the distribution of the returns from an option or an option-affected portfolio can be derived unambiguously. The stock price, S, at time, t, is given by the geometric Brownian motion process:

$$dS = \mu S dt + \sigma S dz \tag{1}$$

where z is a Weiner process, and μ and σ are the instantaneous mean and standard deviation which are assumed constant. Using Ito's lemma, it may be shown that the instantaneous variance of (continuously compounded) stock returns is constant:

$$\text{Var } d \log S = \sigma^2 \tag{2}$$

The price of a put option $P(S,t)$ under the standard Black–Scholes assumptions is:

$$P(S,t) = S \cdot N(d1) - X \cdot e^{-rT} \cdot N(d2) - S + X \cdot e^{-rT} \tag{3}$$

where:

$$d1 = \frac{\ln\left[\dfrac{S}{Xe^{-rT}}\right]}{\sigma\sqrt{T}} + \frac{\sigma\sqrt{T}}{2}$$

$$d2 = d1 - \sigma\sqrt{T}$$

N refers to the cumulative normal distribution, X is the exercise price, r is the riskless interest rate, and T is the term of the option (expressed in years).

Consider the value, $\varphi(S,t)$, of a portfolio consisting of a stock and a protective put:

$$\varphi(S,t) = S + \omega P(S,t) \tag{4}$$

where ω is the proportion of the portfolio protected. The distribution of the value of this portfolio is given by Ito's lemma:

$$d\varphi(S,t) = \left(\omega P_s \mu S + \omega P_t + \frac{\omega P_{ss} \sigma^2 S^2}{2} + \mu S \right) dt + (\omega P_s \sigma S + \sigma S) dz \tag{5}$$

where P_s is the delta of the option, P_t is the theta of the option, and P_{ss} is the gamma of the option.

Applying Ito's lemma to derive the process for (continuously compounded) returns, $(d\log\varphi(S,t))$, shows that the returns on this protected portfolio are conditionally normally distributed with the variance:

$$\text{Var } d \log \varphi(S,t) = \left(\frac{(1 + \omega P_s)\sigma S}{S + \omega P(S,t)} \right)^2 \tag{6}$$

Equation 6 shows that the variance of returns from a protected stock portfolio will vary, even when the variance of stock returns is constant. The variance changes due to both the passage of time and movements in the stock price (both directly and through the behavior of the value of the option and its delta). Since the delta of a put option is bounded by zero and minus unity, the variance of a protected portfolio can never be greater than that of the unprotected portfolio.

Figure 1 illustrates the volatility (standard deviation) of simulated stock portfolios with varying levels of protection. In the first panel, relating to a fully protected portfolio, the true volatility varies significantly from zero to 20% pa. Volatility reaches one of these extreme values at each expiry date. If the put option expires out-of-the-money, the risk of the portfolio is equal to that of the stock, that is, 20% pa. If the put option expires in-the-money, the risk of the portfolio is reduced to zero. At any time prior to expiry, portfolio volatility will lie between these values. Figure 1 also highlights the discontinuities inherent in the protected portfolio which occur when the option expires.

The second panel of Figure 1 illustrates the same simulated portfolio in the case where only 20% of the portfolio is protected, that is, $\omega = 0.20$. Notice that heteroscedasticity and discontinuity in risk for the portfolio is still present, but is greatly reduced in this case.

III. METHODS FOR MEASURING CHANGING RISK

We examine four risk measures that vary in the extent to which they accommodate skewness or changing risk (heteroscedasticity). The characteristics of these meas-

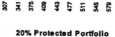

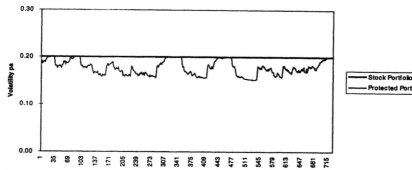

Notes: Shown is the known risk of portfolios under the assumption of constant risk (measured as standard deviation per annum). The simulated stock price path has expected return equal to 8% pa, and standard deviation of 20% pa. The stock, initially valued at $50, is fully or partially protected using quarterly, at-the-money put options, rolled at expiry. The risk of the protected portfolio is calculated using Equation 6.

Figure 1. True Risk of Portfolios Assuming Constant Stock Price Risk

ures are summarized in Table 1. In later sections these risk measures will be assessed for their accuracy in measuring the risk of option-affected portfolios.

A. Fixed Window

We estimate sample variance over the preceding 30 observations. Such a rolling *fixed-window* variance estimator is probably the most commonly used risk measure by practitioners and researchers:

$$\sigma^2_{t+1} = \sum_{i=0}^{m-1} \frac{\varepsilon^2_{t-i}}{m} \tag{7}$$

Table 1.   Characteristics of Risk Measures

Risk Measure	Ability to Accommodate Changes in Risk	Ability to Accommodate Skewness
Fixed Window	Limited	No
Semivariance	Limited	Yes
Exponential Smoothing	Yes[a]	No
GARCH	Yes[a]	No

Note: [a]The parameter estimates for this study suggest that GARCH will react to recent price shocks more rapidly than will exponential smoothing.

where $\varepsilon_t = R_t - (\sum_{i=0}^{m-1} R_{t-i}/m)$, $m = 30$ and R_t = asset return on day t. This measure of risk implicitly assumes that risk is constant for the window of observation. The possibility that risk is changing over time is partially accommodated by using a relatively short observation window. This measure does not specifically account for skewness in portfolio returns and hence implicitly assumes that portfolio returns are normally distributed.

B. Semivariance

Semivariance has been proposed by Sortino and Price (1994) as a more appropriate method for measuring risk in situations where portfolio returns are skewed. This measure focuses on downside risk by considering only returns which are less than the mean for the period. Sortino and Van der Meer (1991) claim that these returns, representing downside risk, are of most concern to investors. Risk is estimated using a rolling window of length 30:

$$\sigma_{t+1}^2 = \sum_{i=0}^{m-1} \frac{Min[0, R_t - \overline{R}]^2}{n} \tag{8}$$

where $\overline{R} = \sum_{t=0}^{m-1} R_{t-i}/m$, $m = 30$ and n is the number of observations within the rolling window where R_t is less than the mean. Note that in the case where returns are distributed symmetrically, sample semivariance and sample variance will be asymptotically equivalent. However, since semivariance includes fewer observations in the sample (that is, only those observations below the mean) the sampling error is likely to be greater.

C. Exponential Smoothing

Exponential smoothing has enjoyed renewed popularity with the distribution of J.P. Morgan's RiskMetrics methodology (Longerstaey and Spencer, 1996). The risk estimate reacts faster to changes in volatility and, as time elapses, the impact of any price shock is reduced. The exponential smoothing estimate for variance in the next period is:

$$\sigma_{t+1}^2 = (1 - \lambda)\varepsilon_t^2 + \lambda\sigma_t^2 \tag{9}$$

where $\varepsilon_t = R_t - (\sum_{i=0}^{t-1} R_{t-i}/t)$ and λ is the smoothing parameter.

When estimating risk for standard asset portfolios, values for λ have normally been selected in the range 0.94–0.97 (Longerstaey and Spencer, 1996). In the case of an option-affected portfolio, however, the appropriate value of λ is not obvious. This study therefore estimates values for λ using an ARIMA(0,1,1) model for the squared returns. For option-affected portfolios values for λ are typically lower than those for standard asset portfolios. In the case of the portfolios described in Section IV, the estimated values of λ typically fall in the range 0.84–0.94.

D. GARCH

GARCH models have become popular over the last decade for modeling changing variance in financial asset returns (see Bollerslev, Chou, and Kroner, 1992). This study uses a simple GARCH(1,1) formulation of risk:

$$\sigma_{t+1}^2 = \gamma_0 + \gamma_1\sigma_t^2 + \gamma_2\varepsilon_t^2 \tag{10}$$

where $\varepsilon_t = R_t - (\sum_{a=0}^{t-1} R_{t-a}/t)$.

The equation expresses the variance of tomorrow's return as a function of today's variance and the news component, ε_t, of today's returns which is conditionally normally distributed. The parameters of the model $(\gamma_0, \gamma_1, \gamma_2)$ are estimated by maximum likelihood procedures. Notice that GARCH and exponential smoothing are similar in form, with exponential smoothing being more constrained and easier to implement.

While GARCH methods have had notable success in measuring the risk of traditional assets, it is not immediately apparent that these methods will perform well in the simulated Black–Scholes environment. Under the Black–Scholes assumptions, the spot price of the stock does not display the real world volatility clustering which GARCH is designed to model. Rather, stock price risk is constant. While the simulated option-affected portfolio returns will exhibit changing risk, it will not be of this volatility clustering type. As noted earlier, there is a discontinuity in the portfolio variance when the option expires or if it is sold. This discontinuity in the portfolio variance creates a once-off "shock" which creates estimation difficulties.

For the option-affected portfolios described in Section IV, parameter estimates for γ_1 are typically in the range 0.70–0.80. Parameter estimates for γ_2 are in the range 0.15–0.35. Thus, in comparison to exponential smoothing, the GARCH(1,1) specification puts more weight on recent price shocks. The weighting on recent price shocks is also higher for option-affected portfolios than for standard asset portfolios discussed in the literature (Bollerslev, Engle, and Nelson, 1994).

IV. EVALUATION OF RISK MEASURES IN SIMULATION

Since the true variance of real world portfolio returns cannot be unambiguously determined, we initially examine a simulated Black–Scholes environment where the true variance of any portfolio return may be determined analytically. Portfolio returns are simulated with varying levels of option protection and therefore different degrees of variation in risk. Since the true variance is known, the most accurate risk measure can be identified.

A. Instantaneous Volatility

Extreme variations in risk associated with protected portfolios create significant risk measurement problems as highlighted in Figure 2. In the case of the fixed window, the risk measure lags the true risk significantly, creating significant measurement error. Similar difficulties apply to semivariance. The GARCH risk measure tracks the true risk closely, but frequently overshoots the mark, creating large discrepancies. This outcome is not unexpected since the GARCH estimation technique is not designed to accommodate the discontinuities found in an option-affected portfolio. In contrast, exponential smoothing, with lower weighting on recent price shocks, minimizes this problem. A visual assessment of Figure 2 suggests that exponential smoothing is the most accurate risk measure, a result that is confirmed by later analysis.

To evaluate the effect of options on portfolio risk, 1,000 stock price paths of 3 years in length are simulated. Simulations are generated using a log-normal, daily discretization of the geometric Brownian motion process[2] with $\mu = 0.08$ and $\sigma = 0.20$. The risk-free interest rate is set at 0.05. A portfolio is constructed consisting of stock overlaid with a protective put. Options are priced using the standard Black–Scholes model which is appropriate for the assumed geometric Brownian motion process. The options are rolled either at expiry, or 20 days prior to expiry. Option strategies vary both in the proportion of the portfolio they protect, and in terms of strike. As portfolio returns are generated under Black–Scholes assumptions, the "true" variance for the portfolio returns can be compared to the estimated variance.

In Table 2 a mean-square error (MSE) criterion determines the most accurate risk measure. The MSE is calculated on a daily basis across all of the 1000 randomly generated portfolio return paths for each of the risk estimates. The strategies are shown in increasing order according to volatility range (see column ^{d}).[3] In each case the most accurate risk measure (that with the lowest MSE) is highlighted in bold type.

First, Table 2 shows that the degree of variability in risk depends on the exact nature of the option strategy. Risk is most variable in cases where a sizeable proportion of the portfolio is protected and the options are held until expiry. Since variance (and therefore standard deviation) is a function of the delta of the option, it is not surprising to see a large range of volatility in such cases.

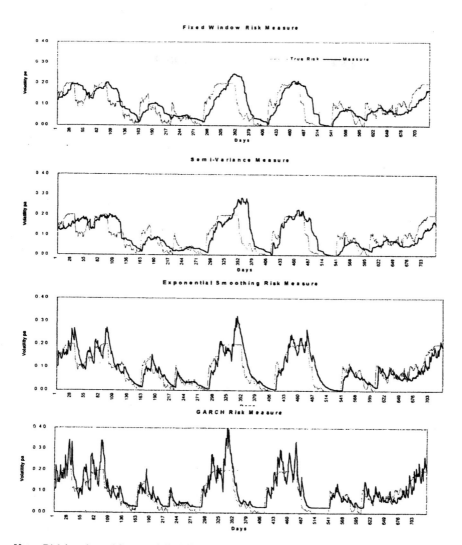

Notes: Risk is estimated for a portfolio fully protected by quarterly, at-the-money put options which are rolled at expiry. Risk is recalculated daily for 3 years. Each panel highlights three risk measures. "Stock only" refers to the risk of the comparable unprotected stock portfolio which is assumed to be constant. "True" refers to the risk derived in Equation 6. The final risk measure in each panel is described in Section III.

Figure 2. Accuracy of Risk Measures Assuming Constant Risk

Table 2. Risk Measure Evaluation: Mean Square Errors

Term[a]	Strike[b]	Protected %[c]	Volatility Range % pa[d]	Moving Semivariance[e]	Moving Variance[e]	Exponential Smoothing[e]	GARCH[e]
Annual	S	20	18.27–18.49	15.60	9.38	5.05	**3.75**
Qtly	S	20	18.08–18.35	15.60	9.60	5.62	**3.61**
Annual[f]	S	40	16.66–17.19	12.80	7.93	5.26	**4.74**
Qtly	S	40	16.25–16.89	14.20	9.61	7.82	**6.03**
Qtly	.9S	100	17.68–18.73	19.60	13.30	10.50	**9.34**
Annual	S	40	16.54–17.70	12.30	7.66	5.67	**4.80**
Qtly	S	60	14.64–15.89	14.30	10.50	9.11	**7.51**
Annual	S	60	15.11–16.45	11.10	7.21	5.56	**5.52**
Annual	0.9S	100	15.82–17.73	13.80	8.97	**7.34**[g]	11.10
Annual[f]	S	100	12.14–15.11	9.65	6.71	**5.72**	10.70
Annual[f]	S	100	11.02–14.66	15.50	12.40	**9.59**	19.20
Qtly	S	100	12.05–15.66	9.62	6.69	**5.74**	23.10
Annual	1.1S	100	3.97–8.72	6.31	4.58	**2.80**	12.90
Qtly	1.1S	100	8.12–12.90	6.02	4.41	**3.88**	10.50

Notes: [a]Options have terms of either one-quarter or one year. At expiry the option is replaced with another having the same initial term.
[b]The strike of the option is determined with reference to the stock price when the option is purchased. For example, a strike of (0.90 × S) indicates that the strike price is 90% of the current stock price and is therefore out-of-the-money.
[c]This column refers to the proportion of the stock portfolio which is protected by the option. For example, 40% indicates that the principal of the option is only 40% of the value of the stock portfolio as at the purchase date of the option.
[d]Volatility range gives the minimum and maximum for true volatility for each simulation (and averaged across 1,000 paths).
[e]The mean-square errors (multiplied by 10^7) of the risk estimates produced by each technique, relative to the true variance.
[f]Rather than holding the option until expiry, the option is sold and replaced 20 days prior to expiry.
[g]Results in bold typeface highlight the most accurate risk measure for each simulation.

Second, the table shows that fixed window and semivariance are *never* optimal risk measures. In every case the methods which give greater weight to more recent events (i.e. exponential smoothing or GARCH) are more suited to measuring risk of option-affected portfolios.[4] In contrast to previous researchers the study finds that skewness, as reflected in semivariance, is not an important consideration.

Third, the choice of risk measure depends on the range of volatility. In cases where the volatility range is low (top of Table 2), GARCH measures risk most accurately. Exponential smoothing is the optimal risk measure in all other cases. This relationship can be explained by the presence of discontinuities. In those cases where changes in risk and discontinuities are more extreme, the GARCH risk measure often overshoots the true level of risk and so exponential smoothing is a superior measure. It should be noted, however, that these simulation results do not fully reflect the value of the GARCH family of models for measuring risk. The simulations consistently apply the same model specifications in all cases, whereas, in a real world case, the model specification could be varied to improve the fit of the model. Thus the results shown here are unavoidably biased against the GARCH measure.

B. Monthly Holding Periods

The simulation analysis shows the efficacy of various risk measures for estimating instantaneous volatility. However, in the funds management industry returns are often calculated using monthly holding periods. Even though instantaneous returns for an option-protected portfolio are conditionally normally distributed, monthly holding period returns may exhibit skewness and heteroscedasticity.[5]

We explore the distribution of holding period returns via simulation. Using the same assumptions as above we generate 1,000 stock price paths of 10 years in length. Quarterly, at-the-money put options are held to expiry. As shown in Table 3, the monthly returns generated in this way often exhibit skewness and heteroscedasticity. The monthly returns are then standardized by dividing by the standard deviation calculated from the exponential smoothing risk measure. Standardized

Table 3. Analysis of Simulated Monthly Holding Period Returns[a]

	Raw Monthly Returns	Standardized Monthly Returns
% Simulations with Skewness	86.5%	4.8%
% Simulations with Heteroscedasticity	13.9%	5.5%

Note: [a]We simulate 1,000 stock price paths of 10 years length, protected by quarterly, at-the-money put options. Monthly returns, before and after standardization, are tested for skewness and heteroscedasticity at the 5% level of significance. Heteroscedasticity is identified using a Lagrange multiplier test for serial correlation (at lags 1–3) in the squared returns. Returns are standardized using the exponential smoothing risk measure.

monthly returns are then retested for skewness and heteroscedasticity, which is eliminated in all but a few cases. After standardization, only around 5% of the simulations exhibit skewness/heteroscedasticity, as expected at the 5% level of significance. This shows that the apparent skewness introduced by option strategies is probably related to changing variance. The results presented in Table 3 suggest that the conclusions relating to instantaneous returns also have some validity when evaluating returns over longer holding periods, such as monthly.

V. EVALUATING OPTION PORTFOLIOS WHEN UNDERLYING VOLATILITY IS CHANGING

All of the preceding analysis assumes that the variance of the underlying asset is constant, consistent with the assumptions of the Black–Scholes model. While such an assumption simplifies the analysis of option affected portfolios, it does not reflect reality. This section considers an unprotected portfolio under a GARCH process and an option-affected portfolio under a GARCH process.

A. Unprotected Portfolios Under a GARCH Process

The extensive GARCH literature surveyed in Bollerslev, Chou, and Kroner (1992) and Bollerslev, Engle, and Nelson (1994) finds evidence of volatility clustering for most asset classes. That is, the variance of returns is positively correlated with past variance and price shocks. Many specifications have been used to describe the process for both stock returns and variance. In this section, these processes are assumed as follows:

$$\ln \frac{S_{t+1}}{S_t} = r + \pi\sqrt{\sigma_t^2} - \frac{\sigma_t^2}{2} + \sqrt{\sigma_t^2}\, \varepsilon_{t+1} \tag{11}$$

$$\sigma_{t+1}^2 = \gamma_0 + \gamma_1\sigma_t^2 + \gamma_2\sigma_t^2\varepsilon_t^2 \tag{12}$$

where ε_{t+1}, conditional on the time t information, is a standard normal random variable, r is the risk-free rate of interest, σ_t^2 is the conditional variance of the logarithmic return, and π is the unit risk premium for the stock.

Stock price returns are simulated according to Equations 11 and 12 where $r = 0.000198$ per day, $\pi = 0.009449$, $\gamma_0 = 0.00000159$, $\gamma_1 = 0.95$, $\gamma_2 = 0.04$. These values are selected such that the steady-state volatility of the stock is 20% pa and $r = 8\%$ pa.

If the underlying volatility process is GARCH, then the best risk measure will logically be the GARCH risk measure. This intuition is confirmed in Table 4 which shows the accuracy of each risk measure over 500 simulated stock price paths. The results confirm that under a GARCH process the best risk measure is GARCH, followed closely by exponential smoothing.

Table 4. Risk Measure Evaluation Mean-Square Errors Stock Portfolio Under GARCH Process[a]

	Fixed Window	Exponential Smoothing	GARCH
Mean-Square Error ($\times 10^7$)	7.10	3.44	2.45

Note: [a]Mean-square errors (multiplied by 10^7) are calculated for each risk estimate, relative to the true risk defined for the GARCH process.

B. Option-Affected Portfolios Under a GARCH Process

Having examined a stock portfolio under a GARCH process, the case of a *protected* portfolio under the same process is analyzed. Consider a stock portfolio protected with an at-the-money put option strategy. The put option has a term of 3 months and is replaced at expiry with another at-the-money put option with the same term. This process continues until 3 years have elapsed.

Since the underlying stock process is GARCH, the put option is priced using the GARCH option-pricing model. Duan (1995) derives an option-pricing mechanism for the process defined in Equations 11 and 12. Under suitable preference restrictions, Duan establishes a local risk neutralized probability measure under which option prices can be computed as simple discounted expected values. The local risk neutralized measure applicable for a GARCH(1,1) process is given by:

$$\ln \frac{S_{t+1}}{S_t} = r_f - \frac{\sigma_t^2}{2} + \sqrt{\sigma_t^2}\, Z_{t+1} \tag{13}$$

$$\sigma_{t+1}^2 = \gamma_0 + \gamma_1 \sigma_t^2 + \gamma_2 \sigma_t^2 (Z_{t+1} - \pi)^2 \tag{14}$$

where Z_{t+1}, conditional on time t information, is a standard normal random variable with respect to the risk-neutralized measure. Following Duan (1995), Monte Carlo simulations[6] are used to reprice the put option, and hence the protected stock portfolio on each business day for the 3-year period.

The true risk for the protected portfolio under a GARCH process is not known, so it is not possible to measure exactly the accuracy of each risk measure. Some insight, however, can be gained by comparing the risk of the protected portfolio under a GARCH process to that under the assumption of constant volatility. Figure 3 draws this comparison for a single realization of the stock process.

Whether the underlying stock process has constant volatility, or whether it follows a GARCH process, the risk measures are almost identical for a fully protected portfolio. This similarity can be explained by the fact that changes in risk resulting from movements in the delta of the option are far more significant than changes in risk which result from the underlying GARCH process. Since the effect

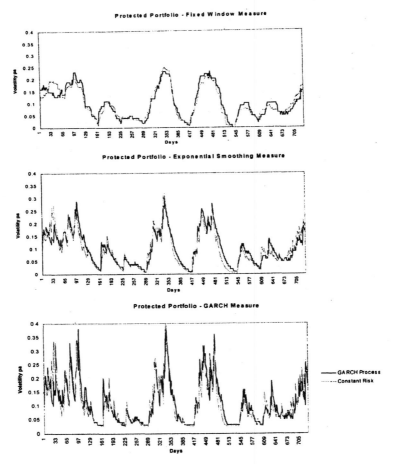

Notes: A simulated price path for a stock portfolio, fully protected with quarterly, at-the-money put options which are rolled at expiry. Risk is measured daily for a 3-year period. Compare risk under two assumptions regarding the underlying stock process, namely, GARCH and constant risk.

Figure 3. How Does Risk Change for a GARCH Process? Protected Portfolio

of the option dominates, the lessons learned in Section IV, and summarized in Table 5, should also apply in the case of a GARCH process. That is, the best risk measures for option-affected portfolios are GARCH and exponential smoothing. Significant discontinuities occur when the option principal is large relative to the portfolio size and when options are held until, or close to, expiry. In such cases, exponential smoothing will outperform GARCH.[7] Figure 4 shows the risk estimates for the stock portfolio under a GARCH process, both protected and unprotected.

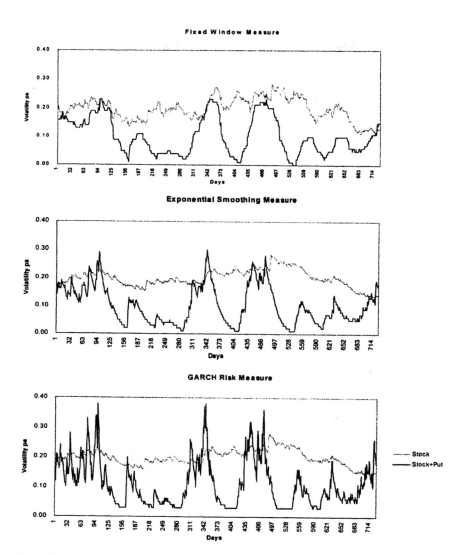

Notes: This figure assumes that the underlying stock process is GARCH. Compare risk for the unprotected stock portfolio and the fully protected portfolio. The protected portfolio uses quarterly, at-the-money put options which are rolled at expiry.

Figure 4. How Does Option Strategy Change Risk? GARCH Process

Table 5. Summary of Lessons from Simulations

Nature of Portfolio	Appropriate Risk Measures
Volatility clustering in underlying assets. No options or other discontinuities	GARCH is superior, followed closely by exponential smoothing. Fixed window and semivariance not suitable
Some use of options (or active asset allocation techniques) which result in changes in risk over time and some minor discontinuities in risk. Underlying asset may display volatility clustering	GARCH is superior, followed closely by exponential smoothing. Fixed window and semivariance not suitable
Significant use of options[a] (or active asset allocation techniques) which result in exaggerated changes in risk over time and significant discontinuities. Underlying asset may display volatility clustering	Exponential smoothing.[b] GARCH, fixed window and semivariance not suitable
Knowledge regarding use of options and discontinuities is unavailable	Exponential smoothing

Notes: [a]Significant use of options refers to portfolios where the principal of options used is greater than, say, 60% of the total portfolio value (see Table 3). The influence of options is exaggerated if the option gamma is high and if they are held until expiry.
[b]For portfolios with significant use of options, a lower value of λ, the smoothing parameter, may be appropriate.

VI. CONCLUSIONS AND IMPLICATIONS

The main objective of this study is to examine the nature of risk for option-affected portfolios and identify suitable risk measures for them. Options potentially present three problems for performance measurement; namely, departures from normality, changes in risk over time, and discontinuities in risk. Since all asset portfolios exhibit these characteristics to some degree, this research has implications for all asset portfolios, not just those containing options. This study finds that capturing changes in risk is the key issue for evaluating option-affected portfolios.

Skewness in portfolio returns has previously been regarded as a key issue for option-affected portfolios. Reflecting this concern, semivariance is suggested by a number of commentators as an appropriate risk measure. This study finds, however, that semivariance is always sub-optimal. The most pressing issue for assessing option-affected portfolios is not skewness, but changing variance. The best measures to take account of changing risk are found to be those that give greater weight to more recent observations and thus adapt quickly to new information about risk (e.g. exponential smoothing and GARCH).

One implication of this finding is that option-affected portfolios may be evaluated (along with all other portfolios) in a mean-variance framework, provided that suitable risk measures are applied. Such an outcome is clearly advantageous since most investors are familiar with this approach and the alternatives involving lower partial moments can be complex.

ACKNOWLEDGMENTS

The authors are from the Centre for Studies in Money, Banking and Finance, Macquarie University. They gratefully acknowledge support from the Australian Research Council, Macquarie Investment Management Limited and Axiom Funds Management Limited under Collaborative Research Grant C595301128.

NOTES

1. The phenomenon of volatility clustering has been well documented in the generalized autoregressive conditional heteroscedasticity (GARCH) literature. This literature is surveyed by Bollerslev, Chou, and Kroner (1992); Bollerslev, Engle, and Nelson (1994).
2. See Hull (1993) Equation 10.7, p. 210.
3. Note that the volatility range is calculated for the average volatility across all 1,000 simulations. Even though the risk in any one simulation could vary between zero and 20% pa, the average volatility is far more stable.
4. Similar results (not reported) are obtained when the portfolios contain call options.
5. The volatility of holding period returns is a function of the instantaneous volatility, change in volatility over the holding period, and the change in mean described in Equation 5 above.
6. Each option price is calculated using 2,000 simulations with a control variate technique to maximize the accuracy.
7. Refer to discussion of Table 2.

REFERENCES

Balzer, L. (1994). Measuring investment risk: A review. *The Journal of Investing*, 47–58.
Bensman, M. (1994). New strategies for selling volatility. *Global Finance, 8(10)*, 30–32.
Bollerslev, T., Chou R., & Kroner, K. (1992). ARCH modelling in finance: A review of the theory and empirical evidence. *Journal of Econometrics 52*, 5–59.
Bollerslev, T., Engle, R., & Nelson, D. (1994). ARCH models. In R. Engle & D. McFadden (Eds.), *Handbook of econometrics* (Vol. 4, pp. 2961–3038). Amsterdam: Elsevier Science B.V.
Bookstaber, R., & Clarke R. (1985). Problems in evaluating the performance of portfolios with options. *Financial Analysts Journal*, 48–62.
Cerulli, K., & Casey, G. (1995). Looking for stable value? Several choices available. *Pension World, 31(5)*, 50–51.
Coopers & Lybrand Banking & Finance Industry Group (1995). Derivatives and funds managers: in control? *On Banking*, 1–6.
Duan, J.C. (1995). The GARCH option pricing model. *Mathematical Finance, 5(1)*, 13–32.
Gastineau, G.L. (1995). The currency hedging decision: A search for synthesis in asset allocation. *Financial Analysts Journal, 51(3)*, 8–17.
Hull, J. (1993). *Options, futures, and other derivative securities*. Prentice Hall.
Layard-Liesching, R. (1994). Currency overlays. *Euromoney* (Currencies Supplement), 69–72.
Lewis, A.L. (1990). Semivariance and the performance of portfolios with options. *Financial Analysts Journal*, 67–76.
Longerstaey, J., & Spencer, M. (1996). *RiskMetrics—technical document* (4th ed.) New York: J.P. Morgan and Reuters.

Millman, G. (1995). Why investors need to understand derivatives. *Global Investor, 81*, 10–13.

Peters, C. (1994). Managed Futures win pension foothold. *Pension World, 30(5)*, 28–30.

Schneeweis, T., Spurgin, R., & Potter, M. (1996). Managed futures and hedge fund investment for downside equity risk management. *Derivatives Quarterly, 3(1)*, 62–72.

Schwimmer, A. (1994). Structured note buyers turn to new exotic plays. *Investment Dealers Digest, 60(34)*, 9.

Simon, R. (1994). Don't get socked by those #?@!* derivatives. *Money, 23(8)*, 26–29.

Sortino, F., & Van der Meer, R. (1991). Downside risk. *Journal of Portfolio Management*, 27–31.

Sortino, F., & Price, L. (1994). Performance measurement in a downside risk framework. *The Journal of Investing*, 59–64.

Sy, W. (1996). Tactical Manoeuvres. *Journal of the Securities Institute of Australia*, 2–9.

CO-MOVEMENT PATTERN OF DAILY STOCK RETURNS:
AN ANALYSIS OF DOW AND JANUARY EFFECTS

Gordon Y. N. Tang

ABSTRACT

Although studies of the day-of-the-week and January effects on stock mean returns and volatility are well documented in the literature, similar studies on correlations between stock returns are rare. This paper examines the day-of-the-week effect on correlations between six industrial indices for the first time in the Hong Kong stock market. Empirical results show that the hypothesis of equal correlation is rejected for all pairs of stock indices across all weekdays, and stock indices are most correlated on Monday, and to a slightly lesser extent for returns after holidays. The results are caused by the fact that more information is accumulated over the weekend (or after the holidays) than just overnight and that industrial sectors adjust to each other with a time lag, resulting in a smaller correlation on Tuesday to Friday. However, this result is valid only in non-January months. A January effect also exists in correlations between sectoral indices, but this anomaly is valid from Tuesday through Friday only, and on Monday a reversed January effect occurs.

Advances in Investment Analysis and Portfolio Management, Volume 7, pages 19–39.
Copyright © 2000 by JAI Press Inc.
All rights of reproduction in any form reserved.
ISBN: 0-7623-0658-0

I. INTRODUCTION

The day-of-the-week and January effects on stock mean returns and volatility have been well documented in the finance literature. Empirical results show that the mean return and variance are different across days of the week. In particular, Monday has the lowest (negative) mean return and the largest variance across all weekdays (for the U.S. evidence, see e.g., Fama, 1965; Cross, 1973; French, 1980; Keim and Stambaugh, 1984; for the Japanese evidence, see Jaffe and Westerfield, 1985; and for international evidence, see Condoyanni, O'Hanlon, and Ward, 1987). Similar studies have also been carried out for Asian Pacific markets (see e.g., Aggarwal and Rivoli, 1989; Ho, 1990; Wong, Hui, and Chan, 1992). Empirical results are in support of those findings in developed markets. Rogalski (1984) further found that the day-of-the-week effect in the U.S. stock market is valid only from February to December. This result is known as Rogalski effect. Ho (1990) also found more day-of-the-week variation in the non-January months than in January for the Asian–Pacific markets. For the January effect (e.g., Rozeff and Kinney, 1976; Gultekin and Gultekin, 1983; Keim, 1983), empirical results found that stock returns are significantly positive and larger than those in non-January months.

Although studies on these anomalies on mean returns and volatilities of stock returns are substantial, similar studies on the co-movement pattern of stock returns are rare. Tang and Kwok (1996) examined the day-of-the-week effect on international portfolio diversification and found that correlations among six international stock markets are most correlated on Monday. It is interesting to investigate if such results can also be found within a domestic market.

On the other hand, much attention has been paid to Pacific Basin markets, particularly the emerging Asian markets recently. They are valuable to international investors because of their available extra investment opportunities and diversification benefits, despite their much smaller market capitalizations. Among those emerging Asian markets, one of the most important markets is the Hong Kong stock market. The Hong Kong stock market is well known by its open, and yet regulated, policies on the securities industry. Most of the studies on the Hong Kong stock market are empirically based, replicating previous studies which employed developed markets (mainly U.S.) data. One of the most widely examined topic is seasonalities of stock returns (see e.g., Ho, 1990; Wong, Hui, and Chan, 1992; Ho and Cheung, 1994). Their results on mean return and volatility support those findings in developed markets in that in Hong Kong, Monday has the lowest (negative) return and also the highest standard deviation. However, no study has been done on the seasonality in the correlation structure of stock returns of industrial sectors in the Hong Kong market. The findings are helpful in better understanding the seasonality patterns and properties of stock returns in this market. This paper tries to fill that gap.

In this paper, we examine whether the day-of-the-week effect exists on correlation between any pair of sectoral stock indices and on the whole correlation matrix.

Correlation between index returns after holidays is also examined. The empirical results may help shed light on the delayed adjustment patterns among industrial sectors. We hypothesize that the correlation between sectoral indices should be rather stable across weekdays if the adjustment process to market information is very similar, if not the same, for different sectors. Statistical tests are used to test the hypothesis of equal correlation between any two indices and between all indices jointly. Our results show that correlations among stock indices differ across days of the week. Daily correlations among stock indices are larger on Monday, probably due to the larger number of calendar days used in calculating returns over the weekend, resulting in smaller risk reduction. Furthermore, our empirical results found that the weekly seasonal pattern in correlations between stock indices only exists in non-January. Also, a January effect exists in correlations among sectoral indices but this anomaly is valid from Tuesday through Friday only, and on Monday a reversed January effect occurs since the January correlations are smaller.

The rest of the paper is organized as follows: Section II describes the data and research methodology; Section III presents the empirical results; and Section IV concludes the paper.

II. DATA AND METHODOLOGIES

A. Data Sources

We use the six sectoral indices and the Hong Kong Index of the Hong Kong stock market. The daily data is collected from *The Securities Journal,* the official publication of The Hong Kong Stock Exchange. The six sectoral stock indices are: Consortium and Enterprise Index (CI), Financial Index (FI), Hotel Index (HI), Industries Index (II), Properties Index (PI), and Utilities Index (UI). Stock index returns are expressed as logarithmic price relatives, i.e., $\ln(P_t/P_{t-1})*100\%$, where P_t and P_{t-1} are the stock indices at time t and time $t - 1$, respectively. To avoid the holiday effect, all returns preceded by a holiday are excluded from this analysis. For example, if Tuesday is a holiday, the return on Wednesday calculated from the closing price of Monday is excluded. This procedure also eliminates the effect of the October stock crash in 1987 as the Hong Kong stock market was suspended for four trading days after "black Monday." This is equivalent to a holiday following our procedures. However, all these holiday returns are included in a separate group for analysis.

The sample period covers January 1984 to March 1992, a total of 8-1/4 years of stock returns. The Hong Kong Index (HKI) and the six sectoral indices are computed by the Hong Kong Stock Exchange. The stock exchange was officially established on April 2, 1986. Before this day, there were four stock exchanges in Hong Kong which unified to form the current stock exchange. Hence, the base day for these indices was April 2, 1986 and the base value for all indices was 1,000.

However, the stock exchange also computed values of all indices before the base day with the earliest index value starting from January 2, 1984.

The HKI consists of around 45 "blue-chip" stocks listed on the stock exchange. The index accounts for around 75% of total market capitalization and around 70% of total trading volume. The HKI and all sectoral indices are value-weighted indices. This is the same as the other popular index in Hong Kong, namely the Hang Seng Index (HSI). Since its launch the HKI has been highly correlated with the HSI (the correlation was 0.998 during our sample period), and hence, the information provided to the market is virtually the same. For this reason, as of April 1992, the Hong Kong Stock Exchange stopped computing the HKI and the six sectoral indices. Our sample period represents a complete data series.

B.   Test on Equality of Correlation

To test the equality of correlation between two weekdays, a *normal distribution test* is used. Each correlation coefficient is first converted into Z, the Fisher transformation, which is defined as:

$$Z_{ij} = 1/2 * \ln[(1 + r_{ij})/(1 - r_{ij})]$$

where r_{ij} is the sample correlation coefficient between stock indices i and j. The hypothesis that the correlation coefficients from two weekdays are equal is then tested by the following statistic, D:

$$D = \frac{Z_{ij}^1 - Z_{ij}^2}{\sqrt{[1/(n_1 - 3)] + [1/(n_2 - 3)]}}$$

where Z_{ij}^k is the Fisher transformation of correlation coefficient between stock indices i and j in weekdays 1 and 2; n_k is the number of observations in weekdays 1 and 2, respectively. Given that the original variables are distributed normally, D also follows a normal distribution, and hence, the level of significance can be inferred from the critical values of a normal distribution.

Similarly, the hypothesis of equal correlation coefficients across different days of the week for all pairs of stock indices is tested by the following procedure (see Snedecor and Cochran, 1976). First, the sample correlation coefficient is converted into Z as defined above. Under the null hypothesis, the Z_i are all estimates of the same mean μ but have different variances $\sigma_i^2 = 1/(n_i - 3)$. The test of significance is based on the result that if k normal deviates have the same mean μ but have different variances σ_i^2, then the quantity, Q is distributed as a Chi-square distribution with $(k - 1)$ degrees of freedom where k is the number of samples:

$$Q = \sum_{i=1}^k (n_i - 3)z_i^2 - \left[\sum_{i=1}^k (n_i - 3)z_i\right]^2 / \sum_{i=1}^k (n_i - 3)$$

and where n_i = number of observations in sample i.

C. Test on Equality of Covariance Matrices

For the hypothesis of equal variance–covariance matrices across different periods, we employ the Box M test (Box, 1949). The Box M statistic is calculated as follows:

$$M = n \ln |C| - \sum_{i=1}^{T} n_i * \ln|C_i|$$

$$C = 1/n \sum_{i=1}^{T} n_i * C_i$$

where C_i is the variance–covariance matrix calculated from sample time period i; T is the number of total subperiods where the equality of matrices is tested; $n = n_1 + n_2 + \ldots + n_T$; and n_i = sample size in time period i minus 1.

Box (1949) showed that the M statistic can be approximated by either a Chi-square statistic or an F statistic. We employ the approximation of the F statistic as it is more accurate (see Pearson, 1969). Box (1949) showed that M/b is distributed approximately as an F distribution with f_1 and f_2 degrees of freedom.

$$D_1 = \frac{2p^2 + 3p - 1}{6(p + 1)(T - 1)} \left[\sum_{i=1}^{T} \frac{1}{n_i} - \frac{1}{n} \right]$$

$$D_2 = \frac{(p - 1)(p + 2)}{6(T - 1)} \left[\sum_{i=1}^{T} \frac{1}{n_i^2} - \frac{1}{n^2} \right]$$

where $b = f_1/(1 - D_1 - f_1/f_2)$; $f_1 = p(p + 1)(T - 1)/2$; p = number of variables (stocks) in the matrix; and $f_2 = (f_1 + 2)/(D_2 - D_1^2)$.

The Box M statistic, the approximate F statistic and the corresponding p value are obtained from the SPSSX computer package.

D. Test of Stability in Correlation Matrices

The Box M test is designed for testing the equality of variance–covariance matrices across different time periods (Mardia, Kent, and Bibby 1979, pp. 140). Several recent studies (Kaplanis, 1988; Meric and Meric, 1989; Wahab and Lashgari, 1993) have used this statistical test to examine the intertemporal stability in international stock market relationships through testing the hypothesis of equal variance–covariance matrices. In testing the hypothesis of equal correlation matrices of stock returns, Kaplanis (1988) used Jennrich's (1970) Chi-square test procedure. In a more recent study, Tang (1995) employed an extension of Box's M test to test the same hypothesis. Tang (1995) directly applied the Box M test on the equality of correlation matrices by first transforming the raw data into standard scores for each time period before applying Box M testing procedures. This useful extension of the Box M statistical test relies on two statistical properties:

1. The correlation between two random variables is the same as that between their respective standard scores, i.e., standardization of variables does not change the correlation structure among these variables.
2. For two standardized random variables, the correlation is the same as the covariance between these two variables.

Hence, testing the equality of variance–covariance matrices of the standard scores of stock returns is the same as testing the equality of correlation matrices of the corresponding stock returns. In our study, we follow Tang's (1995) testing methodologies.

III. EMPIRICAL RESULTS

A. Pairwise Correlations

Table 1 presents the correlation coefficients among all pairs of sectoral stock indices by day of the week. In examining the day-of-the-week effect, returns after holidays are excluded. However, returns after holidays are also studied separately and correlations between stock indices after holidays are shown in the last two columns in Table 1. In our analysis, the 1987 stock market crash is regarded as a holiday because of the 4-day suspension of the stock exchange. The last column differs from the second last column in that the stock crash return is deleted.

The results in Table 1 are shown in two parts. The upper part shows the correlations among the six sectoral indices. The lower part of the table shows the correlation between the Hong Kong Index and each of the sectoral indices. The largest and smallest correlation coefficients on Monday are 0.8799 and 0.7203, respectively. On other weekdays, the corresponding values are 0.8234 and 0.2262 on Tuesday, 0.6612 and 0.1931 on Wednesday, 0.7582 and 0.1849 on Thursday, and 0.7244 and 0.1377 on Friday. The results show that stock indices are more correlated on Monday. In fact, if we look at the average of the 15 possible correlations between stock indices for each weekday, the average correlation coefficient is largest on Monday. Tuesday has the second largest average correlation while the average correlation is roughly the same on the other 3 weekdays. The results can also be applied to the co-movements of individual indices with the market, HKI. The average correlation among the six sectoral indices and HKI is much larger (0.8935) on Monday while the average correlations on Wednesday, Thursday, and Friday are roughly the same and at their smallest (around 0.665).

Table 1. Correlation Between Returns on Stock Indices
by Day of the Week

	Weekday						
	Mon	Tue	Wed	Thu	Fri	Hol[a]	H-87[b]
N[c]	375	380	403	404	401	78	77
CI–FI	0.7839	0.6518	0.4053	0.5589	0.5893	0.9754	0.8183
CI–HI	0.7203	0.2596	0.1931	0.2042	0.1566	0.9638	0.7037
CI–II	0.7855	0.5169	0.3842	0.4909	0.5368	0.9752	0.8050
CI–PI	0.8799	0.8234	0.5187	0.5956	0.7244	0.9924	0.9325
CI–UI	0.8100	0.7104	0.3541	0.4029	0.5205	0.9698	0.7015
FI–HI	0.7296	0.2805	0.2933	0.2481	0.1794	0.9504	0.6396
FI–II	0.8041	0.4807	0.4882	0.6153	0.5073	0.9670	0.7663
FI–PI	0.8397	0.7187	0.6498	0.7582	0.6285	0.9797	0.8515
FI–UI	0.8074	0.6100	0.5047	0.5561	0.5416	0.9693	0.7687
HI–II	0.7947	0.3865	0.2640	0.2646	0.1674	0.9527	0.6409
HI–PI	0.8265	0.3202	0.3354	0.3007	0.1377	0.9668	0.7224
HI–UI	0.7232	0.2262	0.2341	0.1849	0.1612	0.9548	0.5803
II–PI	0.8563	0.6337	0.6612	0.6269	0.5521	0.9759	0.8079
II–UI	0.7818	0.3666	0.4381	0.4239	0.4939	0.9536	0.5898
PI–UI	0.8538	0.7443	0.5877	0.5201	0.5722	0.9725	0.7175
Mean[d]	0.7998	0.5153	0.4208	0.4501	0.4312	0.9680	0.7364
CI–HKI	0.9003	0.8621	0.7297	0.6522	0.8073	0.9919	0.9272
FI–HKI	0.8815	0.7722	0.7105	0.8679	0.7573	0.9846	0.8937
HI–HKI	0.8206	0.3325	0.3460	0.3057	0.2081	0.9640	0.6882
II–HKI	0.8797	0.5968	0.6482	0.6684	0.6444	0.9772	0.8168
PI–HKI	0.9665	0.9341	0.8818	0.8816	0.8627	0.9947	0.9505
UI–HKI	0.9122	0.8508	0.6597	0.6241	0.7292	0.9835	0.8175
Mean[d]	0.8935	0.7248	0.6626	0.6666	0.6682	0.9826	0.8490

Notes: [a]Hol = holiday returns.

[b]H–87 = holiday returns with 1987 stock crash excluded.

[c]N = number of observations.

[d]Mean = simple average.

The large difference is most likely economically significant to investors who concern correlations between stock indices. One implication is that if investors want to diversify across industrial sectors, they are better off in securing risk reduction on Wednesday through Friday rather than on Monday.

The results in Table 1 also suggest that various sectoral stock indices correlate with each other differently across days of the week. The lowest correlations are those correlations between the HI and the other sectoral indices. These correlations are around 0.7 to 0.8 on Monday, but they decrease to less than 0.4 (most of them are less than 0.3) on other weekdays. Hence, the results clearly show that the HI is more correlated with the market on Monday but becomes much less correlated on other weekdays. This is also indicated by the correlation with the HKI. The correlation is 0.82 on Monday but is only 0.35 or less on other weekdays. The same case is applied to all other sectoral indices except that the decrease in the correlation is not as large as that of the HI. On the other hand, the PI has the highest correlation with the HKI across all sectoral indices, supporting the general belief that the Hong Kong stock market is dominated by the properties sector. CI and PI are the most correlated among all pairs of indices on all weekdays except Wednesday and Thursday. On these two weekdays, FI and PI are the most correlated.

One possible explanation for the higher correlation on Monday than on other weekdays is that information accumulated during the weekend can be digested by industrial sectors in three calendar days, causing a general impact on the whole market on Monday. In contrast, for information released during the other weekdays, different industrial sectors may respond with a small time lag. One calendar day is just not long enough for industrial sectors to fully reflect the adjustments necessary. Hence, a delayed adjustment pattern exists across different industrial sectors. The result of this time lag is to cause the sectoral indices apparently to be less correlated during the other weekdays. The results are also supported by the intuition that more information relevant to price formation will be accumulated over the weekend than just overnight for the rest of the week's trading days. One direct implication from this argument is that stock indices should be more correlated after holidays because returns are calculated from more than one calendar day, and hence, a longer period for accumulation of information. This fact is supported by the results presented in Table 1. It is no surprise that the average correlation is highly positive and is around 0.97 with the 1987 stock crash effect included. However, when the crash effect is avoided, the average correlation is 0.74, which is smaller than that on Monday but larger than those on other weekdays. The same result is applied to correlation with HKI. Since most of the holidays in Hong Kong are one calendar day, stock indices adjust to each other after two calendar days. Hence, the returns of stock indices after holidays should be more correlated than those on Tuesday through Friday but less than those on Monday.

In order to formally investigate whether the change in correlation between stock indices is statistically significant with different days of the week, the normal distribution test is used to test the following two hypotheses:

H_{01}:   For each pair of stock indices, the correlation is the same for two adjacent weekdays.

H_{02}:   For each pair of stock indices, the correlation is the same across all weekdays.

Both hypotheses are tested by the normal distribution test for the bivariate and multivariate cases. Empirical results are presented in Table 2. All 15 possible pairs of stock indices rejected the hypothesis of equal correlations across all weekdays (i.e., H_{02}) at the 1% level. The hypothesis of equal correlation between any sectoral

Table 2. Z Values of Testing Equal Correlation Between Adjacent Days of the Week

Stock Index	Mon–Tue	Tue–Wed	Wed–Thu	Thu–Fri	Fri–Mon	Mon & H-87	Weekdays®	Weekdays[a]
CI–FI	3.7895*	4.8546#	−2.8475#	−0.6426	−5.2515#	−0.76848	0.4358#	25.1631#
CI–HI	8.7936#	0.9778	−0.1638	0.6960	−10.4067#	0.2700	150.8809#	2.3109
CI–II	6.6693#	2.3275*	−1.8721+	−0.8820	−6.3753#	−0.4260	93.9375#	8.8644*
CI–PI	2.8484#	8.2551#	−1.5809	−3.2566#	−6.3590#	−2.4131*	169.3325#	80.2188#
CI–UI	3.2712#	7.2139#	−0.8062	−2.1187*	−7.6266#	2.0507*	158.6714#	62.1643#
FI–HI	8.7517#	−0.1946	0.6898	1.0188	−10.3504#	1.3606	139.3176#	3.4647
FI–II	8.0212#	−0.1353	−2.5991*	2.2368*	−7.6415#	0.7894	92.9075#	9.7487*
FI–PI	4.3131#	1.8099+	−3.0691#	3.5745#	−6.6719#	−0.3300	57.1066#	16.3588#
FI–UI	5.6195#	2.1360*	−1.0128	0.2935	−7.1161#	0.8185	78.8392#	4.7167
HI–II	9.2547#	1.9127+	−0.008	41.4424	−12.6892#	2.5904*	206.7597#	11.1188*
HI–PI	11.5653#	−0.2371	0.5472	2.4256*	−14.3999#	2.1116*	252.4100#	11.2311*
HI–UI	9.3622#	−0.1168	0.7282	0.3453	−10.4235#	2.0077*	153.2769#	1.5305
II–PI	7.2762#	−0.6596	0.8299	1.6237	−9.1232#	1.2647	98.9973#	6.4713+
II–UI	9.1047#	−1.1894	0.2475	−1.2549	−7.0537#	2.9757#	108.4720#	4.8201
PI–UI	4.2416#	3.9819#	1.3830	−1.0500	−8.5866#	2.9354#	126.4011#	32.6208#
Avg Cor	7.2260#	1.6893+	−0.5113	0.3301	−8.8268#	1.2415	114.6461#	3.4269

(continued)

27

Table 2. Continued

Stock Index	Mon–Tue	Tue–Wed	Wed–Thu	Thu–Fri	Fri–Mon	Mon & H-87	Weekdays@	Weekdays^a
CI–HKI	2.3535*	5.2030#	2.1077	-4.8068#	-4.9130#	-1.3135	120.1553#	60.3555#
FI–HKI	4.8814#	1.9136+	-6.1714#	4.7290#	-5.4438#	-0.4584	73.9426#	42.2249#
HI–HKI	11.1261#	-0.2121	0.6369	1.4790	-13.1389#	2.5101*	223.2399#	5.4051
II–HKI	9.3875#	-1.1692	-0.5043	0.5952	-8.4389#	1.8147+	116.6693#	2.9296
PI–HKI	4.7479#	4.2663#	0.0114	1.1144	-10.1625#	1.5975	141.9145#	33.4664#
UI–HKI	3.8464#	6.5021#	0.8575	-2.7593#	-8.5027#	3.1235#	178.8736#	64.0812#
Avg Cor	7.1317#	1.6728+	-0.1015	-0.0387	-8.7545#	1.4886	115.1034#	3.7738

Notes: # = significant at the 1% level.

* = significant at the 5% level.

+ = significant at the 10% level.

H-87 = holiday returns with 1987 stock crash excluded.

@ = test of equal correlation across all five weekdays.

a = test of equal correlation across four weekdays. (Tuesday through Friday).

Av. Cor. = average correlation.

index and HKI across all 5 weekdays can also be rejected at the 1% level. Our results clearly show that correlation between stock indices is significantly different across weekdays. The hypothesis H_{02} can be rejected even if we use the average correlation of the 15 individual correlations. For any adjacent weekdays, the hypothesis H_{01} is rejected at the 1% level for all 15 pairs of stock indices for the pair of Monday and Tuesday and the pair of Friday and Monday. The results are the same if we use the average correlation. However, only 6, 3, and 5 pairs of stock indices reject the hypothesis of equal correlation respectively, for the pair of Tuesday and Wednesday, of Wednesday and Thursday, and of Thursday and Friday. In fact, if we use the average correlation, then hypothesis H_{01} cannot be rejected at the 5% level for these three pairs of adjacent weekdays.

The empirical tests confirm our previous findings that the day-of-the-week effect on correlation between stock indices is mainly due to differences between Monday and other weekdays. Correlations on Monday are significantly larger than those on other weekdays. If we exclude Monday returns and retest the hypothesis H_{02} across the other 4 weekdays, only 5 pairs and 4 pairs of indices can still reject the hypothesis at the 1% level and at the 5% level, respectively. However, the hypothesis of equal-average correlation of 15 pairs of indices across all weekdays except Monday cannot be rejected at the 10% level. Our results suggest that there is no day-of-the-week effect from Tuesday through Friday on average, but the effect does exist in some pairs of stock indices across these 4 weekdays.

For the correlations between sectoral indices and the HKI, the results show that four indices (CI, FI, PI, and UI) reject the hypothesis of equal correlation across 4 weekdays from Tuesday through Friday at the 1% level. The results suggest that HI and II have a stable relationship with the HKI from Tuesday through Friday. However, the hypothesis that the average correlation of six sectoral indices and HKI is the same across weekdays from Tuesday through Friday cannot be rejected at the 10% level. Furthermore, Table 2 shows that FI has the most unstable relationship with the HKI among all sectoral indices over the 5 weekdays. The change in correlation is significantly different from zero at least at the 10% level for all five possible pairs of adjacent weekdays.

Results presented in Table 2 show that stock indices are more correlated on Monday than on other weekdays. To further confirm our findings, we test the hypothesis that the correlation between stock indices is the same on Monday and on all other weekdays. That is, we group the daily returns from Tuesday through Friday as a non-Monday group. The average correlation among the six sectoral indices is 0.4436 while that between the HKI and each sectoral index is 0.673. Both values are smaller than the corresponding values on Monday. A normal distribution test on the hypothesis of equal correlation between Monday and non-Monday produces a Z value of 10.7847 and 10.8104 respectively for the average correlation among sectoral indices and that with the HKI. As both Z values are significantly positive at the 1% level, our findings that correlations on Monday are significantly greater than that on non-Monday is supported.

We then examine the correlations between returns on Monday and after holidays. In order to test formally the argument that Monday returns are more correlated than other weekdays returns because of the two more calendar days during the weekend, the following hypothesis is tested:

H_{03}:   Correlation between any pair of index returns on Monday is the same as that occurring in returns after holidays.

Test results are presented in Table 2. Hypothesis H_{03} cannot be rejected at the 10% level by eight pairs of stock indices. Only two pairs of stock indices can reject the hypothesis at the 1% level. Furthermore, the hypothesis of equal average correlation of 15 pairs of indices between Monday and holidays cannot be rejected at the 10% level. Our results suggest that returns after holidays are less correlated than those on Monday only for some pairs of indices but are not significantly different on average. For the correlation with HKI, only HI and UI can still reject the hypothesis of equal correlation between returns on Monday and after holidays at the 5% level. Hence, our prior argument that the longer the holding period in calendar days, the larger is the correlation between stock indices is supported statistically. Our results also suggest that HI and UI may need a longer time period to complete the full adjustment process, and hence, even with an extra calendar day from holiday they still cannot complete the whole adjustment process.

In order to examine further the hypothesis that various industrial sectors apparently correlate with each other differently across weekdays, the difference in correlation coefficients between any two adjacent weekdays are presented in Table 3 for all pairs of sectoral stock indices. Assuming that the mean difference in correlation follows a normal distribution, the mean difference is then tested to see whether it is significantly different from zero. The results show that the mean differences between correlation on Monday and Tuesday and Friday are significantly positive at the 1% level, showing that index returns on Monday are much more correlated than those on Tuesday and Friday. The mean difference in correlation between Monday and holidays is also significantly different from zero but with a smaller t value. However, the mean difference between Wednesday and Thursday, and between Thursday and Friday are not significantly different from zero at the 5% level. Our results support our previous findings that the day-of-the-week effect on correlations is mainly caused by correlations on Monday.

B.   Covariance and Correlation Matrices

Results in Tables 2 and 3 show that correlations among sectoral indices change significantly when the weekday varies from Monday to other weekdays. However, these results are only restricted to pairwise studies. In order to examine the stability of the whole correlation structure among six sectoral indices across weekdays, the following two hypotheses are tested:

Table 3. Differences in Correlation Coefficients Between Two Adjacent Weekdays

Stock Index	Mon–Tue	Tue–Wed	Wed–Thu	Thu–Fri	Fri–Mon	Mon & H-87
CI–FI	0.1321	0.2465	-0.1536	-0.0304	-0.1946	-0.0344
CI–HI	0.4607	0.0665	-0.0111	0.0476	-0.5637	0.0166
CI–II	0.2686	0.1327	-0.1067	-0.0459	-0.2487	-0.0195
CI–PI	0.0565	0.3047	-0.0769	-0.1288	-0.1555	-0.0526
CI–UI	0.0996	0.3563	-0.0488	-0.1176	-0.2895	0.1085
FI–HI	0.4491	-0.0128	0.0452	0.0687	-0.5502	0.0900
FI–II	0.3234	-0.0075	-0.1271	0.1080	-0.2968	0.0378
FI–PI	0.1210	0.0689	-0.1084	0.1297	-0.2112	-0.0118
FI–UI	0.1974	0.1053	-0.0514	0.0145	-0.2658	0.0387
HI–II	0.4082	0.1225	-0.0006	0.0972	-0.6273	0.1538
HI–PI	0.5063	-0.0152	0.0347	0.1630	-0.6888	0.1041
HI–UI	0.4970	-0.0079	0.0492	0.0237	-0.5620	0.1429
II–PI	0.2226	-0.0275	0.0343	0.0748	-0.3042	0.0484
II–UI	0.4152	-0.0715	0.0142	-0.0700	-0.2879	0.1920
PI–UI	0.1095	0.1566	0.0676	-0.0521	-0.2816	0.1363
Mean	0.2845	0.0945	-0.0293	0.0188	-0.3685	0.0634
S.D.	0.1560	0.1239	0.0696	0.0870	0.1699	0.0730
T-value	7.0649*	2.9536*	-1.6298	0.8379	-8.4011*	3.3622*

Notes: S.D. = standard deviation.

T-value = test for mean equal to zero.

H-87 = holiday returns with 1987 stock crash excluded.

* = significant at the 5% level.

GORDON Y. N. TANG

H_{04}:   The variance-covariance matrices of indices are the same across different weekdays.

H_{05}:   The correlation matrices of indices are the same across different weekdays.

The hypothesis of equal variance–covariance matrices (H_{04}) is tested by the Box M statistical test. Table 4 presents the test results and four sets of results are shown. The first set is the joint test of equal variance–covariance matrices across all 5 weekdays jointly. The hypothesis is rejected at the 1% level. The second set is the test of equal variance–covariance matrices between any two adjacent weekdays. All four possible pairs of adjacent weekdays reject the hypothesis at the 1% level. The third set of results is on the test of equal variance–covariance matrices between Monday and the other weekdays. The hypothesis is rejected at the 1% level in all cases. The fourth set of results is the equality of variance–covariance matrices between Monday, Friday, and holidays. Again, the hypothesis is rejected at the 1% level. The empirical results clearly show that the whole variance–covariance matrix among six sectoral indices is very unstable across different weekdays and between holidays and weekdays.

For the hypothesis of equal correlation matrices across different weekdays (H_{05}), the Box M test is used on the standard scores of stock returns. Table 4 presents the

Table 4. Tests of Equal Covariance Matrices and Correlation Matrices Across Different Days of The Week

Weekday	Covariance Matrix			Correlation Matrix		
	M	F	P value	M	F	P value
Mon to Fri[@]	1232.70	14.5790	0.0000*	974.93	11.5310	0.0000*
Mon–Tue	307.91	14.5390	0.0000*	358.74	16.9390	0.0000*
Tue–Wed	275.44	13.0090	0.0000*	159.76	7.5456	0.0000*
Wed–Thu	135.63	6.4076	0.0000*	40.43	1.9098	0.0072*
Thu–Fri	212.66	10.0460	0.0000*	59.32	2.8025	0.0000*
Mon–Wed	418.02	19.7420	0.0000*	597.15	28.2020	0.0000*
Mon–Thu	480.39	22.6880	0.0000*	545.13	25.7460	0.0000*
Mon–Fri	420.05	19.8380	0.0000*	562.43	26.5620	0.0000*
Mon–H-87	121.63	5.6229	0.0000*	50.96	2.3560	0.0004*
Fri–H-87	183.97	8.5061	0.0000*	126.83	5.8643	0.0000*

Notes: M = Box's M statistic.
     F = F statistic (approx. for M distribution).
     * – significant at the 5% level.
     + – significant at the 10% level.
     H-87 = holiday returns with 1987 stock crash excluded.
     Mon to Fri[@] = joint test of equal matrices across all weekdays.

test results on the hypothesis of equal correlation across different weekdays. The hypothesis of equal correlation across all 5 weekdays jointly is rejected at the 1% level. In fact, all four sets of results can reject the hypothesis of equal correlation matrices at the 1% level. Empirical results suggest that both the variance–covariance matrices and correlation matrices are very unstable across different weekdays. Hence, the results from the multivariate joint test confirm that the correlation matrix among stock indices in the Hong Kong market differs significantly across weekdays. As previous results have shown that the instability is caused by the very different properties on Monday from other weekdays, no further analysis is performed on the variance–covariance matrices and the correlation matrices.

C. Rogalski's Effect on Correlations

Our results have found a day-of-the-week effect (or Monday effect) in the correlations among stock indices. Following Rogalski's (1984) idea, we then extend the analysis to see whether a Rogalski effect exists in the correlations among stock indices. Our study is important in explaining the higher correlations found on Monday. If the Rogalski effect does not exist, then the argument based on longer calendar days for the higher correlations on Monday is further supported. However, we should bear in mind that our results on this Rogalski's effect cannot be overemphasized because of the limited number of observations of each weekday in January.

We divided the set of daily data into two groups: the January and non-January groups. For each group, the correlations among stock indices are calculated by day of the week and the hypothesis of equal correlation across weekdays is tested. The results are presented in Table 5. Panel A shows the results among the six sectoral indices. The hypothesis of equal correlation across all weekdays is rejected at the 1% level by all 15 pairs of stock indices in non-January. However, the same hypothesis can only be rejected by two pairs of stock indices (CI and PI, HI, and PI) at the 1% level in January. One other pair of stock indices (HI and II) rejects the hypothesis at the 5% level in January. Our results show that the weekly seasonal pattern in correlation is mainly attributed to the non-January months, suggesting that Rogalski's effect may exist. Looking at the correlations by weekdays, correlations on Monday are still the largest across weekdays in non-January for all 15 pairs of stock indices. In January, only in four pairs of stock indices (FI–HI, FI–PI, HI–II, and HI–PI) is the correlation largest on Monday. Our results show that Rogalski's effect exists in the correlations between stock indices in that the Monday correlation is largest only in February to December. The average correlation of the 15 pairs of stock indices clearly shows this result. In January, the Monday average correlation is only the third largest across all weekdays, and hence, the larger correlation on Tuesday and Thursday cannot be explained by the argument of longer calendar days. This anomaly cannot be explained satisfactory and is left for future research.

Table 5. Correlations Between Returns on Stock Indices By Weekday in January and Non-January

SI		Mon	Tue	Wed	Thu	Fri	All	Q
		Panel A: Correlations Between Returns on Sectoral Indices						
CI–FI	Jan	0.6616	0.5911	0.7680	0.7744	0.7378	0.6538	3.0021
	Non-Jan	0.7935	0.6748	0.3864	0.5532	0.5793	0.6016	87.4021#
	Z-value	−1.5198	−0.7579	3.3894#	2.2765*	1.5631	1.0919	
CI–HI	Jan	0.5551	0.6158	0.6656	0.6035	0.2965	0.5417	4.8968
	Non-Jan	0.7326	0.2520	0.1792	0.1947	0.1546	0.2976	150.5934#
	Z-value	−1.6450+	2.4918*	3.4667#	2.7963*	0.8241	3.7934#	
CI–II	Jan	0.4558	0.4156	0.6574	0.5931	0.5100	0.4809	2.6361
	Non-Jan	0.8105	0.5397	0.3716	0.4864	0.5391	0.5751	108.4954#
	Z-value	−3.3920#	−0.8729	2.2184*	0.8428	−0.2208	−1.6571+	
CI–PI	Jan	0.6282	0.6128	0.9142	0.8938	0.7327	0.6938	20.6129#
	Non-Jan	0.8994	0.8658	0.4991	0.5856	0.7247	0.7110	223.2307#
	Z-value	−3.8931#	−3.2588#	5.6008#	4.2903#	0.0940	−0.4310	
CI–UI	Jan	0.4323	0.5373	0.6831	0.7190	0.6873	0.5607	4.5891
	Non-Jan	0.8405	0.7449	0.3377	0.3896	0.5089	0.5574	196.9607#
	Z-value	−4.0499#	−1.9528+	2.6950*	2.7555*	1.5484	0.0595	
FI–HI	Jan	0.7971	0.5266	0.5438	0.5694	0.3517	0.5824	8.8381+
	Non-Jan	0.7261	0.2740	0.2849	0.2366	0.1782	0.3441	126.2659#
	Z-value	0.9067	1.6459+	1.7650+	2.2612*	1.0300	3.8902#	
FI–II	Jan	0.6435	0.5893	0.4661	0.6825	0.4792	0.5639	2.8165
	Non-Jan	0.8136	0.4731	0.4909	0.6145	0.5101	0.6300	92.8658#
	Z-value	−1.9904*	0.8795	−0.1797	0.6560	−0.2247	−1.3022	
FI–PI	Jan	0.8705	0.8612	0.7542	0.7297	0.6783	0.7755	6.7500
	Non-Jan	0.8385	0.7083	0.6382	0.7612	0.6251	0.7412	54.7293#
	Z-value	0.6348	2.2409*	1.2682	−0.3946	0.5095	1.0233	
FI–UI	Jan	0.6605	0.6456	0.6622	0.6648	0.7036	0.6692	0.2097
	Non-Jan	0.8174	0.6085	0.4891	0.5426	0.5263	0.6236	85.7073#
	Z-value	−1.8934+	0.3309	1.4596	1.0794	1.5913	0.9918	
HI–II	Jan	0.7378	0.6268	0.5255	0.5702	0.1704	0.58481	0.3998*
	Non-Jan	0.7982	0.3814	0.2550	0.2559	0.1688	0.3799	194.2740#
	Z-value	−0.7898	1.8090+	1.8012+	2.1530*	0.0088	3.4148#	
HI–PI	Jan	0.8405	0.6930	0.6072	0.6816	0.2904	0.6575	14.1770#
	Non-Jan	0.8257	0.3096	0.3263	0.2897	0.1355	0.3882	231.6460#
	Z-value	0.2583	2.8858#	2.0391	2.9772#	0.8944	4.7933#	
HI–UI	Jan	0.5242	0.7495	0.4659	0.6274	0.4695	0.5612	5.0670
	Non-Jan	0.7360	0.2070	0.2257	0.1687	0.1562	0.2953	155.0654#
	Z-value	−1.9161+	4.1200#	1.5340	3.1610#	1.9352+	4.1797#	
II–PI	Jan	0.7394	0.7354	0.7619	0.5284	0.5425	0.6678	5.4062
	Non-Jan	0.8637	0.6254	0.6545	0.6313	0.5559	0.7115	98.7221#
	Z-value	−1.9107+	1.1182	1.2135	−0.8682	−0.1059	−1.0548	

(*continued*)

Table 5. Continued

SI		Mon	Tue	Wed	Thu	Fri	All	Q
II–UI	Jan	0.3640	0.7571	0.4140	0.6546	0.6442	0.5246	8.3692+
	Non-Jan	0.8115	0.3316	0.4394	0.4113	0.4863	0.5411	134.2642#
	Z-value	–3.9964#	3.4869#	–0.1730	1.9298+	1.2875	–0.2929	
PI–UI	Jan	0.6856	0.8351	0.6125	0.6090	0.5663	0.6611	6.6142
	Non-Jan	0.8653	0.7352	0.5845	0.5120	0.5742	0.6780	129.2525#
	Z-value	–2.5275*	1.4320	0.2441	0.7913	–0.0646	–0.3873	
Avg	Jan	0.6397	0.6528	0.6334	0.6601	0.5240	0.6119	
	Non-Jan	0.8115	0.5154	0.4108	0.4422	0.4282	0.5384	
	Z-value	–1.9912*	1.1365	1.7314+	1.7733+	0.6828	1.3938	

Panel B: Correlations Between Returns on HKI and Sectoral Indices

SI		Mon	Tue	Wed	Thu	Fri	All	Q
CI	Jan	0.6354	0.5947	0.8667	0.9473	0.9025	0.7147	30.2861#
	Non-Jan	0.9202	0.9161	0.7299	0.6430	0.8009	0.7875	195.7729#
	Z-value	–4.4756#	–4.7554#	2.1811*	5.8073#	2.1157*	–2.1287*	
FI	Jan	0.9045	0.8278	0.7897	0.8441	0.8836	0.8458	3.7243
	Non-Jan	0.8806	0.7706	0.7004	0.8692	0.7467	0.8124	73.4046#
	Z-value	0.6297	0.8621	1.1302	–0.5279	2.3461*	1.3569	
HI	Jan	0.8407	0.6536	0.5936	0.7283	0.4272	0.6752	10.4513*
	Non-Jan	0.8194	0.3248	0.3390	0.2923	0.2056	0.4086	204.6502#
	Z-value	0.3659	2.4051*	1.8408+	3.4799#	1.3635	4.8885#	
II	Jan	0.7891	0.6582	0.5909	0.6425	0.6657	0.6770	2.7466
	Non-Jan	0.8854	0.5931	0.6563	0.6707	0.6454	0.7388	114.2843#
	Z-value	–1.7656+	0.5803	–0.5980	–0.2761	0.1956	–1.5707	
PI	Jan	0.9728	0.8508	0.8656	0.9349	0.8098	0.8885	21.7346#
	Non-Jan	0.9661	0.9448	0.8840	0.8781	0.8680	0.9217	134.8976#
	Z-value	0.5965	–2.8229#	–0.4379	1.8328+	–1.0906	–2.3467*	
UI	Jan	0.7631	0.8121	0.7007	0.7873	0.8620	0.7794	3.4057
	Non-Jan	0.9225	0.8558	0.6562	0.6087	0.7173	0.7682	198.0233#
	Z-value	–3.2069#	–0.7805	0.4603	1.9928*	2.1950*	0.3527	
Avg	Jan	0.8176	0.7329	0.7345	0.8141	0.7585	0.7634	
	Non-Jan	0.8990	0.7342	0.6610	0.6603	0.6640	0.7395	
	Z-value	–1.6925+	–0.0154	0.8026	1.9271+	1.0599	0.6954	

Notes: SI = stock index.
Non-Jan = Non-January.
Z-value = test of equal correlation between Jan and Non-Jan.
Q = Q-statistic for testing equality of correlations across weekdays.
Avg = average correlation.
# - significant at the 1% level.
* - significant at the 5% level.
+ - significant at the 10% level.

Panel B of Table 5 presents the correlations between the HKI and each sectoral index. Again, the hypothesis of equal correlation across all weekdays is rejected at the 1% level for all six sectoral indices in non-January. In January, only two indices (CI and PI) can reject the same hypothesis at the 1% level. HI can reject the hypothesis at the 5% level. The results are similar to those in Panel A. However, for the average correlation between the HKI and the six sectoral indices, Monday correlation is highest in both January and non-January months. For the individual sectoral indices, only CI and UI do not have a larger correlation on Monday in January. The four remaining sectoral indices have the largest correlation occurs on Monday in January, which is the same case as all indices in the non-January months. Hence, Rogalski's effect is weaker in the correlation with the market, HKI.

D. January Effect on Correlations

The previous section has found Rogalski's effect to exist in the correlations among stock indices. As we have found that the weekly seasonal pattern in correlations among stock indices does not exist in January, we extend the analysis to see whether a January effect exists in the correlations. We divided the set of daily data into two groups: the January and non-January groups. The hypothesis of equal correlation between these two groups is tested, and the results are presented in Table 5. Panel A shows the results among the six sectoral indices. For the overall daily returns, the hypothesis of equal correlation is rejected by five pairs of stock indices at the 1% level. In all five cases, the January correlations are larger. The five pairs of indices all include the HI, suggesting that the HI is more correlated with the market in January. The results are supported in Panel B of Table 5. The hypothesis of equal correlation between the HI and HKI in January and in non-January is rejected at the 1% level. The correlation in January is more than 50% higher than that in non-January and the difference is likely economically significant. Panel B also shows that two other indices, CI and PI, are higher correlated with the HKI in non-January, but their correlations in other months are still large. Looking at the average correlation, both Panels A and B show that, although the average correlation is higher in January, the hypothesis of equal correlation cannot be rejected at the 10% level, indicating that the existing January effect in correlation is not market-wide but only industry-specific.

Besides the overall daily returns, we also examine the correlations among stock indices in January and non-January by weekdays. The results presented in Panel A of Table 5 show that the average correlation of the 15 pairs of stock indices is significantly lower in January on Monday at the 5% level but is significantly higher in January on Wednesday and Thursday at the 10% level. On Monday, 12 pairs of stock indices are less correlated in January and of these 12 pairs, 4, 2, and 4 pairs are significant at the 1%, 5%, and 10%, respectively. On Tuesday, 11 pairs (7 pairs are significant at the 10% level) of stock indices are more correlated in January and in the remaining four pairs of indices, two of them are significantly less correlated in January at the 10% level. On Wednesday and Thursday, only two pairs of indices are less correlated in January but none of them are significant at the 10% level. Of the remaining 13 pairs of indices, 7 and 9 pairs are significantly more correlated in January at the 10% level on Wednesday and Thursday, respectively. On Friday, 11 pairs of indices are more correlated in January and of these seven pairs, only one is significant at the 10% level. Our results suggest that a January effect in correlations between sectoral indices exists but this anomaly is valid from Tuesday through Friday only and on Monday, a reversed January effect occurs since the January correlations are smaller.

Panel B of Table 5 presents the correlations between the HKI and each sectoral index by weekday. The hypothesis of equal average correlation in January and in non-January is rejected at the 10% level on Monday and Thursday only. However, the result is just the opposite on the 2 weekdays. On Monday, the average correlation is lower while on Thursday it is higher in January. The results confound those presented in Panel A on correlations among sectoral indices. However, this January effect differs significantly across sectoral indices. CI is significantly less correlated with the HKI in January on Monday and Tuesday but is significantly more correlated on the other 3 weekdays at the 5% level. FI is significantly more correlated with the HKI in January only on Friday while HI is significantly more correlated in January on Tuesday, Wednesday, and Friday. II and UI are significantly less correlated with the HKI in January on Monday while PI is significantly less correlated on Tuesday. PI is significantly more correlated with the HKI in January on Thursday and UI is significantly more correlated in January on both Thursday and Friday.

V. CONCLUSIONS

This paper has examined the day-of-the-week effect on correlations among the six sectoral indices for the first time in the Hong Kong stock market. Empirical results show that stock indices are most correlated on Monday, and to a slightly lesser extent for returns after holidays. The results support the argument that the degree of correlation is directly related to the number of calendar days used in calculating stock returns. The results are caused by the fact that more information is accumulated over the weekend (or after the holidays) than just overnight and that industrial sectors adjust to each other with a time lag, resulting in a smaller correlation on Tuesday to Friday. However, this explanation can only be applied to the non-January months since, in January, Monday correlation is no longer largest for most pairs of stock indices. This effect on correlation cannot be explained satisfactory and more research using longer sample periods is needed in the future.

The Hotel Index is the least correlated with other indices, particularly on weekdays other than Monday, showing that the hotel industry is very different from the other sectoral industries. The hypothesis of equal correlation is rejected for all pairs of stock indices across all weekdays. Furthermore, the hypothesis of equal variance–covariance matrices across all weekdays, and of equal correlation matrices can also be rejected at the 1% level. Empirical results suggest that the degree of diversification benefits changes across weekdays. Our results further show that a January effect in correlations among sectoral indices exists but this anomaly is valid from Tuesday through Friday only and, on Monday, a reversed January effect occurs since the January correlations are smaller. Hence, our empirical results provide new evidence on the existence of anomalies in returns in the industrial sectors of the Hong Kong stock market.

ACKNOWLEDGMENTS

An earlier version of this paper was presented at the Sixth Conference on Pacific Basin Business, Economics and Finance on 28–29 May, 1998 in Hong Kong. The author thanks the participants and two anonymous referees of this journal for their comments and suggestions.

REFERENCES

Aggarwal, R., & Rivoli, P. (1989). Seasonal and day-of-the-week effects in four emerging stock markets. *The Financial Review, 24*, 541–550.

Box, G.E.P. (1949). A general distribution theory for a class of likelihood criteria. *Biometrika, 36*, 317–346.

Condoyanni, L., O'Hanlon, J., & Ward, C. (1987). Day of the week effects on stock returns: international evidence. *Journal of Business Finance and Accounting, 14*, 159–174.

Cross, F. (1973). The behavior of stock prices on Fridays and Mondays. *Financial Analysts Journal, 29*, 67–69.

Fama, E. F. (1965). The behavior of stock market prices. *Journal of Business, 38*, 34–105.

French, K. R. (1980). Stock returns and the weekend effect. *Journal of Financial Economics, 8*, 55–69.

Gultekin, M.N., & Gultekin, N.B. (1983). Stock market seasonality: international evidence. *Journal of Financial Economics, 12*, 469–481.

Ho, Y.K. (1990). Stock return seasonalities in Asia Pacific markets. *Journal of International Financial Management and Accounting, 2*, 44–77.

Ho, Y.K., & Cheung, Y.L. (1994). Seasonal pattern in volatility in asian stock markets. *Applied Financial Economics, 4*, 61–67.

Jaffe, J., & Westerfield, R. (1985). The week-end effect in common stock returns: the international evidence. *Journal of Finance, 40*, 433–454.

Jennrich, R.I. (1970). An analytical examination of the intervalling effect on skewness and other moments. *Journal of Financial and Quantitative Analysis, 15*, 1121–1127.

Kaplanis, E.C. (1988). Stability and forecasting of the comovement measures of international stock market returns. *Journal of International Money and Finance, 7*, 63–75.

Keim, D.B. (1983). Size-related anomalies and stock return seasonality: empirical evidence. *Journal of Financial Economics, 12*, 13–32.

Keim, B.D., & Stambaugh, R.F. (1984). A further investigation of the weekend effect in stock returns. *Journal of Finance, 39*, 819–840.

Mardia, K.V., Kent, J.T., & Bibby, J.M. (1979). *Multivariate analysis*, Academic Press.

Meric, I., & Meric, G. (1989). Potential gains from international portfolio diversification and intertemporal stability and seasonality in international stock market relationships. *Journal of Banking and Finance, 13*, 627–640.

Pearson, E.S. (1969). Some comments on the accuracy of Box's approximation to the distribution of M. *Biometrika, 56,* 219–220.

Rogalski, R.J. (1984). New findings regarding day-of-the-week returns over trading and non-trading periods: a note. *Journal of Finance, 39,* 1603–1614.

Rozeff, M.S., & Kinney, W.R. (1976). Capital market seasonality: the case of stock returns. *Journal of Financial Economics, 3,* 397–402.

Snedecor, G. W., & Cochran, W.G. (1976). *Statistical methods.* Ames, IW: Iowa State University Press.

Tang, G.Y.N. (1995). Intertemporal stability in international stock market relationships: a revisit. *Quarterly Review of Economics and Finance, 35,* 579–593.

Tang, G.Y.N., & Kwok, J.K.H. (1996). Seasonality in international portfolio diversification. *Advances in Pacific Basin Business, Economics and Finance, 2.*

Wahab, M., & Lashgari, M. (1993). Covariance stationarity of international equity markets returns: recent evidence. *Financial Review, 28,* 239–260.

Wong, K.A., Hui, T.K., & Chan, C.Y. (1992). Day-of-the-week effects: evidence from developing stock markets. *Applied Financial Economics, 2,* 49–56.

PORTFOLIO ALLOCATION AND THE LENGTH OF THE INVESTMENT HORIZON

R. Douglas Van Eaton

ABSTRACT

We model an investor's asset allocation decision for an investment horizon of variable length with a (mean-variance) utility function that is more general than those of previous models. We demonstrate that such an investor may rationally prefer larger equity allocations early in his working years and smaller equity allocations as retirement approaches, in contrast to the frequent claim that portfolio allocations to equities should be invariant to the length of the investment horizon. The model provides a theoretic basis for common practitioner and institutional advice and a rational basis for observed investor behavior. The model is easily extended to account for other factors that may influence equity allocations such as labor supply flexibility and mean reversion in returns.

Advances in Investment Analysis and Portfolio Management, Volume 7, pages 41–54.
Copyright © 2000 by JAI Press Inc.
All rights of reproduction in any form reserved.
ISBN: 0-7623-0658-0

I. INTRODUCTION

Debate about the effect of the length the investment horizon on an investor's optimal equity allocation has continued for almost 30 years. We present new analysis of the issues involved and model the asset allocation decision for a mean-variance utility maximizing investor. The model results demonstrate that an investor may rationally prefer a larger risky asset allocation when faced with a longer investment horizon. This is contrary to frequent claims that the length of the investment horizon should have no effect on optimal asset allocations, but is consistent with actual investor behavior and offers theoretic support for common practitioner advice. The model captures the intuition of the practitioner argument that preferred equities allocations may be larger at longer horizons if the increased attractiveness of larger expected (holding period) returns outweighs the investor aversion to the increase in returns variance.

Arguably, the most influential author in the ongoing debate about the effect of the investment horizon on asset allocation has been Samuelson (1969, 1974, 1989, 1991, 1994). Samuelson (1969)[1] presents a model of asset allocation over several discrete periods with the result that the investment horizon has no effect on the optimal risky asset allocation. The contrary position, that larger risky asset allocations are preferable when investment horizons are longer, is commonly espoused by practitioners and in mutual fund sales literature.[2] Bodie and Crane (1997) present empirical evidence that investors tend to hold larger equity allocations in retirement accounts early in their working years, consistent with practitioner advice and inconsistent with the claim that preferred equity allocations are invariant to the length of the investment horizon.

Several theoretical arguments have been made in support of the practitioner view of the horizon effect. The claim that equities are less risky at longer horizons because the variance of geometric mean return decreases, was criticized by those who argued that the variance of holding period returns is the appropriate risk measure.[3] A separate argument for the view that equity allocations should be larger when investment horizons are longer is based on the decreased probability that equity returns will fall short of some benchmark rate of return (shortfall risk) when anticipated holding periods are longer.[4] Portfolio rankings based on shortfall probabilities, however, are sensitive to the benchmark chosen and imply plunging behavior—100% allocations to either equities or the risk-free asset.[5]

A preference for smaller equities allocations at shorter horizons, due to greater equities shortfall probabilities, is at the heart of related argument as well. Tversky and Kahneman (1991) have labeled investor sensitivity to the probability of negative nominal returns as "loss aversion." Benzarti and Thaler (1995) employ this concept in a proposed explanation of the size of the equilibrium equity-risk premium. They argue that investors' aversion to nominal losses combined with a tendency to focus on returns over (irrationally) short investment horizons tend to reduce equity allocations in the aggregate and consequently increase the equilibrium equity-risk premium.

Samuelson (1991) and Bodie, Merton, and W. Samuelson (1992) present alternative explanations for rational expected utility maximizing investors to prefer larger equity allocations at longer horizons. Samuelson (1991) presents a two-period example in which the introduction of mean reversion in risky asset returns affects investors' preferred risky asset allocations differently depending on their degree of risk aversion. Bodie, Merton, and W. Samuelson (1992) present a model in which an investor's ability to adjust the amount of labor supplied (in response to investment outcomes that are better or worse than expected) drives a preference for larger equity allocations early in investors' working years when labor supply flexibility is assumed to be greater. The authors also argue that early in investors' working years their capital is concentrated in relatively safe human capital, so that adequate portfolio risk is only achieved by placing a large fraction of their investable wealth in equity securities, the more risky asset in the model.

While these various explanations for an investor preference for larger equities allocations at longer horizons are plausible, whether and to what extent they actually motivate investor behavior is an open question. We present alternative analysis, based on mean-variance utility, that provides a rational basis for such an investor preference without introducing changes in labor supply flexibility over time, assuming that human capital is a relatively safe asset, or focusing on the probability of nominal losses as a portfolio selection criterion. If investors are indeed myopic, as Benzarti and Thaler (1995) argue, the results here are consistent with decreased aggregate equity allocations as a consequence. That is, loss aversion need not be assumed to support their conclusion. The effect of labor supply flexibility on investor preferences for risk and expected return can be incorporated in the model through investor-specific risk aversion parameters.

The remainder of the paper is organized as follows: In the next section we present a model of a mean-variance utility maximizer's asset allocation decision for an investment horizon of variable length. We then derive a necessary and sufficient condition for investor indifference to changes in the length of the investment horizon, and show that a rational investor may prefer either an increased or a decreased risky asset allocation in response to a longer anticipated holding period. Following that, we present analysis of the effects of mean reversion in returns and of the effect of an investor preference for returns skewness on the model results. Conclusions are in a final section.

II. A MODEL OF THE ASSET ALLOCATION DECISION

We model an investor's portfolio allocation decision for an investment horizon of variable length. In order to focus solely on the effect of the length of the investment horizon, we consider changes in an investor's anticipated holding period while holding preferences constant. Just as the utility of an investor with a 1-year horizon is commonly assumed to be unaffected by hourly or daily expected returns and variances, we assume that an investor's utility is a function of the means and variances of returns over his anticipated holding period.

We assume initially that returns are independent across periods so that the horizon effect can be examined separately from any effect of autocorrelation in periodic returns. Under these conditions we examine the effects of a change in the length of the investment horizon (anticipated holding period) on optimal asset allocations. While an investor may have multiple motives for saving and several investment accounts with different anticipated holding periods, we focus on the effect of the length of the investment horizon for a single account and assume that allocation decisions in such accounts are independent of each other. The model construction is arguably appropriate for an investor's decision about the allocation of retirement funds, as these funds are, to a large extent, not commingled with other savings. Given the penalties and tax consequences of early withdrawal, it is likely that retirement account funds are expected to be used for consumption beginning only at retirement.

Consider an investor who maximizes utility over the first two moments of the portfolio returns distribution by selecting α, the proportion of portfolio wealth invested in a risky asset. The remaining fraction of the account $(1 - \alpha)$ is invested in a riskless alternative asset. For a holding period of length t the expected return of the risky asset is denoted $\mu_{Rm(t)}$, the standard deviation of the risky asset return is $\sigma_{Rm(t)}$, and the (certain) return on the riskless asset is $Rf(t)$.

For any particular choice of α, expected portfolio return over horizon t is then:

$$\mu_{Rp(t)} = \alpha \mu_{Rm(t)} + (1 - \alpha)Rf(t) \tag{1}$$

and the standard deviation of portfolio returns over horizon t is

$$\sigma_{Rp(t)} = \alpha \sigma_{Rm(t)} \tag{2}$$

The investor's utility function is assumed to be of the form:

$$U = \mu_{Rp(t)} - \frac{A}{2\gamma}(\sigma_{Rp(t)})^{2\gamma} \tag{3}$$

The commonly used (quadratic) mean-variance utility function

$$U = \mu_{Rp} - \frac{A}{2}(\sigma_{Rp}^2) \tag{4}$$

is equivalent to this more general form with t and γ both set to 1.

Explicitly introducing t allows for comparative statics analysis with respect to the length of the anticipated holding period. Allowing γ to take values different from one permits changes the curvature of utility isoquants in mean-standard deviation space. Of interest here, using values of γ less than 1 reduces the curvature of utility isoquants compared to the quadratic utility case, and reduces the change in the trade-off between risk and return for movement along a particular utility isoquant. $\gamma = 1/2$ corresponds to the case of linear utility isoquants. The restriction that $\gamma > 1/2$ excludes the linear case and insures that investors' preferences will be convex, as is required under standard rationality assumptions. One feature of mean-variance portfolio choice that is unchanged by the more general specification of investor utility is that preferred portfolio allocations are invariant to changes in wealth, since rankings are based on percentage returns and variances, rather than dollar returns and variances.

Under the above assumptions we will prove the theorem that an investor who maximizes utility of the form:

$$U = \mu_{Rp(t)} - (A/2\gamma)(\sigma^{2\gamma}_{Rp(t)})$$

by his choice of α, the percentage portfolio allocation to a risky asset will have an optimal risky asset allocation which is invariant to the length of the anticipated holding period (t), if and only if:

$$\frac{[\mu_{Rm(t)} - Rf(t)]'}{\mu_{Rm(t)} - Rf(t)} \frac{\delta^2_{Rm(t)}}{[\delta^2_{Rm(t)}]'} = \gamma \tag{5}$$

We also prove a corollary that the optimal risky asset allocation will be increasing (decreasing) at longer horizons as:

$$\frac{[\mu_{Rm(t)} - Rf(t)]'}{\mu_{Rm(t)} - Rf(t)} \frac{\delta^2_{Rm(t)}}{[\delta^2_{Rm(t)}]'} > (<)\gamma \tag{6}$$

The problem faced by the investor is:

$$\max U = \mu_{Rp(t)} - (A/2\gamma)(\sigma_{Rp(t)})^{2\gamma}$$

where $\mu_{Rp(t)} = \alpha\mu_{Rm(t)} + (1 - \alpha)Rf(t)$ and $\sigma_{Rp(t)} = \alpha\sigma_{Rm(t)}$ for $A > 0$ (risk aversion) and $\gamma > 1/2$ (convex preferences).

This is equivalent to:

$$\max U = \alpha\mu_{Rm(t)} + (1 - \alpha)Rf(t) - \alpha^{2\gamma}(\sigma_{Rm(t)})^{2\gamma} \tag{7}$$

A necessary FOC for a maximum w.r.t. α is:

$$U'_\alpha = [\mu_{Rm(t)} - Rf(t)] - A \, \alpha^{(2\gamma-1)}(\sigma_{Rm(t)})^{2\gamma} = 0 \tag{8}$$

so that for the optimal risky asset allocation α^*:

$$\alpha^{*(2\gamma-1)} = \frac{\mu_{Rm(t)} - Rf(t)}{A\delta^2_{Rm(t)}} \tag{9}$$

The SOC for a maximum at α^* is:

$$U''_\alpha = -(2\gamma - 1)A(\sigma_{Rm(t)})^{2\gamma}\alpha^{*(2\gamma-2)} < 0 \tag{10}$$

which is satisfied for positive values of α^*, since $A > 0$ and $\gamma > 1/2$. For negative values of α^* that satisfy the FOC (Equation 8), the sign of the SOC is changed and α^* is the solution for a minimum utility portfolio. A negative α corresponds to a net short position in the risky asset. Such a (short equities) portfolio is dominated in mean/standard deviation space by the risk-free asset, and by any portfolio with a risky asset allocation between 0 and the absolute value of α^*.

If the optimal risky asset allocation (α^*) is to be constant with respect to the length of the investment horizon (t); it must also be the case that $\alpha^{*(2\gamma-1)}$ (the left-hand term in Equation 9) is invariant to changes in the length of the investment horizon. We can derive the condition for such invariance by differentiating the right-hand side of Equation 9 with respect to t and setting it equal to zero. This yields:

$$\frac{\partial\alpha^{*(2\gamma-1)}}{\partial t} =$$

$$\frac{\{2A(\sigma_{Rm(t)})^{2\gamma}[\mu'_{Rm(t)} - Rf(t)'] - [\mu_{Rm(t)} - Rf(t)]2A\gamma(\sigma_{Rm(t)})^{2\gamma-2}(\sigma^2_{Rm(t)})'\}}{[A(\sigma_{Rm(t)})^{2\gamma}]^2} = 0 \tag{11}$$

which reduces to:

$$\frac{[\mu'_{Rm(t)} - Rf(t)'] - [\mu_{Rm(t)} - Rf(t)]\gamma(\sigma_{Rm(t)})^{-2}(\sigma^2_{Rm(t)})'}{0.5A(\sigma_{Rm(t)})^{2\gamma}} = 0 \tag{12}$$

Since the denominator of Equation 12, is positive, the numerator of Equation 12 must equal zero and we can derive the condition for invariance of the optimal risky asset allocation to the investor's time horizon (t), as:

$$\frac{\dfrac{[\mu_{Rm(t)} - Rf(t)]'}{\mu_{Rm(t)} - Rf(t)}}{\dfrac{[\delta^2_{Rm(t)}]'}{\delta^2_{Rm(t)}}} = \gamma \tag{13}$$

which proves the theorem.

The corollary follows from an examination of Equation 11. Since the denominator is positive, the sign of $\alpha^{*2\gamma-1}/\partial t$ is $>$ or < 0 as:

$$\frac{[\mu_{Rm(t)} - Rf(t)]'}{\mu_{Rm(t)} - Rf(t)} \frac{\delta^2_{Rm(t)}}{[\delta^2_{Rm(t)}]'} > (<)\gamma \tag{14}$$

III. IMPLICATIONS OF THE THEOREM FOR OPTIMAL ASSET ALLOCATION

The term in the left-hand side of the allocation invariance condition (Equation 13) is the ratio of the percentage change in market excess returns to the percentage change in the variance of the market (excess) return in response to an incremental increase in the investment horizon. The parameter γ in utility functions of the form:

$$U = \mu_{Rp(t)} - (A/2\gamma)(\sigma_{Rp(t)})^{2\gamma}$$

determines the curvature of the utility isoquants in mean-standard deviation space and also affects the orientation of the curves by entering the scalar $A/2\gamma$. Overall, a larger γ means that greater increases in expected returns are required to hold utility constant for successive (incremental) increases in portfolio returns variance.

Since the utility function itself is assumed to be independent of the length of the investment horizon, the convexity assumption ($\gamma > 1/2$) together with the fact that expected returns and returns variances are larger at longer horizons, insures that the investor's risk return tradeoff (marginal rate of substitution) changes with the length of the investment horizon. For larger values of γ, the subjective trade-off between expected return and standard deviation changes more rapidly with increases in the investment horizon, as both expected returns and returns variance increase.

The result has strong intuitive appeal. The effect of the investment horizon on preferred portfolio proportions is seen to depend on both the change in expected returns/variance opportunities presented by the market at incrementally longer horizons and on the change in the investor's subjective trade-off between expected return and returns variance. For optimal risky asset allocations to remain constant over longer horizons, expected excess return and return variance must change in proportions which (fortuitously) match the change in an investor's subjective trade-off between expected returns and returns variance at the higher levels of both associated with the longer horizons.

The corollary has an intuitive interpretation as well. When the ratio of the percentage increase in excess returns to the percentage increase in variance is greater than γ, the opportunities presented by longer holding periods are more attractive to an investor (according to his preferences as express in γ). In response to this increase in the relative attractiveness of risky asset returns, an investor will choose a larger allocation to the risky asset.

If we consider a discrete rebalancing period, the results are unaffected. By construction, the investor's level of wealth does not affect his allocation decision. Only the change in risk–return opportunities, due to the decreased length of the (remaining) holding period at each rebalancing, will impact an investor's allocation decision. As retirement, approaches, investors' preferences may dictate that their risky asset allocations decrease, consistent with actual investor behavior and common practitioner advice.

For illustration, we consider some numerical values for the ratio in the left-hand side of the horizon invariance condition (Equation 13). For stable independent returns distributions, expected compound returns increase more slowly than returns variance.[6] Using values of 10% for expected risky asset returns, 20% for their standard deviation, and 5% for the riskless rate, the value of the ratio in Equation 13 is approximately 0.89 at a 1-year horizon.

An investor with $\gamma = 1$ (quadratic utility) will optimally select smaller risky asset allocations as the investment horizon is increased incrementally beyond 1 year.[7] By the corollary, investors with γ less than 0.89 will prefer larger risky asset allocations for horizons incrementally longer than 1 year. The same cannot be said, however, for all longer horizons. For the assumed returns distribution, the ratio in Equation 13 decreases at longer horizons and is less than 0.5 at a horizon of 18 years.[8] This value is significant since γ must be greater than 0.5 for rational preferences. The implication is that (for these assumed returns parameters) no rational mean-variance utility maximizing investor will increase his preferred risky asset allocation beyond the 18-year levels. With γ greater than 0.5, the horizon at which this change in the sign of the effect of longer horizons on the optimal risky asset allocation takes place is less than 18 years. The intuition of this example is that at some relevant horizons, rational investors may find that the increase in expected returns for longer holding periods does not compensate for the increase in returns variance and equities are becoming a less attractive alternative.

One objection to mean-variance analysis is that it fails to consider the skewness of the returns distribution. One example of such an objection in the current context is argument in Hodges and Yoder (1996). The authors argue that stochastic dominance analysis is superior to mean-variance analysis for addressing the effect of the investment horizon on risk and for addressing the time diversification question in general. They present simulation evidence that equity returns do not stochastically dominate the returns of other asset classes. The authors are correct in arguing that if equities returns stochastically dominate those of other asset classes at sufficiently long horizons, any rational investor would prefer a 100% allocation to equities at that horizon. However, the converse does not logically follow. The fact that equities returns do not stochastically dominate those of other asset classes at longer horizons does not preclude a rational preference for increased equities allocations at longer horizons. As Hodges and Yoder (1996) do not consider possible changes in allocations, but only the dominance condition, their analysis does not address this point.

Several authors have examined the role of returns skewness and skewness preference on efficient portfolio construction for moment based utility functions.[9] While consideration of additional moments of the returns distribution increases the complexity of the analysis, the implications are not qualitatively different from those of the mean-variance utility model. For illustration of this point, assume that equity returns skewness is increasing at longer horizons, as it is in the Hodges and Yoder (1996) simulations, and also that investors prefer greater positive skewness.

Under these assumptions the increased attractiveness of equities at longer horizons due to larger expected returns is augmented by the expectation of increasingly (positively) skewed returns for a mean-variance-skewness utility maximizer. Although returns variance is increased for longer assumed holding periods, an investor who found that the concomitant increase in expected returns more than compensates for this increase in variance, will find equities returns even more attractive at longer horizons due to the increase in skewness. The three-moment equivalent of our allocation invariance condition would thus equate an investor's marginal disutility from increased returns variance to the marginal utility derived from increases in both expected returns and returns skewness at longer horizons. The main result of the mean-variance analysis, that an investor may rationally prefer larger equities allocations at longer horizons, is not invalidated by introducing a preference for returns skewness.

It is clear that the difference between the Samuelson (1969) allocation invariance result and the current result cannot be explained by preferences for skewness. We need only consider the case of normally distributed returns to illustrate this point. The assumption of normally distributed returns, while violated in practice, is theoretically admitted in both models. Since the implications of the two models are unchanged when returns are assumed to be normally distributed, it follows that changes in returns skewness at longer horizons cannot explain the difference in model results.

The assumption in the Samuelson (1969) model that drives the allocation invariance result is that investor preferences are characterized by constant relative risk aversion. The class of utility functions characterized by constant relative risk aversion is the class of power utility functions:

$$U(W) = \frac{W^\gamma}{\gamma}$$

where W is end-of-period wealth. This class of utility functions is defined for $0 < \gamma < 1$ and $\gamma < 0$. The special case of $\gamma = 0$ is defined in the limit and is equivalent to log utility, $U(W) = \log W$.[10]

The assumption that investors have power utility of wealth functions, together with the assumption of returns independence, leads directly to the Samuelson (1969) result. To see this clearly, consider a two-period investor who will realize portfolio outcomes (wealth relatives) $W_1(x_1)$ and $W_2(x_2)$ that depend on the choices of risky asset weights x_1 and x_2. That is, the investor is assumed to rebalance the portfolio at the end of the first period, selecting x_2. As optimal portfolio allocations are invariant to initial wealth, beginning wealth can be normalized to 1 so that the two-period wealth outcome is $W_1(x_1)W_2(x_2)$. The expected (power) utility of wealth at the end of two periods is then:

$$E\left(\frac{W_1'(x_1)W_2'(x_2)}{\gamma}\right) = \frac{1}{\gamma}E[W_1'(x_1)W_2'(x_2)] \tag{15}$$

Since $W_1(x_1)$ and $W_2(x_2)$ are assumed to be independently distributed, it is equivalent to maximize $E[W_1'(x_1)]E[W_2'(x_2)]$.

Under the independence assumption, the maximization decisions are separable for the two horizons. Since any change in wealth at the end of the first period does not affect the optimal portfolio allocations at the second horizon; preferences, returns distributions, and optimal allocations are identical for each choice of X_i. The expected utility of the portfolio is maximized by selecting the same risky asset weight for any single period; the number of remaining periods has no effect on the allocation decision and the Samuelson (1969) horizon invariance result obtains.

In the (special) case of log utility, independence of periodic returns is not required for the allocation invariance result to obtain. The investor's problem is to maximize:

$$E[\log(W_1(x_1)W_2(x_2))] = E(\log W_1(x_2) + \log W_2(x_2)) = E[\log W_1(x_1)] + E[\log W_2(x_2)]$$

Again we can see that the two-period maximization problem can be represented as two separate single-period maximization problems. These two problems are solved by the same optimal risky asset allocation as long as W_1 and W_2 are identically distributed. Independence is not required for the optimal risky asset allocation to be the same at each rebalancing opportunity in this case. Consequently, as in Samuelson (1991), a log utility investor's optimal risky asset allocation is invariant to the number of investment periods remaining, even when the assumption of independent returns is relaxed in favor of mean reversion in periodic returns.

This second result emphasizes the fact that the assumed form of the investor utility function can drive the model results. We argue that the Samuelson (1969) result should be much more narrowly interpreted than it often has been. The model does not suggest how an investor's risky asset allocation *should* be adjusted when investment horizons are longer; it indicates how an expected utility maximizing investor with power utility would behave. The model does not suggest that there is no rational expected utility function for which larger risky asset allocations are preferred at longer horizons. Although expected utility analysis has been criticized for producing results and implications inconsistent with actual investor behavior, it is not expected utility analysis per se, but the assumption of power utility that leads to the conflict between the model results and actual investor behavior.

IV.   MEAN REVERTING RETURNS AND THE HORIZON EFFECT

For power utility functions other than log utility, Samuelson (1991) demonstrates that the introduction of mean reversion in returns does not have a predicable effect on risky asset allocations. As shown above, a log utility investor's optimal allocation will be unaffected by the introduction of mean reversion in returns. Specifically, Samuelson (1991) shows that for an investor who is less (more) risk-averse than a log-utility investor, the optimal risky asset allocation is increased (decreased) by the introduction of mean reversion in returns.

The present model yields stronger and more intuitively appealing results. Consider initially a situation where periodic returns are independently distributed and the equality in Equation 13 holds for some horizon $t > 1$ and some $\gamma_0 < \gamma_1$. If we then introduce mean reversion in returns, the growth rate of returns variance (the denominator of the ratio in Equation 13) will be decreased compared to the case of independently distributed returns, as multiperiod returns will be more concentrated around the mean. As Samuelson (1991) demonstrates, the introduction of mean reversion into a risky asset returns process may, in fact, decrease the growth rate of expected returns as well as the growth rate of returns variance when the investment horizon is lengthened. However, as long as the growth rate of variance is decreased more than the growth rate of expected (excess) returns, the effect of introducing mean reversion in returns is unambiguous. Under these conditions, the ratio in Equation 13 tends to increase so that it is greater than γ_0. By the corollary, optimal risky asset allocations will be larger for anticipated holding periods incrementally longer than t. If we denote the new (larger) value of the ratio in Equation 13 as γ_1, the effect of introducing mean reversion in returns is to induce investors characterized by values of γ between γ_0 and γ_1 to select larger risky asset allocations at incrementally longer horizons. In the absence of mean reversion, such an investor would prefer decreased risky asset allocations at incrementally longer horizons.

Variance ratio tests of historical returns have shown that holding period returns variances do grow more slowly at longer horizons than they would if periodic returns were independent. Lee (1990) presents evidence that mean returns for longer holding periods are approximately equal to compound mean annual rates, while returns variance at longer horizons are significantly lower than those that would obtain if annual returns were independently distributed. He argues, without reference to preferences, that this smaller decrease in returns variances at longer horizons is the sole explanation for investors to hold larger equity proportions when facing longer investment horizons.

V. CONCLUSIONS

We have presented a model of the portfolio allocation decision over a variable investment horizon that is more general than previous mean-variance utility models in that there are fewer restrictions on investor preferences. This more general specification of an investor's preference function allowed us to derive the optimal risky asset allocation as a function of the mean and variance of the returns distribution and of a second, investor-specific risk aversion parameter, γ. Incorporating a variable investment horizon allowed us to derive a necessary condition for an investor's optimal asset allocation to be invariant to the length of the investment horizon.

The model provides a rational theoretic basis for a preference for larger equities allocations at longer horizons. The model also captures well the intuition of practitioner argument that the increased attractiveness of equities at longer horizons from higher expected returns may outweigh the disutility of larger returns variances. In this regard, our results offer some resolution to the longstanding debate about the effect of the length of the anticipated holding period on optimal risky asset allocations. The variance of the geometric mean return, the probability of a returns shortfall, and investor loss aversion need not be explicitly considered to explain observed investor behavior. Importantly, the assumption of investor rationality need not be relaxed. By introducing a parameter that allows the curvature of investor utility isoquants to vary across investors, we provide a more general result than earlier analysis based on quadratic mean-variance utility.

Our results are not at odds with claims that investors' abilities to vary their labor supply or their expectations about future retirement account contributions may influence their preferred equities allocations (as a percent of investable wealth). We have argued only that in the absence of such effects an investor may still rationally prefer to increase risky asset allocations in response to longer anticipated investment horizons. Further, we argued that the influential Samuelson (1969, 1991) allocation-invariance result depends on assumptions about the form of the investor utility function and cannot, therefore, be considered to be a result of expected utility analysis in general. The effect of introducing mean reversion in returns in a manner that slows the growth rate of returns variance at longer horizons more than the growth rate of expected returns is unambiguous under the current analysis. Some investors will prefer increased risky asset allocations at longer horizons over a range of holding periods for which they previously did not.

Finally, we note that one of the crucial assumptions of the analysis presented here is that investor utility is maximized with respect to the mean and variance of returns for the anticipated holding period. If investors are myopic, in that they base decisions on interim holding period returns distributions, the effect of the investment horizon on risky asset allocations may be less. In the case of extreme myopia (decisions based on single period returns and variances), the length of the anticipated holding period will have no effect on asset allocations. Shortsightedness should, of course, be avoided by investors and fiduciaries. Given the relevant horizon and the opportunities presented over that horizon, advisors and fiduciaries must, as always, consider the preferences or loss functions of their clients and advise them accordingly.

NOTES

1.   Merton (1969) presents the analogous result in continuous time. Related results can be found in Merton (1971), Mossin (1968), and Hakansson (1970, 1974).

2. Examples are Vanguard Funds literature cited in Bodie (1995) and sales literature for Fidelity Freedom® Funds, introduced in 1996 and designed with different equity allocations to suit investors with different times to anticipated retirement.

3. An example of this argument is in Lloyd and Haney (1980) with a response in McEnally (1985).

4. Examples are Leibowitz and Kogelman (1991), Seigel (1994), and Reichenstein and Dorsett (1995).

5. Single period implications of such ranking criteria are summarized in Elton and Gruber (1995).

6. Tobin (1965) showed that for stationary, mutually independent, periodic returns, the t period expected return relative is R^t and its variance is $(R^2 + \sigma^2)^t - R^{2t}$, where R and σ^2 are the single-period return relative and returns variance. The partial derivative of the holding period rate of return, with respect to t, is $R^t \ln(R)$ and the partial derivative of the holding period variance is $(R^2 + \sigma^2)^t \ln(R^2 + \sigma^2) - 2R^{2t}\ln(R)$. We have verified numerically that the percentage rate of change of holding period (excess) returns variance is greater than the percentage rate of change of holding period returns at all horizons conceivably relevant to retirement investors, although we do not present an analytic proof that this relation will hold for all values of t.

7. Gressis, Philippatos, and Hayya (1976) examine the horizon effect of longer investment horizons with $\gamma = 1$ (quadratic mean-variance utility). Under this assumption, optimal risky asset allocations are *decreasing* at all longer investment horizons.

8. The horizon at which the ratio decreases to less than 0.5 is sensitive to the excess returns assumption and is approximately 11 years for annual *excess* risky asset expected returns of 10%.

9. Arditti (1967) presents evidence of an investor preference for positive skewness. Examples of analysis of portfolio efficiency when three returns moments are considered are: Samuelson (1958), Jean (1971), Arditti and Levy (1972), and Kraus and Litzenberger (1976).

10. Ingersoll (1987, pp. 39–41) presents a useful summary of several utility of wealth functions and their characteristics.

REFERENCES

Arditti, F., (1967). Risk and the required return on equity. *Journal of Finance, 22(1)*, 19–36.

Arditti, F., & Levy, H. (1975). Portfolio efficiency analysis in three moments: The multiperiod case. *Journal of Finance, 30(3)*, 797–809.

Benzarti, S., & Thaler, R.H. (1995). Myopic loss aversion and the equity premium puzzle. *Quarterly Journal of Economics, 110(1)*, 73–91.

Bodie, Z., & Crane, D.B. (1997). Personal investing: advice, theory, and evidence. *Financial Analysts Journal, 53(6)*, 13–23.

Bodie, Z., Merton, R., & Samuelson, W.M. (1992). Labor supply flexibility and portfolio choice in a life-cycle model. *Journal of Economic Dynamics and Control, 16(3/4)*, 427–449.

Elton, E., & Gruber, M. (1995). *Modern portfolio theory and investment analysis.* 5th Ed. New York: John Wiley.

Gressis, N., Philippatos, G.C., & Hayya, J. (1976). Multiperiod portfolio analysis and the inefficiency of the market portfolio. *Journal of Finance, 40(4)* 1115–1126.

Hakansson, N. H. (1970). Optimal Investment and consumption strategies under risk for a class of utility functions. *Econometrica 38*, 587–607.

Hakansson, N.H. (1974). Convergence to isoelastic utility and policy in multiperiod portfolio choice. *Journal of Financial Economics, 1*, 201–224.

Hodges, C., & Yoder, J.A. (1996). Time diversification and security preferences: A stochastic dominance analysis. *Review of Quantitative Finance, and Accounting, 7(3)*, 289–298.

Ingersoll, J. (1987). *Theory of investments.* Tolowa, NJ: Rowman & Littlefield.

Jean, W. (1971). The extension of portfolio analysis to three or more parameters. *Journal of Financial and Quantitative Analysis, 6(4)*, 505–515.

Kraus, A., & Litzenberger, R. (1976). Skewness preference and the valuation of risky assets. *Journal of Finance, 21(4)*, 1085–1094.

Lee, W.Y. (1990). Diversification and time: do investment horizons matter? *The Journal of Portfolio Management, 16(3)*, 24–26.

Leibowitz, M., & Kogelman, S. (1991). Asset allocation under shortfall constraints. *The Journal of Portfolio Management, 17(2)*, 18–23.

Lloyd, W., & Haney, Jr., R. (1980). Time diversification: surest route to lower risk. *The Journal of Portfolio Management, 6(3)*, 5–9.

McEnally, R.W. (1985). Time diversification: surest Route to Lower Risk? *The Journal of Portfolio Management, 11(4)*, 24–26.

Merton, R.C. (1969). Lifetime portfolio selection under uncertainty: the continuous-time case. *Review of Economic Statistics, 51(3)*, 247–257.

Merton, R.C. (1971). Optimum consumption and portfolio rules in a continuous-time model. *Journal of Economic Theory 3*, 374–413.

Reichenstein, W., & Dorsett, C. (1995). *Time diversification revisited.* The Research Foundation of the Institute of Chartered Financial Analysts, Charlottesville, VA.

Samuelson, P.A. (1958). The fundamental approximation theorem of portfolio analysis in terms of means, variances and higher moments. *Review of Economic Studies, 25*, 65–86.

Samuelson, P.A. (1969). Lifetime portfolio selection by dynamic stochastic programming. *Review of Economics and, Statistics, 51(3)*, 239–246.

Samuelson, P.A. (1974). Challenge to judgment. *The Journal of Portfolio Management, 1(1)*, 17–19.

Samuelson, P.A. (1989). The judgment of economic science on rational portfolio management: timing and long horizon effects. *The Journal of Portfolio Management, 16(1)*, 4–12.

Samuelson, P.A. (1991). Long run-risk tolerance when equity returns are mean regressing: pseudoparadoxes and vindication of "businessman's risk." In W.C. Brainard, W.D. Nordhaus, & H.W. Watts (Eds.). *Money, Macroeconomics and Economic Policy.* Cambridge, MA: The MIT Press.

Samuelson, P.A. (1994). The long term case for equities and how it can be oversold. *The Journal of Portfolio Management, 21(1)*, 15–24.

Seigel, J. (1994). *Stocks for the Long Run.* Homewood, IL: Irwin.

Tobin, J. (1965). Theory of portfolio selection. F. Hahn & F. Breeching (Eds.), *In Theory of Interest Rates.* London: Macmillan.

Tversky, A., & Kahneman, D. (1991). Loss aversion and riskless choice: a reference dependent model. *Quarterly Journal of Economics, 106(4)*, 1039–1061.

MARKOWITZ MODELS OF PORTFOLIO SELECTION:
THE INVERSE PROBLEM

Michael J. Hartley and Gurdip S. Bakshi

ABSTRACT

Predictions about investor portfolio holdings can provide powerful tests of asset pricing theories. In the context of Markowitz portfolio selection problem, this paper develops an algorithm which determines the structural parameters in both the investor's return-generating process and the utility function based upon the actual portfolio choices made by each investor. We refer to this problem as the inverse of portfolio selection. Furthermore, through the introduction of a set of investor-specific characteristics, the methodology accommodates either homogeneous or heterogeneous anticipated rates of return—a contribution over the existing returns-generating models. Generalization of the algorithm to Black (1972) and Tobin (1965) models where the efficiency frontier is known in closed form is direct and immediate. The methodology is useful for understanding the investor risk-return trade-offs and, in particular, can be considered as the microlevel counterpart of the determination of the "taste parameters" in Hansen–Singleton (1982) and the simultaneous determination of the parameters driving the forcing process and the "taste parameters" in Duffie–Singleton (1993).

Advances in Investment Analysis and Portfolio Management, Volume 7, pages 55–89.
Copyright © 2000 by JAI Press Inc.
All rights of reproduction in any form reserved.
ISBN: 0-7623-0658-0

I. INTRODUCTION

The portfolio selection model of Markowitz (1952, 1959) consists of two interrelated modules:

- A nonlinear programming problem where risk-averse investors solve a utility maximization problem involving the risk and the expected rate of return of any portfolio, subject to the constraint of an efficiency frontier. The latter is defined *pointwise*, as a sequence of solutions to a quadratic programming problem which minimizes the risk associated with each possible portfolio's expected rate of return subject to the constraint that the elements of the portfolio be non-negative and sum to unity.
- A parametric stochastic returns-generating process by which, in each period, the investors determine the requisite vector of expectations and the variance–covariance matrix of the investors anticipated rates of return on all risky assets.

Thus, given the inputs from above—that is, expected rates of return and their associated covariance inputs, along with knowledge of the parameters in the investor's specific mean-variance utility function—the investor's optimal portfolio can be computed, but only *numerically*, as a solution to the nonlinear programming problem. We refer to these two steps as the *forward solution* to the portfolio selection problem in which all the above parameters are determined, *ex ante*.

Our present interest, however, is to offer an algorithm for the *inverse* of the portfolio selection problem which confronts an external investigator. That is, given:

- a time series of actual portfolios for a sample of investors;
- a time series of preceding observed prices and dividends of the relevant set of risky assets; and
- a set of socioeconomic characteristics for each investor in the sample.

The above is in conjunction with a well-behaved specification of the parametric form of the investor's utility function and returns-generating process; one can infer or otherwise determine the parameter values in each investor's utility function and, where also of interest, the associated parameters in the returns-generating process based on their reflection in the *actual* portfolio choices of investors?

Once the parameters in the complete system have been determined, forward solutions of the model may be employed to compute the optimal portfolio for particular investors in subsequent time periods.

For several reasons, the inverse of the portfolio selection has proved to be a difficult task when approached by conventional econometric methods. First, while the portfolio selection problem is a specialized form of consumer demand model couched in budget–share form, the fact that the optimal portfolio, relative to any feasible configuration of parameter values, can only be computed numerically, and is not representable as a closed-form system of seemingly unrelated regression (SUR) equations, has been problematic. This creates fundamental problems of model specification for the investigator under standard econometric practices.

Second, and more importantly, the fact that certain assets are *not* selected in the investor's optimal portfolio causes serious difficulties.[1] The traditional econometric approach to accommodating the presence of non-negativity constraints is to formulate an underlying *stochastic* limited dependent variable (LDV) model, in which there is an accumulation of probability mass at all boundary values—each requiring the evaluation of multiple numerical integrals (Maddala, 1983). In the present generic case, not only are such models extremely difficult to formulate in a logically consistent manner; but, even if possible, suffer from three remaining fundamental flaws:

1. The functional form of each of the asset equations is ad hoc, in the sense that, while the domain restrictions on the dependent variable, in principle, may be accommodated; the *functional form* of the asset-demand relationships are not "derived" from the posited underlying constrained optimization problem.
2. The mechanism by which infeasible values of the "latent-dependent variables" are mapped back onto the boundary of the feasible decision space is ad hoc.
3. Even if the issues in the above can be resolved satisfactorily, present computer limitations (see Hausman and Wise, 1978; Quandt, 1983) restrict the analysis to no more than four multiple numerical integrations. Unfortunately, any realistic analysis of portfolio selection would encompass substantially more than four risky assets.

In order to circumvent the above problems, we have formulated a deterministic version of the portfolio selection problem.[2] Specifically, the use of deterministic neoclassical econometric methods advanced in Hartley (1986, 1988, 1994) permits the calibration of the structural parameters in a specified constrained optimization model in cases where the optimal solution, relative to any feasible parameter vector, can only be computed numerically. This contrasts with the requirement of closed-form analytic solution for the optimal portfolio under traditional econometric practice. The occurrence of "corner solutions", which arise when one or more assets are added to or removed from the prevailing portfolio in the course of the implementation of the proposed algorithm, causes the elements in the prevailing Jacobian matrix of partial derivatives of the currently predicted optimal portfolio with respect to the current structural parameters to exhibit "jump discontinuities" in the neighborhood of a corner solution. Such cases frequently arise, and avoiding these problems in the context of our algorithm, requires various possible "smoothing" techniques (Hardle, 1990). Moreover, the fact that the model formulation is deterministic implies that we do not have to concern ourselves with the accumulation of probability mass that would otherwise be associated with all boundary solutions for the portfolio problem, whether corner or not.

Only some special cases of the inverse of the portfolio-selection problem have been previously examined in the asset-pricing literature. For instance, take as an example the Euler equation tests of the consumption-based asset-pricing model (Hansen-Singleton, 1982; Ferson, 1994; Bakshi and Chen, 1996). Using the generalized methods of moments of Hansen (1982), the "taste parameters" in the representative agent's utility function and his subjective discount factor have been inferred using aggregate consumption and asset-pricing data. In addition, Mehra and Prescott (1985) and Constantinides (1990), among many others, calibrated the mean and the standard deviation of the aggregate consumption process and observed that aggregate consumption is "too smooth" to fit the aggregate market risk premium and the risk-free real interest rate without resorting to implausibly high values of the risk aversion parameter. In the context of an intertemporal asset-pricing model, Merton (1980), Harvey (1991), and Bakshi and Chen (1994), calculate the reward-to-risk ratio to infer the economy-wide risk aversion.

The simulated moments estimators of Duffie and Singleton (1993) and McFadden (1989) are important contributions, and are appealing on the grounds that the methodology jointly determines the unknown parameters driving the time-homogeneous stochastic forcing process as well as the structural parameters in the agents utility function. However, in the case of portfolio selection, a drawback of the simulated moments estimator is that it cannot avoid the "curse of dimensionality". Furthermore, as demonstrated in Section IV, the calibration methods are computationally much simpler and the proposed quasi-Newton algorithm is able to accommodate the corner solutions and the associated discontinuities, which are likely to be troublesome in simulated moment estimators.

The rest of the paper proceeds as follows: Section II outlines the basic features of the Markowitz portfolio selection problem; Section III introduces a simple autoregressive model as the basis for the stochastic returns generating process, and permits the parameters to vary with the set of investor characteristics—thus, in any period in which investment decision is called for, we may accommodate either homogeneous or heterogeneous expected rates of return across all investors, along with a homogeneous covariance matrix; Section IV presents the neoclassical econometric methods applicable to the inverse of the portfolio selection problem for given structural parameters in the returns-generating process obtained *ex ante* from historical data—in this case, only the structural parameters in the utility function require determination. This section also illustrates how the unknown efficiency frontier can be determined using numerical methods and offers an analytically tractable procedure to evaluate the Jacobian matrix of partial derivatives that serves as a basic input to the modified Newton algorithm (Hartley, 1961); Section V tackles the more demanding task of calibrating the structural parameters of the investor's utility function and the returns-generating process, as reflected ex post in the actual portfolios of investors. We explain, in Section VI, how the proposed framework extends in a simple way to the Black (1972) and Tobin (1965) portfolio selection models. Concluding remarks are offered in Section VII. Mathematical details relating to the algorithm are sketched in Appendices A, B, and C.

II. THE MARKOWITZ MODEL OF PORTFOLIO SELECTION

This section is devoted to the Markowitz theory of portfolio selection for a set of risky assets.[3] Markowitz postulated that each investor generates a vector of expected returns, denoted μ, and an associated covariance matrix, Σ, for the set of risky assets under consideration. Given these inputs, he assumed that a risk-averse investor will trade-off between the portfolio expected rate of return and risk as embodied in the utility function. Consequently, the optimal Markowitz portfolio may be computed from an optimization problem in which the mean-variance utility function is maximized, subject to the constraint that all prospective portfolio's lie on an "efficiency frontier". However, the latter is defined *pointwise* from a set of solutions to a series of quadratic programming problems in which, for each specified rate of return, the variance of the portfolio is minimized, subject to the conditions that:

- The proportions invested in each risky asset are proper weights, that is, are non-negative and sum to unity.
- The rate of return on a feasible portfolio equals a specified value, ranging from the smallest to the largest rate of return on all individual assets.

Specifically, let $\pi \equiv \pi_a$, for $a = 1 \cdots A$ denote the vector of portfolio weights for any risky asset portfolio for a given investor. The expected rate on any portfolio, ϕ, is therefore given by:

$$\phi = \pi' \mu = \sum_{a=1}^{A} \pi_a \mu_a \tag{1}$$

and the standard deviation of the portfolio is defined as:

$$\omega = (\pi' \Sigma \pi)^{\frac{1}{2}} = \left[\sum_{a=1}^{A} \sum_{a'=1}^{A} \pi_a . \sigma_{aa'} . \pi_{a'} \right]^{\frac{1}{2}} \tag{2}$$

for any portfolio, π. These have an admissible domain:

$$\Pi = \{\pi : \pi \geq 0 \text{ and } \mathbf{i}' \pi = 1\} \tag{3}$$

where $\mathbf{i}'$ denotes the unit vector. Hence, the elements, π_a of π are proper weights.

From mean-variance mathematics referred to, among many others, in Merton (1972) and Roll (1977), it is clear that the image of Π under the transformations,

Equations 1 and 2, to (ϕ, ω)-space is an "umbrella-shaped" region, which we can write as:

$$F^M = \left\{ (\phi, \omega) \equiv (\pi'\mu, (\pi'\Sigma\pi)^{\frac{1}{2}}) : \pi \in \Pi \right\}$$

The "northwest" boundary function:

$$b^M(\phi, \omega) \doteq b^M\left(\pi'\mu, (\pi'\Sigma\pi)^{\frac{1}{2}} \right) = 0 \tag{4}$$

of F^M is a *piecewise-continuous*, concave function or concave spline in (ϕ, ω)-space, and defines the set of all efficient portfolios of risky assets for a risk-averse investor, where the "join-points" arise when one or more assets are either introduced or deleted from the prevailing portfolio.

Following Markowitz (1959), one can represent the arbitrary investors utility function in risk-return space or in terms of the portfolio space as follows:[4]

$$u(\phi, \omega; \mathbf{x}, \xi) = u\left((\pi'\mu, (\pi'\Sigma\pi)^{\frac{1}{2}}; \mathbf{x}, \xi) \right), \tag{5}$$

where we have introduced the K-element vector, $\mathbf{x}$, of the investor's socioeconomic characteristics to capture differences in risk aversion, age, household income, size of investment fund, sex, wealth, and so on. This allows us to incorporate heterogeneity in an individual or institutional investor population. Accordingly, ξ is a P-element vector of unknown "taste parameters" which is to be determined through our calibration exercises in the next sections.

The portfolio selection can now be stated as a nonlinear programming problem in risk-return or portfolio space:

$$\max_{\pi} u(\phi, \omega; \mathbf{x}, \xi), \quad \text{s.t.} \quad b^M(\phi, \omega) = 0, \tag{6}$$

where as previously mentioned, $b^M = 0$ denotes the *unknown* efficiency frontier to be determined pointwise and embodying the constraints, $\pi \geq 0$ and $\mathbf{i}'\pi = 1$.

As is well known, "efficiency" for any portfolio with a specified rate of return, say ϕ^*, is defined as that portfolio which minimizes the variance, subject to the conditions that π represents a set of proper portfolio weights. Thus, an associated portfolio satisfying $b^M = 0$ obtains as the solution to the quadratic programming problem:[5]

$$\min_{\pi} \frac{1}{2} \pi'\Sigma\pi \quad \text{s.t.} \quad \mathbf{i}'\pi = 1, \quad \mu'\pi = \phi^*, \quad \pi \geq 0. \tag{7}$$

Thus, the solution associated with a specific value of ϕ^* defines an efficient portfolio, $\pi^* = \pi(\phi^*)$, which, in turn, defines the associated mean, $\pi^{*'}\mu$, and the standard deviation, $\omega^* = (\pi^{*'}\Sigma\pi^*)^{1/2}$ of this efficient portfolio.

Let $\phi_{min} = \min_a\{\mu_a\}$ denote the smallest element of μ and analogously let ϕ_{max} denote the largest element. Then, by spanning the range $[\phi_{min}, \phi_{max}]$, over a set of successively-finer one-dimensional grids of ϕ values, for any investor, one can calculate the corresponding efficient portfolios and the standard deviations. Consequently, for any investor, the efficiency frontier, $b^M = 0$, is defined pointwise. Accordingly, by evaluating the utility function in Equation 5 at each point along the efficiency frontier, the optimal Markowitz portfolio, π^{*M}, and the associated optimal expected return, ϕ^{*M}, and the standard deviation, ω^{*M}, may be determined by one-dimensional grid search methods which are explained in detail in Section IV.B and V.B.

Observe that in traversing the efficiency frontier over the values $\phi \in [\phi_{min}, \phi_{max}]$, the associated efficient portfolio's, π^*, will be one of the three types:

1. an interior solution, or,
2. a boundary, non-corner solution, or,
3. a boundary, corner solution.

In the case of interior solutions, the prevailing portfolio includes all of the A risky assets with $i'\pi^* = 1$, and $\pi^* > 0$. With a large number of risky assets, this will rarely occur. Instead, a boundary solution, in which certain risky assets are not held, is more typical. Here, again $i'\pi^* = 1$; but, upon reordering the assets as $\pi^* \equiv [\pi_1^{*\prime}, \pi_2^{*\prime}]'$, we find that $\pi_1^* > 0$, but $\pi_2^* = 0-$ thus defining a boundary solution portfolio. Of these, we may encounter a boundary corner portfolio, in which one or more risky assets have been deleted from or added to the neighboring portfolios associated with a slightly smaller or larger rate of return than ϕ^*.

Obviously, the optimal Markowitz portfolio will also be one of the three types noted above. While this causes no particular difficulty in calculating π^{*M}, the optimal Markowitz portfolio in the forward solution, it poses some difficulties in the inverse problem. In particular, the cases (1) and (2) represent "tangency solutions", π^{*M}, relative to either the universe of risky assets, A, or the smaller dimensional problem involving $A_1 < A$ risky assets in π_1^{*M}. However, the case of a corner solution in (3) gives rise to "jump-discontinuities" in the associated Jacobian matrix of partial derivatives of the prevailing portfolio with respect to the structural parameters, as shown in Section IV, requiring the use of "smoothing techniques" to implement the portfolio selection algorithm.

III. INPUTS TO THE MARKOWITZ MODEL: THE RETURNS-GENERATING PROCESS

Before discussing the algorithm for the inverse selection problem, this section considers a simple prototype model for the underlying stochastic returns-generating process which embodies both homogeneous and heterogeneous expected rate of return. However, in both cases, on grounds of parsimony, we retain a homogeneous covariance matrix across individuals in any investment period.

A. A Homogeneous Returns-Generating Process

Let L denote the maximum number of lagged time-periods of actual data considered by each investor in assessing future expected rate of return and the associated covariance matrix. It follows that the observed rate of return for any asset a, $a = 1, \cdots, A$, during time t is calculable as:

$$r_{a,t} = \frac{p_{a,t} + d_{a,t} - p_{a,t-1}}{p_{a,t-1}}, \quad \forall a = 1 \cdots A; \ \forall t = -L + 1, \cdots, 1, \cdots T$$

where d_t and p_t, respectively, denotes the time t dividends and prices for the risky asset a.

Consider first a simple constant-coefficient autoregressive model for the one-period ahead anticipated rate of return for each investor:[6]

$$r_{i,a,t} = \alpha_{0,a} + \sum_{l=1}^{L} \alpha_{l,a} \cdot r_{i,a,t-l} + e_{i,a,t}; \ a = 1, \cdots, A; \ t = 1, \cdots, T \tag{8}$$

Note that the "systematic" part on the right-hand-side of Equation 8 is independent of the socioeconomic characteristics of the individual investor; and thus defines a set of homogeneous returns-generating process where the covariance matrix associated with $\{e_{i,a,t}\}$, denoted Σ, is a constant over all investors and time periods. Further assume that, $e_{i,t} \equiv (e_{i,a,t})$ which denotes the $A \times 1$ vector of random disturbances follows the probability density function:

$$e_{i,t} \sim NID(0, \Sigma) \tag{9}$$

In this case, Equation 9 defines a linear vector autoregressive (VAR) process for the vector of anticipated rates of return, $r_{i,t} \equiv (r_{i,a,t})$, involving $A \cdot (L + 1)$ autoregressive parameters, $\{\alpha_{l,a}: l = 0, 1, \cdots, L; a = 1, \cdots, A\}$.[7,8] This implies that we may obtain consistent and asymptotically normal (CAN) estimates, $\{\hat{\alpha}_{l,a}\}$, from which we may calculate the homogeneous expected rates of return for each risky asset, as:[9]

$$\hat{\mu}_{i,a,t} = \hat{\alpha}_{0,a} + \sum_{l=1}^{L} \hat{\alpha}_{l,a} \cdot r_{i,a,t-l}; \quad a = 1, \cdots, A, \quad t = 1, \cdots, T \tag{10}$$

This model can be updated for each investment period t; and results in the sequence, $\{\hat{\mu}_{i,a,t}: i = 1, \cdots, N; a = 1, \cdots A; t = 1, \cdots T\}$, of expected rates of return that are identical across each investor. Finally, the $A \times A$ covariance matrix, Σ can be estimated by its sample analog,

$$\hat{\Sigma} = \frac{1}{NT} \sum_{i=1}^{N} \sum_{t=1}^{T} (r_{i,t} - \hat{\mu}_{i,t})(r_{i,t} - \hat{\mu}_{i,t})'$$

provided that $NT > A$.

Observe that the homogeneous inputs imply that, in any period, all investors have identical, *ex ante* beliefs regarding the expectations and the covariance matrix of future anticipated rates of return on all risky assets. Were this be so, it is difficult to imagine a viable market for *any* risky asset. This requires, at a minimum, different expected rates of returns, in which some investors expect the expected returns on a given risky asset to be lower than currently prevailing, while others, presumably with the same information, expect them to be higher in the future. This motivates our discussion of the heterogeneous returns generating process in the next section.

B. A Heterogeneous Returns-Generating Process

This section discusses the econometric implementation of a heterogeneous returns generating process which is more characteristic of the diversity in investors beliefs and of portfolio selection in the "real world".[10]

The generic approach is to utilize the vector of observable investor characteristic, $\mathbf{x}_{i,t}$, to generate a parsimoniously parameterized, investor-specific, returns-generating process for the anticipated rates of return for each investor, $i = 1, \cdots, N$, in each time period. We write this below as:

$$r_{i,a,t} = \alpha_{0,a}(\mathbf{x}_{i,t}; \gamma_0) + \sum_{l=1}^{L} \alpha_{l,a}(\mathbf{x}_{i,t}; \gamma_l) \cdot r_{i,a,t-l} + e_{i,a,t}; \, a = 1, \cdots, A; t = 1, \cdots, T \quad (11)$$

where again, $e_{i,t} \equiv (e_{i,a,t})$ is a normal random disturbance with p.d.f given in Equation 9. Here, both the intercept and the L autoregressive "slope coefficients" vary with the vector of socioeconomic characteristics, $\mathbf{x}_{i,t}$. One plausible specification is to define the $\{\alpha_{l,a}\}$ as linear function of the $\mathbf{x}_{i,t}$ values, that is:

$$\alpha_{l,a}(\mathbf{x}_{i,t}; \gamma_l) = \alpha_{i,0,l} + \sum_{k=1}^{K} \gamma_{i,k,l} \cdot \mathbf{x}_{i,k,t}$$

separately for each investor, $i = 1, \cdots, N$, with $l = 0, \cdots, L$ and $a = 1, \cdots, A$. This formulation yields the following investor-specific returns-generating process which will be extensively exploited in our investigation:

$$r_{i,a,t} = \left(\alpha_{i,0,0} + \sum_{k=1}^{K} \gamma_{i,k,0} \cdot \mathbf{x}_{i,k,t} \right) + \sum_{l=1}^{L} \left(\gamma_{i,0,l} + \sum_{k=1}^{K} \gamma_{i,k,l} \cdot \mathbf{x}_{i,k,t} \right) r_{i,a,t-l} + e_{i,a,t} \quad (12)$$

The above model involves $(K + 1) \cdot (L + 1)$ parameters, and not only captures the investor's "bullish" or "bearish" anticipations of future asset prices relative to the current state of the market, as manifest in the intercept of Equation 12; but also permits each investor to place different "weights" $\sum_{l=1}^{L} (\gamma_{i,0,l} + \sum_{k=1}^{K} \gamma_{i,k,l} \cdot \mathbf{x}_{i,k,t})$, on the preceding rates of return. Thus, if feasible on grounds of dimensionality, we would fit the model in Equation 11 jointly to all risky assets. This again involves formulating a linear VAR model for estimating the parameters, $\{\gamma_{i,k,l}: a = 1, \cdots, A; k = 0, 1, \cdots, K; l = 1, \cdots, L\}$, for each investor. The resulting heterogeneous returns-generating process may then be defined as:[11]

$$\hat{\mu}_{i,a,t} = \left(\hat{\alpha}_{i,0,0} + \sum_{k=1}^{K} \hat{\gamma}_{i,k,0} \cdot \mathbf{x}_{i,k,t} \right) + \sum_{l=1}^{L} \left(\hat{\gamma}_{i,0,l} + \sum_{k=1}^{K} \hat{\gamma}_{i,k,l} \cdot \mathbf{x}_{i,k,t} \right) r_{i,a,t-l} \qquad (13)$$

and applies to each investor, i.

There are clearly innumerable alternative model specifications for the returns-generating process. In particular, the empirically attractive single-index model of Sharpe (1963) and the multiple index models, especially Ross (1976), which have been considered in the existing literature on portfolio selection can be analyzed separately, and used in the calibration of portfolio choice.

IV. DIRECT *EX ANTE* CALIBRATION OF PORTFOLIO CHOICE

Having discussed the portfolio selection problem and the specification of the returns-generating process, let us focus our attention on the inverse selection problem. Taking parametrically, the time series of actual portfolio's for a sample of investors, the returns-generating process for the relevant set of risky assets, and the set of socioeconomic characteristics of each investor; one can determine the parameter values in each investor's utility function and the associated parameters in the returns-generating process based upon their reflections in the *actual* portfolio choices of investors. Having determined these structural parameters, the optimal portfolios can be computed using the techniques described in Section II.[12] The goal in this section is, therefore, to discuss the econometric methods associated with *ex ante* calibration of the "taste parameter" within the utility function of a Markowitz model based upon actual portfolio decisions of investors.[13]

A. The Quasi-Newton Algorithm

Recall that the heterogeneous autoregressive model for the anticipated rates of return outlined in Equation 11 involves estimating the parameters $\{\hat{\gamma}_{i,k,l}: i = 1, \cdots, N; k = 1, \cdots, K; l = 0, 1, \cdots, L\}$, which can be denoted $(K + 1) \cdot (L + 1) \cdot N \times 1$ element vector, $\hat{\gamma}$. Given $\hat{\gamma}$, we can define, for each investor, the expected rate of return vectors $\{\hat{\mu}_{i,t}: i = 1, \cdots, N\}$, and the estimated covariance matrix, $\hat{\Sigma}$ for each time period, $\{t = 1, \cdots, T\}$. These serve as inputs to the portfolio selection problem; and, in turn, permit the computation of the optimal Markowitz portfolios, $\{\pi_{i,t}^{*M}: i = 1, \cdots, N, t = 1, \cdots, T\}$, via the methods of Section II. Thus, each investor at time t will confront a different efficiency frontier; and in the *ex ante case*, the only remaining problem is to calibrate the vector of "taste parameters", ξ in the investors utility function, $u(\pi'\mu, (\pi'\Sigma\pi)^{1/2}; \mathbf{x}, \xi)$.

For this purpose, consider the following formulation for the actual portfolio held by investor i at time t,

$$\pi_{i,t} = \pi_{i,t}^{*M} + v_{i,t} \equiv \pi_{i,t}^{*M} (\mathbf{x}_{i,t}, \hat{\mu}_{i,t}, \hat{\Sigma}) + v_{i,t}; \tag{14}$$

where $\pi_{i,t}$ is an $A \times 1$ vector denoting the actual portfolio held by investor in period t; and $\pi_{i,t}^{*M}$ denotes the $A \times 1$ vector defining the corresponding "optimum" Markowitz portfolio. The latter is, however, defined relative to the prevailing set of taste parameters, ξ, with given values for the inputs, $\hat{\mu}_{i,t}$, $\hat{\Sigma}$ and $\mathbf{x}_{i,t}$. Here, since $\pi \geq 0$, $\pi_{i,t}^{*M}$ can only be determined numerically, the functional form the right-hand side will not be known to the investigator, though the variables which affect the numerical value of $\pi_{i,t}^{*M}$ can be specified. Finally, $v_{i,t}$ is defined as an A element vector of discrepancies between the actual value of the ith investor's portfolio, $\pi_{i,t}$, and the predicted value, $\pi_{i,t}^{*M}$, relative to a given value of parameter vector, ξ.

In the present context, we must distinguish between the calibration of the structural parameters, ξ, where the $\{v_{i,t}\}$ are treated as *constant discrepancies*, and the estimation of the "true" parameters, in which $\{v_{i,t}\}$, are regarded as *random disturbances*. Here, the presence of A inequality domain restrictions, $\pi \geq 0$, gives rise to A^{th} order multiple integral in implementing a *stochastic* limited dependent variable approach. However, since no more than four multiple numerical integrals can at present be accommodated (Hausman and Wise, 1978; Quandt, 1983), we opt for the specified deterministic approach outlined in Hartley (1984, 1986, 1994). This implies that we must forego the customary rituals of statistical inference and hypothesis testing, but in turn, as we show below, may determine the parameter values for a much larger number of assets, A.

Having defined *constant discrepancies* as the difference between actual investor portfolio's and the prevailing Markowitz portfolio, we define the quadratic loss function as:

$$Q^1(\xi) = \frac{1}{2} |\Omega^1|^{\frac{1}{TN}} \sum_{t=1}^{T} \sum_{i=1}^{N} \left(\pi_{i,t} - \pi_{i,t}^{*M} \right)' \cdot [\Omega^1]^+ \left(\pi_{i,t} - \pi_{i,t}^{*M} \right) \tag{15}$$

which has to be minimized with respect to, ξ, where $[\Omega^1]^+$ is the $A \times A$ weighting matrix,[14]

$$\Omega^1 = \frac{1}{TN} \sum_{t=1}^{T} \sum_{i=1}^{N} \left(\pi_{i,t} - \pi_{i,t}^{*M} \right) \cdot \left(\pi_{i,t} - \pi_{i,t}^{*M} \right)' \tag{16}$$

representing the Mahalanobis distance criterion which may be obtained by solving $\partial Q^1/\partial \Omega^1 = 0$, for Ω^1.

Note from Equation 14 that $i'\pi_{i,t} = 1 = i'\pi_{i,t}^{*M}$, so that $i'\Omega^1 i = 0$ and the $A \times A$ matrix, Ω, is of rank, $A - 1$. Consequently, we must delete one of the risky assets from the model. Without loss of generality, let the deleted risky asset be the Ath.[15] Accordingly, using the symbol, $-$, to denote an $(A - 1)$-dimensional vector or matrix extracted from an A-dimensional one, we may implicitly define the following $(A - 1)$-dimensional expressions:

$$\pi_{i,t} \equiv [\overline{\pi}_{i,t}' \mid \pi_{i,t,A}]'; \; \pi_{i,t}^{*M} \equiv [(\overline{\pi}_{i,t}^{*M})' \mid \pi_{i,t,A}^{*M}]'; \; v_{i,t} \equiv [\overline{v}_{i,t}' \mid v_{i,t,A}]'; \; \hat{\mu}_{i,t} \equiv [\hat{\overline{\mu}}_{i,t}' \mid \mu_{i,t,A}]'$$

Other variables are similarly defined. In this situation, we must definite the basic budget-share model as one involving only the first $A - 1$ risky assets as in:

$$\overline{\pi}_{i,t} = \overline{\pi}_{i,t}^{*M} + \overline{v}_{i,t} \equiv \overline{\pi}_{i,t}^{*M}(x_{i,t}, \hat{\mu}_{i,t}, \hat{\Sigma}) + \overline{v}_{i,t} \tag{17}$$

and, in the next step, the loss function as:

$$\overline{Q}^1(\xi) = \frac{1}{2} |\overline{\Omega}^1|^{-\frac{1}{TN}} \sum_{t=1}^{T} \sum_{i=1}^{N} (\overline{\pi}_{i,t} - \overline{\pi}_{i,t}^{*M})' \cdot [\overline{\Omega}^1]^+ \cdot (\overline{\pi}_{i,t} - \overline{\pi}_{i,t}^{*M}). \tag{18}$$

Relative to the loss function in Equation 18, and holding $\overline{\Omega}^1$, the first-order conditions are defined by:

$$\frac{\partial \overline{Q}^1}{\partial \xi} = -\sum_{t=1}^{T} \sum_{i=1}^{N} \{\overline{J}_{i,t}^1\}' \cdot [\overline{\Omega}^1]^+ \cdot (\overline{\pi}_{i,t} - \overline{\pi}_{i,t}^{*M}) = 0 \tag{19}$$

where $\overline{J}_{i,t}^1 \equiv \frac{\partial \overline{\pi}^{*M}}{\partial \xi}$ is an $(A - 1) \times P$ Jacobian matrix of partial derivatives with respect to the parameter vector, ξ. Since Equation 19 is highly nonlinear in ξ, we must resort to iterative methods to obtain a solution, ξ, for ξ.

Let $n = 0, 1, \ldots$ denote an iteration index, and consider the standard quasilinearization (Bellman and Roth, 1983) of the optimal portfolio vector, $\overline{\pi}_{i,t}^{*M}$, around the current iterate, $[\overline{\pi}_{i,t}^{*M}]^n$, that is:

$$\overline{\pi}_{i,t}^{*M} = [\overline{\pi}_{i,t}^{*M}]^n + \overline{J}_{i,t}^1 (\xi - [\xi]^n) \tag{20}$$

Then, substituting, Equation 20 into Equation 19 with both $\overline{J}_{i,t}^1$ and $\overline{\Omega}^1$ evaluated at $[\xi]^n$, and solution for $\xi = [\xi]^{n+1}$, leads to the *modified* quasi-Newton algorithm (Hartley, 1961),

$$[\xi]^{n+1} = [\xi]^n - [\psi]^n \cdot [\overline{H}^1]^n \cdot [\overline{g}^1]^n \tag{21}$$

Here,

$$[\overline{H}^1]^n = \sum_{t=1}^{T} \sum_{i=1}^{N} \left[\{\overline{J}_{i,t}^1\}' \right]^n \cdot \left[\overline{\Omega}^{1n} \right]^+ \cdot \left[\overline{J}_{i,t}^1 \right]^n \tag{22}$$

will be referred as the $P \times P$ Hessian matrix under the method of quasilinearization:

$$[\overline{g}^1]^n = -\sum_{t=1}^{T}\sum_{i=1}^{N}\left[\{\overline{J}_{i,t}^1\}'\right]^n \cdot \left[\overline{\Omega}^{1n}\right]^+ \cdot \left(\overline{\pi}_{i,t} - \left[\overline{\pi}_{i,t}^{*M}\right]^n\right) \tag{23}$$

denotes the $P \times 1$ gradient vector; and $0 \le [\psi]^n \le 1$ denotes a suitable step-size parameter (see Dennis and Schnabel, 1983) chosen to ensure that in each iteration:

1. ξ^{n+1} is feasible.
2. $[\overline{Q}^1]^{n+1} \le [\overline{Q}^1]^n$ which ensures monotonicity.

Given $[\xi]^n$, $[H^1]^n$ and $[g^1]^n$, along with an initial value of $[\psi]^n = 1$, Equation 21 determines the "full-step" parameter value of $[\xi]^{n+1}$. In particular, a line-search algorithm is then employed—first to establish feasibility, and then to establish monotonicity within any iteration.[16] Finally, assuming that we can determine the elements in the Jacobian matrix, $[\overline{J}_{i,t}^1]^n$, in each iteration, n, the quasi-Newton algorithm, described in Equation 21, will converge to the limit point:

$$\hat{\xi} = \lim_{n \to \infty} [\xi]^n \tag{24}$$

To implement the above algorithm, we determine the optimal portfolio, $\overline{\pi}^{*M}$, and seek an expression for the elements of the $(A - 1) \times P$ Jacobian submatrix, $\overline{J}_{i,t}^1 \equiv \partial \overline{\pi}^{*M}/\partial \xi$. We discuss these in turn in the next sections. These steps are critical, since in each iteration, $[\overline{J}_{i,t}^1]$ determines the Hessian matrix, $\overline{H}^1$, and the gradient vector, $\overline{g}^1$.

B. Efficiency Frontier Approximations

Our discussion in Section II emphasized that the efficiency frontier in either portfolio or risk-return space is only defined *pointwise* when $\pi_{i,t} \ge 0$. In particular, such points $\pi_{i,t}^{*M}$ in portfolio space or $(\phi_{i,t}^*, \omega_{i,t}^*)$ in risk-return space, lie on the unknown efficient boundary function:

$$b_{i,t}^M(\phi_{i,t}^*, \omega_{i,t}^*) \equiv b_{i,t}^M\left(\pi_{i,t}^*\hat{\overline{\mu}}_{i,t}, (\pi_{i,t}^*\hat{\overline{\Sigma}}\pi_{i,t}^*)^{\frac{1}{2}}\right) = 0$$

These are obtained by solving the quadratic programming problem, in Equation 7, over a succession of finer grids, each being (say) one-tenth of the grid size, G, of the former. More specifically, we begin by evaluating the utility function:

$$u_{i,t}^* \equiv u\left(\phi_{i,t}^*, \omega_{i,t}^*\right) \equiv u\left(\pi_{i,t}^*\hat{\overline{\mu}}_{i,t}, (\pi_{i,t}^*\hat{\overline{\Sigma}}\pi_{i,t}^*)^{\frac{1}{2}}; x_{i,t}, \xi\right) \tag{25}$$

relative to the prevailing value of ξ, over the initial grid $[\phi_{min}, \phi_{min} + \delta_0, \phi_{min} + 2.\delta_0, \cdots, \phi_{max} - \delta_0, \phi_{max}]$, involving (say) eleven ϕ^* values, where, in the initial grid, $\delta_0 = \phi_{max} - \phi_{min}/10$. This defines an initial "optimal" utility function value, $u_{i,t}^{*1}$, at $\phi_{i,t}^{*1}$, with associated values for $\omega_{i,t}^{*1}$ and $\pi_{i,t}^{*1}$.

The values of $\phi_{i,t}^{*1}$ and δ_0 define our initial grid conditions. Let $m = 1, \cdots, M$ define the index number of each successive grid search and let $\delta_m = \delta_{m-1}/G$ define the density of each such grid. Then we may define the points within arbitrary m^{th} grid as follows:

$$[\phi_{i,t}^{*m} - \delta_{m-1} + \delta_m, \phi_{i,t}^{*m} - \delta_{m-1} + 2.\delta_m, \ldots, \phi_{i,t}^{*m}, \ldots,$$

$$\delta_{m-1} - 2.\delta_m, \phi_{i,t}^{*m} - \delta_{m-1} - \delta_m].$$

Thus, for example, the choice of $G = 10$ would result in each successive grid size being one-tenth of the preceding one and bounded by the points, $[\phi_{i,t}^{*m} - \delta_{m-1}, \phi_{i,t}^{*m} + \delta_{m-1}]$, which have already been evaluated. The successive evaluation of these grids stops when $\phi_{i,t}^{M}$ has been determined with prespecified accuracy, and, in turn, permits the evaluation of the associated values of $u_{i,t}^{*M}$, $\omega_{i,t}^{*M}$ and $\pi_{i,t}^{*M}$, the Markowitz portfolio.

For subsequent purposes, the succession of all grid values then should be rank-ordered from ϕ_{min} to ϕ_{max}. Thus, for each value of the expected rate of return, $\phi_{i,t}^*$, employed in the preceding succession of grid searches, these may be associated tabularly with the corresponding values of the standard deviation, $\omega_{i,t}^*$, the value of the maximum utility level, $u_{i,t}^*$, and the "optimal" portfolio vector, $\pi_{i,t}^*$. We note that the design of the grid search we have advocated "bunches" many evaluation points around the $\phi_{i,t}^{*M}$ of interest. Two criteria are relevant to the choice of M and G in the succession of grids:

1. The grid-size, G, must be small enough to determine $\pi_{i,t}^{*M}$ to a prespecified level of accuracy.

2. The succession of grids, M, must be sufficiently dense around $\pi_{i,t}^{*M}$ that is possible to fit a polynomial of suitable order (cases 1 and 2 below) or a "polynomial spline" (case 3 below) to the expected rates of return and standard deviations, $(\phi_{i,t}^*, \omega_{i,t}^*)$ in the neighborhood of the point, $(\phi_{i,t}^{*M}, \omega_{i,t}^{*M})$, which determines the optimal Markowitz portfolio, $\pi_{i,t}^{*M}$.

As we show next and in Appendixes A and B, these points will prove helpful in evaluating the elements of the Jacobian matrix. Our procedure for the optimal portfolio selection can be contrasted with the algorithm in Lewis (1988) which maximizes a concave utility function but only with linear constraints. Alexander (1976, 1977) and Elton–Gruber (1991) also discuss quadratic programming algorithms applicable to the Markowitz (1959) and related models.[17]

Suppose, for instance, we have completed the aforementioned grid search to determine the optimal Markowitz portfolio. Then, a simple inspection of the optimal Markowitz portfolio would immediately reveal to the investigator, whether or not we have an interior optimum, i.e., $\pi_{i,t}^{*M} > 0$, or, alternatively, whether a boundary portfolio, $\pi_{1i,t}^{*M} > 0$ and $\pi_{2i,t}^{*M} = 0$, has been obtained; but not immediately inform the investigator whether or not the prevailing optimal boundary portfolio is a noncorner or a corner solution. This, however, requires that we inspect the composition of the closest adjacent portfolios associated with the values, $\phi^{*M} - \delta_M$ and $\phi^{*M} + \delta_M$, to reveal whether one or more risky assets have been introduced or deleted relative to the optimal portfolio, $\pi_{i,t}^{*M}$. Now we investigate each of the possible cases for the prevailing portfolio and the associated boundary function approximations in turn.[18]

1. Interior Solutions

Suppose we have an interior solution for $\pi_{i,t}^{*M}$, involving all the risky assets. In the next step, inspect all of the adjacent portfolios, $\pi_{i,t}^* > 0$, in the neighborhood of $\pi_{i,t}^{*M}$ to identify which of them are also interior points. This will include portfolios from each of the current $(m = M)$ and preceding $(m = 1, \cdots, M - 1)$ grids that have already been rank-ordered by their expected rate of return, $\phi_{i,t}^*$. Let $\phi_{i,t}^{min}$, and $\phi_{i,t}^{max}$, respectively, denote the smallest and largest expected rate of return associated with an interior portfolio. Suppose that this includes a total of $S_1 + 1$ interior points—one of which is $\phi_{i,t}^{*M}$. Then over the range, $[\phi_{i,t}^{min}, \phi_{i,t}^{max}]$, we have the set of efficient boundary points, $\{(\phi_{i,t}^s, \omega_{i,t}^s): s = 0, 1, \cdots, S_1\}$ in risk-return space, and we can approximate the unknown efficient boundary frontier by an interpolation polynomial of degree S_1. This algorithm permits us to replace the unknown efficient frontier, $b^M(\phi_{i,t}^*, \omega_{i,t}^*) = 0$, by a known polynomial approximation that passes through each of the $S_1 + 1$ grid points and is twice continuously differentiable. For further details refer to Appendix A.

2. Boundary Noncorner Solution

Consider, next, the case of boundary noncorner solution, $\phi_{i,t}^{*M}$, resulting from a succession of grid searches. Inspection of the composition of $\phi_{i,t}^{*M}$, upon reordering the elements, reveals that the A_1-element subvector $(A_1 < A)$ $\phi_{1,i,t}^{*M} > 0$, whereas the A_2-element subvector, $\phi_{2,i,t}^{*M} = 0$, with $A_1 + A_2 = A$. We may therefore proceed exactly as before and approximate the unknown implicit efficient boundary frontier by an interpolation polynomial of degree S_2. Again, for further details, refer to Appendix A.

3. Boundary Corner Solution

It remains to consider the case where $\phi_{i,t}^{*M}$ is a boundary *corner* solution. In this case, the two portfolios associated with $\phi_{i,t}^{*M} - \delta_M$ and $\phi_{i,t}^{*M} + \delta_M$ will be of different types, reflecting the fact that one or more assets have been deleted from and/or added to the portfolio $\phi_{i,t}^{*M}$, associated with the expected rate of return, $\phi_{i,t}^{*M}$.[19] It follows that a *different* polynomial approximation function to the efficient boundary function, $b_{i,t}^M(\phi_{i,t}^*, \omega_{i,t}^*) = 0$, must be fit to the common portfolio types that have expected rates of return that are greater or equal to $\phi_{i,t}^{*M}$, as opposed to those with expected returns that are less than or equal to $\phi_{i,t}^{*M}$. Moreover, the two approximation functions must be coincident at the common "joint point," $(\phi_{i,t}^{*M}, \omega_{i,t}^{*M})$. Thus, in the case of the corner solution, we assume that there are S_{31} points with smaller ϕ-values than $\phi_{i,t}^{*M}$ and S_{32} relevant grid points greater than $\phi_{i,t}^{*M}$—plus the inclusion of $\phi_{i,t}^{*M}$, itself, in each.

In short, at this juncture, the approximation function is a concave spline with a joint point at $(\phi_{i,t}^{*M}, \omega_{i,t}^{*M})$, where the "left-hand" derivative of the approximation function associated with smaller expected rates of return evaluated at the value, $\phi_{i,t}^{*M}$, will be larger than the "right-hand" derivative of the corresponding portfolio with larger expected rates of return (see Figure 1). This results in "jump continuities" in the derivative of the original function and the approximating polynomial function to the left and the right of the value, $\phi_{i,t}^{*M}$, at which point the derivative is not defined. Our approach to this dilemma is to replace the approximating polynomials in the immediate vicinity of $(\phi_{i,t}^{*M}, \omega_{i,t}^{*M})$ by a circle of sufficiently small radius in $(\phi_{i,t}, \omega_{i,t})$-space, and to evaluate the requisite derivative relative to $\phi_{i,t}^{*M}$ as the slope of the "circular approximant" (see Appendix A for details).

C. Evaluation of the Jacobian Matrix

The burden of the preceding subsection has been to argue that in the neighborhood of the optimal portfolio, $\phi_{i,t}^{*M}$, the unknown efficient frontier, $b^M(\phi_{i,t}^*, \omega_{i,t}^*) = 0$, may be approximated by an analytic, twice-continuously differentiable function, $b^{*M}(\phi_{i,t}^*, \omega_{i,t}^*) = 0$, regardless of which type of portfolio is encountered. Thus at this junction, we may exploit the fact that both the utility function, $u_{i,t}$, and the boundary function, b^{*M}, are known differentiable functions.

Since the optimal Markowitz portfolio, $\pi_{i,t}^{*M}$, can only be computed by numerical methods, it may be tempting to conclude that its partial derivatives, $J_{i,t}^1 \equiv \partial \pi_{i,t}^{*M} / \partial \xi$, must also be computed by numerical approximation. This would involve perturbing each element of ξ in turn by a small $\varepsilon > 0$, and using finite-difference approximations, relative to the prevailing value of ξ (see, e.g., Quandt, 1983 to evaluate each of the partial derivatives required in $J_{i,t}^1$). This would entail repeating the same steps required to calculate $\pi_{i,t}^{*M}$ a further $p = 1, \cdots, P$ times, as each parameter in ξ is successively perturbed by ε and the optimal portfolio is recomputed. In the context of our algorithm, therefore, it is of considerable importance to note that, even though $\pi_{i,t}^{*M}$ must be computed by numerical methods, once $\pi_{i,t}^{*M}$ is known, its Jacobian matrix may be calculated directly using a closed-form expression. Since this must be done for each (i, t) in the sample over the iterations, $n = 0, 1, \cdots$, this saves vast amounts of computer time.

Given our twice continuously differentiable approximation, $b^{*M}(\phi_{i,t}^*, \omega_{i,t}^*) = 0$, to the efficient boundary function in the neighborhood of $\pi_{i,t}^{*M}$, to derive this expression, recast the utility maximization problem as:

$$\max_{\pi} u\left(\pi'_{i,t}\hat{\mu}_{i,t},\ (\pi'_{i,t}\hat{\Sigma}_t\pi_{i,t})^{\frac{1}{2}};\ x_{i,t},\ \xi\right), \quad \text{s.t.} \quad b^{*M}_{i,t}\left(\pi'_{i,t}\hat{\mu}_{i,t},\ (\pi'_{i,t}\hat{\Sigma}_t\pi_{i,t})^{\frac{1}{2}}\right) = 0 \quad (26)$$

Formulate a Lagrange function and denote the Lagrange multiplier as $\lambda_{i,t}$. Elementary total differentiation of the two first-order conditions with respect to $\pi_{i,t}$, $\lambda_{i,t}$, ξ, with all the partials evaluated at ξ^n, leads to the following set of equations:

$$\left[J^{1*}_{i,t}\right]^n \cdot dz_{i,t} \equiv \begin{bmatrix} S^{1n}_{i,t} & s^{1n}_{i,t} \\ s^{1n\prime}_{i,t} & 0 \end{bmatrix} \cdot \begin{bmatrix} d\pi_{i,t} \\ d\lambda_{i,t} \end{bmatrix} = \begin{bmatrix} -R^{1n}_{i,t} \cdot d\xi \\ 0 \end{bmatrix}, \quad (27)$$

where $z_{i,t} \equiv [\pi'_{i,t} \mid \lambda_{i,t}]'$; and the expression of $S^1_{i,t}$, $s^1_{i,t}$, and $R^1_{i,t}$ are quite complicated, and relegated to Appendix B. It follows that using the formula for partitioned inverses (see, e.g., Rao, 1973, p. 73), we may solve Equation 27 for a closed-form expression for the full Jacobian matrix,

$$[J^1_{i,t}]^n \equiv \frac{\partial[\pi^{*M}_{i,t}]^n}{\partial\xi} = -[R^1_{i,t}]^n\left[\{S^{1n}_{i,t}\}^{-1} - \frac{\{S^{1n}_{i,t}\}^{-1} \cdot s^{1n}_{i,t} \cdot s^{1n\prime}_{i,t} \cdot \{S^{1n}_{i,t}\}^{-1}}{s^{1n\prime}_{i,t} \cdot \{S^{1n}_{i,t}\}^{-1} \cdot s^{1n}_{i,t}}\right] \quad (28)$$

Thus the desired sub-matrix $\bar{J}^{1n}_{i,t}$ can be extracted from $J^{1n}_{i,t}$, and inserted into the algorithm in Equation 21.

V. INDIRECT *EX POST* CALIBRATION OF PORTFOLIO CHOICE

Tests based on predictions about investor portfolio holdings can provide powerful tests of asset pricing theories. The previous section described one such econometric method by which parameters in the investor's utility function can be determined on the basis of their reflections in the actual portfolio decisions of investors. It is, however, arguable as to whether investors' expectations of future rates of returns are best modeled as manifestations of the preceding, historical behavior of actual prices, or whether such investor expectations are better reflected in the actual portfolio decisions that investors make. Accordingly in this section, we generalize the econometric problem to the case in which *both* the parameters in the investors utility function *and* those in the model adopted for the expected rates of return are simultaneously determined, *ex post*, from the actual portfolios selected by investors.

Specifically, in this section, we generalize our calibration methods to include not only the $P \times 1$ vector of taste parameters, ξ, in the investors utility function, but also include the $(K + 1) \cdot (L + 1) \cdot N$ parameters in the variable-coefficient autoregressive models that surrogates for heterogeneity in the investor population. However, it is important to emphasize that the proposed calibration methodology is general enough to accommodate any reasonably parameterized heterogeneous forcing process for asset returns. We proceed as before in three steps: describing first the quasi-Newton algorithm, then characterizing the optimal Markowitz portfolio relative to the prevailing parameter values and the associated boundary function approximation using numerical methods, and finally evaluating the elements of the Jacobian matrix.

A. The Quasi-Newton Algorithm

Let the $\hat{\mu}_{i,t}(\gamma_i) \equiv (\hat{\mu}_{i,a,t}(\gamma_i))$ denote the A-element vector of expected rates of return for investor i in period t. It has previously been noted that the parameters, $\{\gamma_{i,k,l}: k = 0, 1, \cdots, K; l = 0, 1, \cdots, L\}$, are independent of the particular asset "a" and the time period t. Consequently, let

$$\gamma_i = [\gamma_{i,0,0}, \gamma_{i,1,0}, \cdots, \gamma_{i,K,0} \,|\, \gamma_{i,0,1}, \gamma_{i,1,1}, \cdots, \gamma_{i,K,1} \,|\, \cdots \,|\, \gamma_{i,0,L}, \gamma_{i,1,L}, \cdots, \gamma_{i,K,L}]' \tag{29}$$

denote the $(K + 1) \cdot (L + 1)$ autoregressive parameters applicable to the ith investor. Furthermore let $\theta \equiv [\xi' \,|\, \gamma_1', \cdots, \gamma_i', \cdots, \gamma_N']'$ denote the $B \equiv P + (K + 1) \cdot (L + 1) \cdot N$ parameters in the complete model, and note that for any investor i and time period t, the portfolio model contains only the parameters, ξ and γ_i, the former common to each observation in the sample. Thus, we have the complete model which can be written, as before as:

$$\pi_{i,t} = \pi_{i,t}^{*M} + \nu_{i,t} \equiv \pi_{i,t}^{*M}\left(\mathbf{x}_{i,t}, \hat{\mu}_{i,t}(\gamma_i), \hat{\Sigma}; \xi\right) + \nu_{i,t} \tag{30}$$

and define the quadratic loss function as:

$$Q^2(\theta) = \frac{1}{2} \sum_{t=1}^{T} \sum_{i=1}^{N} \left(\pi_{i,t} - \pi_{i,t}^{*M}\right)' \cdot \left[\Omega^2\right]^{\dagger}\left(\pi_{i,t} - \pi_{i,t}^{*M}\right) \tag{31}$$

which now has to be minimized with respect to, θ, where Ω^2 is the $A \times A$ weighting matrix:

$$\Omega^2 = \frac{1}{TN} \sum_{t=1}^{T} \sum_{i=1}^{N} \left(\pi_{i,t} - \pi_{i,t}^{*M}\right) \cdot \left(\pi_{i,t} - \pi_{i,t}^{*M}\right)' \tag{32}$$

Again, using the same arguments as before, Ω^2 must be of rank $A - 1$, so one of the risky assets must be deleted—say the Ath. Accordingly, this results in the modified model:

$$\overline{\pi}_{i,t} = \overline{\pi}_{i,t}^{*M} + \overline{\nu}_{i,t} \equiv \overline{\pi}_{i,t}^{*M}\left(\mathbf{x}_{i,t}, \hat{\mu}_{i,t}(\gamma_i), \hat{\Sigma}; \xi\right) + \overline{\nu}_{i,t} \tag{33}$$

Form a quadratic loss function, $\overline{Q}^2$ analogous to $\overline{Q}^1$, and consider the first-order conditions with respect to the parameter vector θ:

$$\frac{\partial \overline{Q}^2}{\partial \theta} = -\sum_{t=1}^{T} \sum_{i=1}^{N} \{\overline{J}_{i,t}^2\}' \cdot \left[\overline{\Omega}^2\right]^{\dagger} \cdot \left(\overline{\pi}_{i,t} - \overline{\pi}_{i,t}^{*M}\right) = 0 \tag{34}$$

where now $\overline{J}_{i,t}^2 \equiv \partial \overline{\pi}^{*M}/\partial \theta$ is an $(A-1) \times B$ Jacobian matrix of partial derivatives. Following the same quasilinearization procedure in Section IV.A, we are lead to the *modified* quasi-Newton algorithm:

$$[\theta]^{n+1} = [\theta]^n - [\psi]^n \cdot [\overline{H}^2]^n \cdot [\overline{g}^2]^n \tag{35}$$

where:

$$[\overline{H}^2]^n = \sum_{t=1}^{T} \sum_{i=1}^{N} \left[\{\overline{J}_{i,t}^2\}' \right]^n \cdot \left[\overline{\Omega}^{2n} \right]^{+} \cdot \left[\overline{J}_{i,t}^1 \right]^n \tag{36}$$

denotes the $B \times B$ Hessian matrix under the method of quasilinearization:

$$[\overline{g}^2]^n = -\sum_{t=1}^{T} \sum_{i=1}^{N} \left[\{\overline{J}_{i,t}^2\}' \right]^n \cdot \left[\overline{\Omega}^{2n} \right]^{+} \cdot \left(\overline{\pi}_{i,t} - \left[\overline{\pi}_{i,t}^{*M} \right]^n \right) \tag{37}$$

denotes the $B \times 1$ gradient vector; and $[\psi]^n$ denotes a suitable step-size parameter defined over the unit interval, $[0,1]$, and chosen to ensure the feasibility and the monotonicity of θ^{n+1}. Then by similar arguments presented to obtain Equation 24, the sequence of the parameter values, $\{\theta^n\}$, will converge to a limit point:

$$\hat{\theta} = \lim_{n \to \infty} [\theta]^n \tag{38}$$

The next two sections discuss the derivation and evaluation of the Jacobian matrix used above in the context of optimal portfolio choice.

B. Efficiency Frontier Approximations

Consider the arbitrary investor i in period t, and seek an expression for the $(A-1) \times B$ sub-matrix, $\overline{J}_{i,t}^2 \equiv \partial \overline{\pi}^{*M}/\partial \theta$, of the complete Jacobian matrix $J_{i,t}^2$. As before, the unknown efficiency frontier which is only defined *pointwise*, where, for any specified $\phi_{i,t}^*$, with associated $\omega_{i,t}^*$ and $\pi_{i,t}^*$, we have:

$$b_{i,t}^M(\phi_{i,t}^*, \omega_{i,t}^*) \equiv b_{i,t}^M \left(\pi_{i,t}^{*} \hat{\mu}_{i,t}(\gamma_{i,t}), (\pi_{i,t}^{*} \hat{\Sigma} \pi_{i,t}^*)^{\frac{1}{2}} \right) = 0 \tag{39}$$

We proceed in analogous fashion to Section IV.B and define a sequence of grids at which $\omega_{i,t}^*$, $\pi_{i,t}^*$, and $u_{i,t}^*$ are evaluated. These, in turn, lead to the determination of the optimal portfolio, $\pi_{i,t}^{*M}$ relative to the prevailing parameter values, ξ, and γ_i. Moreover, by inspection of the composition of $\pi_{i,t}^{*M}$ and its two adjacent portfolios $\{\phi^{*M} - \delta_M\}$ and $\{\phi^{*M} + \delta_M\}$, we may again determine whether $\pi_{i,t}^{*M}$ is an interior solution (case 1), a boundary noncorner solution (case 2), or a boundary corner solution (case 3). Consequently, for the boundary function approximations, a similar procedure to those advanced in Section IV.B applies to each of the possible types of portfolio for $\pi_{i,t}^{*M}$.

1. Interior Solutions

Using the points, $\{(\phi_{i,t}^s, \omega_{i,t}^s): s = 0, 1, \cdots, S_1\}$ obtained from tabular presentation of the ordered $\phi_{i,t}^{*s}$-values, Appendix A provides the methods by which the unknown efficient boundary function, $b^M(\phi_{i,t}^*, \omega_{i,t}^*) = 0$, of Equation 39 can be replaced by a twice continuously differentiable approximation function, $b^{*M}(\phi_{i,t}^*, \omega_{i,t}^*) = 0$, in the neighborhood of $\pi_{i,t}^{*M}$.

2. Boundary Noncorner Solution

Apart from the fact that now we are dealing with $A_1 < A$ assets, the same procedures as discussed in Section IV.B apply to fitting an interpolation polynomial approximation to the efficient boundary function to a boundary noncorner solution involving the points, $\{(\phi_{i,t}^s, \omega_{i,t}^s): s = 0, 1, \cdots, S_2\}$—see Appendix A.

3. Boundary Corner Solution

In the case of a boundary corner solution, as before, we must fit a spline which is piecewise twice continuously differentiable to the "left" and the "right" of the "join point" value, $\phi_{i,t}^{*M}$. This involves $S_{31} + 1$ points, $(\phi_{i,t}^*, \omega_{i,t}^*)$, for expected rates of return with values less than or equal to $\phi_{i,t}^{*M}$, and $S_{32} + 1$ points with greater than or equal expected rates of return than $\phi_{i,t}^{*M}$. For details, the reader can refer to Appendix A and C.

C. Evaluation of the Jacobian Matrix

With the approximation to the efficient boundary function in hand, we may reformulate the investors utility maximization problem as follows:

$$\max_{\pi_{it}} u\left(\pi_{i,t}'\hat{\mu}_{i,t}(\gamma_{i,t}), (\pi_{i,t}'\hat{\Sigma}_t\pi_{i,t})^{\frac{1}{2}}; x_{i,t}, \xi \right), \quad \text{s.t.} \quad b_{i,t}^{*M}\left(\pi_{i,t}'\hat{\mu}_{i,t}(\gamma_{i,t}), (\pi_{i,t}'\hat{\Sigma}_t\pi_{i,t})^{\frac{1}{2}} \right) = 0$$

which differs from Equation 26 in that dependence of $\hat{\mu}_{i,t}$ on γ_i is now explicit. Denote the Lagrange multiplier for this maximization problem as $\lambda_{i,t}$. Total differentiation of the first-order conditions with respect to $\pi_{i,t}$, $\lambda_{i,t}$, and θ can be written instructively as:

$$\left[J_{i,t}^{2*} \right]^n \cdot dz_{i,t} \equiv \begin{bmatrix} S_{i,t}^{2n} & s_{i,t}^{2n} \\ s_{i,t}^{2n\prime} & 0 \end{bmatrix} \cdot \begin{bmatrix} d\pi_{i,t} \\ d\lambda_{i,t} \end{bmatrix} = \begin{bmatrix} -[R_{i,t}^2]^n \cdot d\theta \\ 0 \end{bmatrix} \tag{40}$$

where the $A \times A$ matrix, $S_{i,t}^2$, the $A \times 1$ vector, $s_{i,t}^2$, and the $A \times P + (K + 1) \cdot (L + 1)$ matrix, $R_{i,t}^2$ are defined in Appendix C, and are evaluated at the prevailing parameter value, θ^n. Here, the last of these, $R_{i,t}^2$, exhibits a patterned structure due to the fact that only γ_i appears in the $(i,t)^{\text{th}}$ term. It follows from the use of partitioned inversion of the leading matrix, $[J_{i,t}^{2*}]^n$, in Equation 40 that a closed-form expression for the full Jacobian matrix can be derived as:

$$J_{i,t}^{2n} \equiv \frac{\partial \pi_{i,t}^{*Mn}}{\partial \xi} = -R_{i,t}^{2n} \left[\{S_{i,t}^{2n}\}^{-1} - \frac{\{S_{i,t}^{2n}\}^{-1} \cdot s_{i,t}^{2n} \cdot s_{i,t}^{2n\prime} \cdot \{S_{i,t}^{2n}\}^{-1}}{s_{i,t}^{2n\prime} \{S_{i,t}^{2n}\}^{-1} \cdot s_{i,t}^{2n}} \right] \qquad (41)$$

Thus the sub-matrix $\overline{J}_{i,t}^{2n}$, of interest in the algorithm may simply be inserted into Equation 35.

VI. EXTENSIONS AND RELATED ISSUES

The proposed calibration methods are potentially useful in several other asset-pricing applications, especially in situations where it is important to introduce institutional restriction. Consider first the portfolio selection model due to Tobin (1958, 1965), who explored the consequence of introducing a risk-free asset into an otherwise risky portfolio. As is well known, in this case of riskless borrowing and lending, the Sharpe portfolio or the market portfolio, denoted s, can be defined as the point on the efficiency frontier at which a line emanating from the point, $(r^f, 0)$, in risk-return space, has maximum slope. This reflects the fact that any convex combination of the risk-free asset and a portfolio of risky assets is feasible. Apart from the increase in dimensionality of the portfolio selection problem, the econometric accommodation of the Tobin model poses no new substantive issues. For instance, the algorithm discussed in Sections IV.B, V.B, and Appendix A must now simply be modified to locate that point $(\phi_{i,t}^s, \omega_{i,t}^s)$, on the efficiency boundary that maximizes the slope, $\phi_{i,t}^s r_t^f / \omega_{i,t}^s$, of the line,

$$\phi_{i,t} = r_t^f + \left[\frac{\phi_{i,t}^s - r_t^f}{\omega_{i,t}^s} \right] \omega_{i,t} \qquad (42)$$

Under homogeneous returns, this search determines the Sharpe (market) portfolio; and then it is straightforward to determine the optimal utility maximizing portfolio, $[w \mid (1 - w) \cdot s']'$, where w is the proportion of the risk-free asset held and $(1 - w)$ is the proportion held in the form of the Sharpe risky asset portfolio.

The institutional distinction that borrowing rates (r^{fB}) must be greater than the lending rates (r^{fL}), i.e., $r^{fB} > r^{fL}$, as emphasized in Brennan (1971), can be similarly handled. Let s^L and s^B, respectively, denote the Sharpe portfolios relative to the lending and borrowing rates. The Brennan efficient boundary function, $b^{BR}(\phi, \omega) = 0$, consists of three pieces: (1) a straight line connecting the point, $(r^{fL}, 0)$, to the point, (ϕ^{sL}, ω^{sL}), where $(\phi^{sL} = s^{L\prime}\mu$, and $\omega^{sL} = (s^{L\prime}\Sigma s^L)^{1/2}$; (2) the Markowitz efficient boundary function, $b^M(\phi, \omega) = 0$, for (ϕ, ω) values between (ϕ^{sL}, ω^{sL}) and (ϕ^{sB}, ω^{sB}); and (3) a straight line emanating from the point, (ϕ^{sB}, ω^{sB}), with slope $\phi^{sB} - r^{fB}/\omega^{sB}$. With this set-up, the calibration procedures are essentially the same: the forward solution, the Brennan efficient boundary function, is searched for the value which maximizes utility, subject to any institutional restrictions on lending and borrowing which may also restrict the domain of w. In the inverse problem, however, problem arise with possible corner solutions at either of the two join points, which as discussed before, can be handled by circular approximants.

Suppose now, the non-negativity restriction on the portfolio's is removed as in Black (1972). This implies that the Black efficiency frontier, $b^B(\phi, \omega)$, is defined as a solution to the following quadratic programming problem:

$$\min_{\pi} \frac{1}{2} \pi' \Sigma \pi \quad \text{s.t.} \quad i'\pi = 1, \ \mu'\pi = \phi^* \tag{43}$$

This leads to a closed-form hyperbolic expression for the investor's efficiency frontier (Alexander-Francis, 1986; Ingersoll, 1987; Huang and Litzenberger, 1988; Elton-Gruber, 1991):

$$b^B(\phi, \omega) = \omega - \left\{ [\phi \ i] \cdot D^{-1} \cdot \begin{bmatrix} \phi \\ i \end{bmatrix} \right\}^{\frac{1}{2}} = 0; \quad D = \begin{bmatrix} \mu' \\ i' \end{bmatrix} \cdot \Sigma \cdot [\mu \ i]; \tag{44}$$

and, by standard solution of the first-order conditions or by numerical grid-search methods, the utility function may be maximized. In the *mixed* Markowitz–Black model, short sales without margin requirements are permitted on only a subset, π_1, of the A risky assets, with no forward markets for the remainder, π_2. Thus, the optimization problem confronting the investor is identical to Equation 6, except that the number of non-negativity constraints in $\pi \geq 0$ is replaced by $\pi_1 \geq 0$. Thus, the Black (1972) model and the mixed Markowitz–Black models permits calibration of the structural parameters as discussed above, as would be expected from a special case.

In situations where short selling of risky assets is permitted but typical margin required are imposed, the analysis of Dyl (1975), Ross (1977), and Sharpe (1991) leads to the following relationship between realized long (r^{lo}), and short rates (r^{sh}):

$$r^{sh}_{a,t} = -\frac{r^{lo}_{a,t}}{c_{a,t}}$$

where $c_{a,t}$ is proportion of the short-sale proceeds deposited with the broker. This mixed Markowitz–Black case is straightforward application of our econometric methodology and involves an increase in the dimensionality of the problem to $2 \cdot A$ risky assets.

Observe that the market-based capital asset pricing model (CAPM) and its multibeta interpretations in Merton (1973) only exploit the homogeneous input assumptions. This assumption implies that all the optimal portfolio's will lie on the same linear function in the risk-return space and the proportion of the risky assets contained in the Sharpe or "market portfolio," s, will be identical across all investors, so that the optimal portfolio's will only differ in the proportions, $w_{i,t}$, of risk-free versus risky assets that are held. But surely, the essence of a stock market is that different investors arrive at different expectations as to the future course of prices and dividends, and that is why there are both buyers and sellers to "make a market" and, consequently, motivated the econometric implementation of portfolio choice under heterogeneous expectations.

VII. CONCLUDING REMARKS

In this paper, we have developed an econometric methodology associated with the inverse of the portfolio selection problem. In particular, given a time series of actual observed portfolio of risky assets for a sample of investors, a set of socioeconomic characteristics for each investor in the sample, and a time series of preceding rates of return for the set of risky assets, the algorithm determines the parameter values in each investor's utility function and the associated parameters in the returns-generating process. It also determines the optimal current portfolios at the same time for all sample members. The proposed econometric framework can, therefore, accommodate either homogeneous or heterogeneous expected returns and covariance matrix. Specifically, in the context of market-based CAPM, note that heterogeneous expectations causes investors to face different efficiency frontiers and destroys the linearity of the *security market line* and this forces the analysis into the domain of searching for the *structural* parameters which underlies the economic system, rather than just the "α" and "β" parameters.

This paper makes two important methodological contributions in terms of the algorithm for portfolio selection and its inverse.[20] First, since the efficient boundary function can only be determined pointwise, we have employed Lagrange interpolation polynomials fitted to the points on an increasingly finer, one-dimensional grids. This permits the approximating polynomials to pass through each of the grid points, and preserves the concavity of the efficient boundary function. However, in cases where the calibration algorithm encounters a "corner solution" which results in "jump discontinuities" in the partial derivatives efficiency frontier, our approach is to use "circular approximants". This allows us to approximate the efficiency frontier by embedding a small circle into the immediate vicinity of the corner point. Second, whereas only *numerical* solutions can be computed for the optimal Markowitz portfolio, we demonstrate that given this optimal portfolio, the Jacobian matrix of partial derivatives required to implement the quasi-Newton procedure can be derived as a closed-form analytic expression. This avoids the need for the use of numerical approximations to the derivatives in each iteration and, therefore, saves vast amounts of computer time.

Clearly, the existing asset-pricing theories such as the market-based CAPM and the consumption-based CAPM have the distinct advantage that they can be fitted to aggregate-time series data. However, predictions about individual or panels of portfolio holdings can provide powerful tests of asset pricing theories. Consequently, a natural question, in the present framework, is how to go from a microtheory of the individual or institutional investor's asset–portfolio mix to the aggregate behavior of the market for risky and risk-free assets. If the set of panel data represents a stratified sample of individual/institutional investors, then by applying suitable sampling weights to the numerical solution values in the sample, one may develop an internally consistent micro–macro model with no further restrictions on the functional forms of the underlying functional relationships—the investor's returns-generating process and the utility function—than the customary stipulations of "well-behavedness".

APPENDIX A: APPROXIMATIONS TO THE EFFICIENT BOUNDARY FUNCTION

A.   Interior Solutions and Boundary Noncorner Solutions

Both the interior and boundary noncorner portfolios require fitting a polynomial to the set of (say) $S + 1$ points, $\{(\phi_{i,t}^{*s}, \omega_{i,t}^{*s}): s = 0, 1, \ldots, S$, in risk-return space. It will be convenient for our purposes to employ Lagrange interpolation polynomials (Isaacson and Keller, 1966, p. 189), defined as:

$$\omega_{i,t} \equiv f_S(\phi_{i,t}) = \sum_{s=0}^{S} \omega_{i,t}^{*s} \prod_{r=0,r\neq s}^{S} \frac{(\phi_{i,t} - \phi_{i,t}^{*r})}{(\phi_{i,t}^{*s} - \phi_{i,t}^{*r})} \tag{45}$$

Note that at any of the grid points, $\phi_{i,t} = \phi_{i,t}^{*s}$, we have $\omega_{i,t} = \omega_{i,t}^{*s}$ for $s = 0, 1, \ldots, S$, hence the Lagrange interpolation polynomial is of degrees; and it passes through each of the $(S + 1)$ grid points, $(\phi_{i,t}^{*s}, \omega_{i,t}^{*s})$. Equivalently, the approximation to the unknown efficiency frontier in the neighborhood of $\phi_{i,t}^{*M}$ can be rewritten for present purposes as the implicit function:

$$b_{i,t}^{*M}(\phi_{i,t}, \omega_{i,t}) = \omega_{i,t} - \sum_{s=0}^{S} \omega_{i,t}^{*s} \prod_{r=0,r\neq s}^{S} \frac{(\phi_{i,t} - \phi_{i,t}^{*r})}{(\phi_{i,t}^{*s} - \phi_{i,t}^{*r})} = 0 \equiv \omega_{i,t} - f_S(\phi_{i,t}) \tag{46}$$

As we demonstrate in Appendices B and C, to calculate the elements of the Jacobian matrix in either the direct *ex ante* or direct *ex post* cases, we require various expressions for the partial derivatives of $b_{i,t}^{*M}(\phi_{i,t}, \omega_{i,t})$, with respect to $\phi_{i,t}$ and $\omega_{i,t}$, which we can write below as:

$$\frac{\partial b_{i,t}^{*M}(\phi_{i,t}, \omega_{i,t})}{\partial \phi_{i,t}} = \sum_{s=0}^{S} \omega_{i,t}^{*s} \frac{\sum_{u=0}^{S} \prod_{r=0,r\neq u}^{S}(\phi_{i,t} - \phi_{i,t}^{*r})}{\prod_{r=0,r\neq s}^{S}(\phi_{i,t}^{*s} - \phi_{i,t}^{*r})} = \frac{\partial f_S(\phi_{i,t}, \omega_{i,t})}{\partial \phi_{i,t}}; \quad \frac{\partial b_{i,t}^{*M}(\phi_{i,t}, \omega_{i,t})}{\partial \omega_{i,t}} = 1$$

$$\tag{47}$$

Similarly, the second partial derivatives are given by:

$$\frac{\partial^2 b_{i,t}^{*M}}{\partial \phi_{i,t}^2} = \sum_{s=0}^{S} \omega_{i,t}^{*s} \frac{\Sigma_{u=0}^{S} \Sigma_{v=0, v \neq u}^{S} \Pi_{r=0, r \neq u, r \neq v}^{S} (\phi_{i,t} - \phi_{i,t}^{*r})}{\Pi_{r=0, r \neq s}^{S} (\phi_{i,t}^{*s} - \phi_{i,t}^{*r})}; \quad \frac{\partial^2 b_{i,t}^{*M}}{\partial \omega_{i,t} \partial \phi_{i,t}} = \frac{\partial^2 b_{i,t}^{*M}}{\partial \omega_{i,t}^2} = 0 \quad (48)$$

These expressions, along with the first and second partial derivatives of the utility function specified by the investigator with respect to $\phi_{i,t}$ and $\omega_{i,t}$, are required to define the elements of the Jacobian matrix, as outlined in Appendices B and C.

B. Boundary Corner Solutions

It remains to approximate the efficient boundary by a twice continuously differentiable function when a corner solution obtains. As noted earlier, such situations occur when one or more assets are introduced into or deleted from the prevailing portfolio. In risk-return space, the presence of a corner solution is revealed to the investigator by the adjacent portfolio with slightly smaller or larger expected rate of return than that associated with $\phi_{i,t}^{*M}$ being of different types.

Suppose that, in the neighborhood of $\phi_{i,t}^{*M}$, there are $S_1 + 1$ grid points, $\{(\phi_{i,t}^{*s}, \omega_{i,t}^{*s}): s = 0, 1, \ldots, S_1\}$, associated with the adjacent portfolios with expected rates of return less than or equal to $\phi_{i,t}^{*M} = \phi_{i,t}^{*S_1}$ of (say) type 1; and suppose there are $S_2 + 1$ grid points, $\{(\phi_{i,t}^{*s}, \omega_{i,t}^{*s}): s = 0, 1, \ldots, S_2\}$, associated with the adjacent portfolios with expected rates of return less than or equal to $\phi_{i,t}^{*M} = \phi_{i,t}^{*0}$ of (say) type 2. By the analysis above, we may fit two separate Lagrange interpolation polynomials, $\omega_{i,t} = f_{S_1}(\pi_{i,t})$ and $\omega_{i,t} = g_{S_2}(\pi_{i,t})$ to the $\{\phi_{i,t}^{*s}, \omega_{i,t}^{*s}\}$-values associated with the portfolio of each type—including the corner portfolio. However, since each Lagrange interpolation polynomial passes through each of the grid points, $\{\phi_{i,t}^{*s}, \omega_{i,t}^{*s}\}$, it follows that the two approximation polynomials have the common "joint point", $\{\phi_{i,t}^{*M}, \omega_{i,t}^{*M}\}$—that is $\omega_{i,t}^{*M} = f_{S_1}(\pi_{i,t}^{*M}) = g_{S_2}(\pi_{i,t}^{*M})$. However, since $b_{i,t}^{M}(\phi_{i,t}, \omega_{i,t}) = 0$ is strictly concave, then so will be the approximation, $b_{i,t}^{*M}(\phi_{i,t}, \omega_{i,t}) = 0$, in the neighborhood of $\phi_{i,t}^{*M}$. Moreover, since $\phi_{i,t}^{*M}$ is associated with a corner portfolio, $\pi_{i,t}^{*M}$, it follows that the partial derivatives of the "left", $\partial f_{S_1}/\partial \phi_{i,t}$, and "right", $\partial g_{S_2}/\partial \phi_{i,t}$, of $\phi_{i,t}^{*M}$—the joint point—are not equal. This results in a "jump-discontinuity" in the associated elements of the Jacobian matrix, $J_{i,t}$; and we must resort to the use of various possible "smoothing techniques" to avoid the fact that the derivative, $\partial b_{i,t}^{*M}/\partial \phi_{i,t}$, does not exist at $\phi_{i,t}^{*M}$, which we describe below.

C. Circular Approximants

A comprehensive treatment of the smoothing techniques is given in Hardle (1990). Our development of the circular approximant is dictated by its simplicity when restricted to two-dimensional risk-return space. Essentially, circular approximants involve embedding a simple circle of pre-specified data, ρ, into the immediate vicinity of the corner point $(\phi_{i,t}^{*M}, \omega_{i,t}^{*M})$, which is tangent to both Lagrange interpolation polynomials, f_{S_1} and g_{S_2}; and the requisite partial derivatives at the corner solution value, $\phi_{i,t}^{*M}$, can then be taken relative to the "circular approximant".

The circular approximant is displayed in Figure 1. The two Lagrange interpolation polynomials, f_{S_1} and g_{S_2}, intersect at the corner solution, $(\phi_{i,t}^{*M}, \omega_{i,t}^{*M})$, in risk-return space. The problem in two dimensions is to smooth the approximation function by inserting a circle of suitably small radius so that it is tangent to both f_{S_1} and g_{S_2}, and then to define the approximating function between the two points of the tangency as the circle itself. Let this circular approximant be defined as:

$$(\phi_{i,t} - a)^2 + (\omega_{i,t} - b)^2 = \rho^2 \tag{49}$$

where (a, b) is the unknown center of the circle with specified radius, ρ. Then, the problem is to determine (a, b) from the knowledge of the two functions, f_{S_1} and

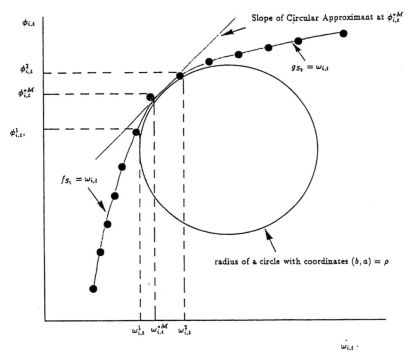

Notes: ●—curve denotes the points $\{(\phi_{i,t}^{*s}, \omega_{i,t}^{*s}): s = 0, 1, \cdots, S_1\}$ and $\{(\phi_{i,t}^{*s}, \omega_{i,t}^{*s}): s = 0, 1, \cdots, S_2\}$ on the functions, $\omega_{i,t} = f_{S_1}(\phi_{i,t})$ and $\omega_{i,t} = g_{S_2}$ respectively.

Figure 1. Circular Approximation in the Neighborhood of a Corner Solution

g_{S_2}, along with a given value for ρ. Despite, the apparent simplicity of this problem, unfortunately there does not appear to be a general closed-form solution.

Let $(\phi^1_{i,t}, \omega^1_{i,t})$ and $(\phi^2_{i,t}, \omega^2_{i,t})$ denote the points at which the circle is both tangent to and coincident with the functions $\omega_{i,t} = f_{S_1}(\phi_{i,t})$ and $\omega_{i,t} = g_{S_2}(\phi_{i,t})$, respectively. Then the equivalence of the two functions implies that:

$$(\phi^1_{i,t} - a)^2 + \left(f_{S_1}(\phi^1_{i,t}) - b\right)^2 = \rho^2; (\phi^2_{i,t} - a)^2 + \left(g_{S_2}(\phi^2_{i,t}) - b\right)^2 = \rho^2 \qquad (50)$$

whereas the equivalence of the slopes at these two points implies that:

$$\frac{(\phi^1_{i,t} - a)}{\left(f_{S_1}(\phi^1_{i,t}) - b\right)} = \frac{\partial f_{S_1}(\phi^2_{i,t})}{\partial \phi_{i,t}}; \frac{(\phi^2_{i,t} - a)}{\left(g_{S_2}(\phi^2_{i,t}) - b\right)} = \frac{\partial g_{S_2}(\phi^2_{i,t})}{\partial \phi_{i,t}} \qquad (51)$$

Here, f_{S_1} and g_{S_2} are Lagrange polynomials of order, $(S_1 + 1)$ and $(S_2 + 1)$; whereas the first partials of with respect to $\phi_{i,t}$ are given in Equation 47 and are polynomials of order S_1 and S_2, respectively. Thus, the four-equation system, Equations 50 and 51, must be solved numerically for the four variables: a, b, $\phi^1_{i,t}$, and $\phi^2_{i,t}$.

Thus given a solution to the above problem, the boundary function, $b^{*M}_{i,t}(\phi_{i,t}, \omega_{i,t}) = 0$, is then approximated by the values assumed by the circle over the arc from $(\phi^1_{i,t}, \omega^1_{i,t})$ to $(\phi^2_{i,t}, \omega^2_{i,t})$. Consequently, the approximation to the boundary function is given by:

$$b^{*M}_{i,t}(\phi_{i,t}, \omega_{i,t}) = (\phi_{i,t} - a)^2 + (\omega_{i,t} - b)^2 - \rho^2 = 0 \qquad (52)$$

over the specified arc; and the requite partial derivatives are given by:

$$\frac{\partial b^{*M}_{i,t}}{\partial \phi_{i,t}} = 2 \cdot (\phi^{*M}_{i,t} - a); \frac{\partial b^{*M}_{i,t}}{\partial \omega_{i,t}} = 2 \cdot (\omega^{*M}_{i,t} - b) \qquad (53)$$

and:

$$\frac{\partial^2 b^{*M}_{i,t}}{\partial \phi^2_{i,t}} = \frac{\partial^2 b^{*M}_{i,t}}{\partial \omega^2_{i,t}} = 2; \frac{\partial^2 b^{*M}_{i,t}}{\partial \phi_{i,t} \partial \omega_{i,t}} = 0 \qquad (54)$$

Clearly, the method of "circular approximants" can be extended to other conic section—for example, the use of ellipse.

APPENDIX B: EVALUATION OF THE JACOBIAN MATRIX IN THE DIRECT *EX ANTE* CASE

Regardless of the type of the optimal portfolio encountered by the algorithm in the direct *ex ante* case, this appendix demonstrates that given the restriction that the utility function be twice continuously differentiable, and given our twice continuously differentiable approximation to the efficient boundary function shown in Appendix A, the elements of the Jacobian matrix will be known in closed-form.

To prove this assertion, consider the constrained maximization problem from Section IV.C, which we can formulate as:

$$\max_{\pi_{i,t}} \Lambda_{i,t}(\pi_{i,t}, \lambda_{i,t}) = u\left(\pi'_{i,t}\hat{\mu}_{i,t}, (\pi'_{i,t}\hat{\Sigma}_t\pi_{i,t})^{\frac{1}{2}}; x_{i,t}, \xi\right) + \lambda_{i,t} \cdot b^{*M}_{i,t}\left(\pi'_{i,t}\hat{\mu}_{i,t}, (\pi'_{i,t}\hat{\Sigma}_t\pi_{i,t})^{\frac{1}{2}}\right)$$

(55)

The first order conditions for this maximization are:

$$\frac{\partial \Lambda_{i,t}}{\partial \pi_{i,t}} = \left(\frac{\partial u_{i,t}}{\partial \phi_{i,t}} + \lambda_{i,t} \cdot \frac{\partial b^{*M}_{i,t}}{\partial \phi_{i,t}}\right)\hat{\mu}_{i,t} + \left(\frac{\partial u_{i,t}}{\partial \omega_{i,t}} + \lambda_{i,t} \cdot \frac{\partial b^{*M}_{i,t}}{\partial \omega_{i,t}}\right)\left(\pi'_{i,t}\hat{\Sigma}_t \cdot \pi_{i,t}\right)^{-1/2} \cdot \hat{\Sigma}_t \cdot \pi_{i,t} = 0$$

(56)

and:

$$\frac{\partial \Lambda_{i,t}}{\partial \lambda_{i,t}} = b^{*M}_{i,t}(\phi_{i,t}, \omega_{i,t}) = 0$$

(57)

Consider total differentiation of the first-order conditions in Equations 56 and 57, with respect to $\pi_{i,t}$, $\lambda_{i,t}$, and ξ, which implicitly defines the expressions for the $A \times A$ matrix, $S^1_{i,t}$; the $A \times P$ matrix, $R^1_{i,t}$; and the $A \times 1$ vector, $s^1_{i,t}$:

$$S^1_{i,t} \cdot d\pi_{i,t} + s^1_{i,t} \cdot d\lambda_{i,t} + R^1_{i,t} \cdot d\xi = 0$$

where:

$$s^1_{i,t} = \frac{\partial b^{*M}_{i,t}}{\partial \phi_{i,t}} \cdot \hat{\mu}_{i,t} + \frac{\partial b^{*M}_{i,t}}{\partial \omega_{i,t}} \cdot \left(\pi'_{i,t}\hat{\Sigma}_t \cdot \pi_{i,t}\right)^{-1/2} \cdot \hat{\Sigma}_t \cdot \pi_{i,t}$$

$$R^1_{i,t} = \frac{\partial^2 u_{i,t}}{\partial \phi_{i,t}\partial \xi'_{i,t}} \cdot \hat{\mu}_{i,t} + \left(\hat{\pi}'_{i,t}\hat{\Sigma}_t \cdot \hat{\pi}_{i,t}\right)^{-1/2} \cdot \hat{\Sigma}_t \cdot \hat{\pi}_{i,t} \cdot \frac{\partial^2 u_{i,t}}{\partial \omega_{i,t}\partial \xi'_{i,t}}$$

and:

$$S^1_{i,t} = \left[\frac{\partial^2 u_{i,t}}{\partial \phi_{i,t}\partial \phi_{i,t}} + \lambda_{i,t} \cdot \frac{\partial^2 b^{*M}_{i,t}}{\partial \phi_{i,t}\partial \phi_{i,t}}\right] \cdot \hat{\mu}_{i,t} \cdot \hat{\mu}'_{i,t} +$$

$$\left[\frac{\partial^2 u_{i,t}}{\partial \phi_{i,t}\partial \omega_{i,t}} + \lambda_{i,t} \cdot \frac{\partial^2 b^{*M}_{i,t}}{\partial \phi_{i,t}\partial \omega_{i,t}}\right] \cdot \left(\hat{\pi}'_{i,t}\hat{\Sigma}_t \cdot \hat{\pi}_{i,t}\right)^{-1/2} \cdot \hat{\Sigma}_t \cdot \pi_{i,t}\hat{\mu}_{i,t} +$$

$$\left[\frac{\partial^2 u_{i,t}}{\partial \omega_{i,t}\partial \phi_{i,t}} + \lambda_{i,t} \cdot \frac{\partial^2 b^{*M}_{i,t}}{\partial \omega_{i,t}\partial \phi_{i,t}}\right] \cdot \left(\pi'_{i,t}\hat{\Sigma}_t \cdot \pi_{i,t}\right)^{-1/2} \cdot \hat{\Sigma}_t \cdot \pi_{i,t}\hat{\mu}_{i,t} +$$

$$\left[\frac{\partial^2 u_{i,t}}{\partial \omega_{i,t} \partial \omega_{i,t}} + \lambda_{i,t} \cdot \frac{\partial^2 b_{i,t}^{*M}}{\partial \omega_{i,t} \partial \omega_{i,t}}\right] \cdot \left(\pi_{i,t}' \hat{\Sigma}_t \cdot \pi_{i,t}\right)^{-1/2} \cdot \hat{\Sigma}_t \cdot \pi_{i,t} \cdot \pi_{i,t}' \cdot \hat{\Sigma}_t +$$

$$\left\{\frac{\partial u_{i,t}}{\partial \omega_{i,t}} + \lambda_{i,t} \cdot \frac{\partial b_{i,t}^{*M}}{\partial \omega_{i,t}}\right\} \cdot \left\{\left(\pi_{i,t}' \hat{\Sigma}_t \cdot \pi_{i,t}\right)^{-1/2} \cdot \hat{\Sigma}_t - \left(\pi_{i,t}' \hat{\Sigma}_t \cdot \pi_{i,t}\right)^{-3/2} \cdot \hat{\Sigma}_t \cdot \pi_{i,t} \cdot \pi_{i,t}' \cdot \hat{\Sigma}_t\right\}$$

and each of these are to be evaluated at the prevailing parameter vector, $[\xi]^n$.

It is important to note that, given the twice continuously differentiable approximation, $b_{i,t}^{*M}(\phi_{i,t}, \omega) = 0$, to the efficient boundary function in the neighborhood of the expected rate of return, $\phi_{i,t}^{*M}$, evaluation of the terms above require expressions for the first and second partial derivatives of the utility function specified by the investigator, as well the use of corresponding expressions with respect to the Lagrange interpolation polynomials for $b_{i,t}^{*M}$.

Note that in the case of the interior or boundary noncorner solutions for the optimal portfolio, the use of Equations 47 and 48 simplifies the above expressions; whereas, in the case of corner solutions, simplifications obtains from applying Equations 53 and 54.

APPENDIX C: EVALUATION OF THE JACOBIAN MATRIX IN THE INDIRECT *EX POST* CASE

This appendix shows that the elements of the Jacobian matrix will be known in closed-form. For this purpose, consider the constrained maximization problem from Section V.C, which we can rewrite as:

$$\max_{\pi_{i,t}} \Lambda_{i,t}(\pi_{i,t}, \lambda_{i,t}) = u\left(\pi_{i,t}' \hat{\mu}_{i,t}(\gamma_i), (\pi_{i,t}' \hat{\Sigma}_t \pi_{i,t})^{\frac{1}{2}}; x_{i,t}, \xi\right) + \lambda_{i,t} \cdot b_{i,t}^{*M}\left(\pi_{i,t}' \hat{\mu}_{i,t}(\gamma_i), (\pi_{i,t}' \hat{\Sigma}_t \pi_{i,t})^{\frac{1}{2}}\right)$$

$$(58)$$

The first order conditions for this maximization are:

$$\frac{\partial \Lambda_{i,t}}{\partial \pi_{i,t}} = \left(\frac{\partial u_{i,t}}{\partial \phi_{i,t}} + \lambda_{i,t} \cdot \frac{\partial b_{i,t}^{*M}}{\partial \phi_{i,t}}\right) \hat{\mu}_{i,t}(\gamma_i) + \left(\frac{\partial u_{i,t}}{\partial \omega_{i,t}} + \lambda_{i,t} \cdot \frac{\partial b_{i,t}^{*M}}{\partial \omega_{i,t}}\right) \left(\pi_{i,t}' \hat{\Sigma}_t \cdot \pi_{i,t}\right)^{-1/2} \cdot \hat{\Sigma}_t \cdot \pi_{i,t} = 0$$

$$(59)$$

and:

$$\frac{\partial \Lambda_{i,t}}{\partial \lambda_{i,t}} = b_{i,t}^{*M}(\phi_{i,t}, \omega_{i,t}) = 0 \qquad (60)$$

Consider total differentiation of the first-order conditions in Equations 59 and 60, with respect to $\pi_{i,t}$, $\lambda_{i,t}$, and $\theta \equiv [\xi' \mid \gamma'_1, \cdots, \gamma'_i, \cdots, \gamma'_N]'$, which results in:

$$S^2_{i,t} \cdot d\pi_{i,t} + s^2_{i,t} \cdot d\lambda_{i,t} + P^2_{i,t} \cdot d\xi + h^2_{i,t} \cdot G^2_{i,t} \cdot d\gamma_i = 0;$$

where the following expressions define the $A \times A$ matrix, $S^2_{i,t}$; the $A \times P$ matrix, $P^2_{i,t}$; the $A \times 1$ vector, $s^2_{i,t}$; and the scaler, $h^2_{i,t}$:

$$s^2_{i,t} = \frac{\partial b^{*M}_{i,t}}{\partial \phi_{i,t}} \cdot \hat{\mu}_{i,t}(\gamma_i) + \frac{\partial b^{*M}_{i,t}}{\partial \omega_{i,t}} \cdot (\pi'_{i,t}\hat{\Sigma}_t \cdot \pi_{i,t})^{-1/2} \cdot \hat{\Sigma}_t \cdot \pi_{i,t},$$

$$P^2_{i,t} = \frac{\partial^2 u_{i,t}}{\partial \phi_{i,t} \partial \xi'_{i,t}} \cdot \hat{\mu}_{i,t}(\gamma_i) + \left(\hat{\pi}'_{i,t}\hat{\Sigma}_t \cdot \hat{\pi}_{i,t}\right)^{-1/2} \cdot \hat{\Sigma}_t \cdot \pi_{i,t} \cdot \frac{\partial^2 u_{i,t}}{\partial \omega_{i,t} \partial \xi'_{i,t}},$$

and,

$$S^2_{i,t} = \left[\frac{\partial^2 u_{i,t}}{\partial \phi_{i,t} \partial \phi_{i,t}} + \lambda_{i,t} \cdot \frac{\partial^2 b^{*M}_{i,t}}{\partial \phi_{i,t} \partial \phi_{i,t}}\right] \cdot \hat{\mu}_{i,t}(\gamma_i) \cdot \hat{\mu}_{i,t}(\gamma_i)' +$$

$$\left[\frac{\partial^2 u_{i,t}}{\partial \phi_{i,t} \partial \omega_{i,t}} + \lambda_{i,t} \cdot \frac{\partial^2 b^{*M}_{i,t}}{\partial \phi_{i,t} \partial \omega_{i,t}}\right] \cdot \left(\pi'_{i,t}\hat{\Sigma}_t \cdot \pi_{i,t}\right)^{-1/2} \cdot \hat{\Sigma}_t \cdot \pi_{i,t}\hat{\mu}_{i,t}(\gamma_i) +$$

$$\left[\frac{\partial^2 u_{i,t}}{\partial \omega_{i,t} \partial \phi_{i,t}} + \lambda_{i,t} \cdot \frac{\partial^2 b^{*M}_{i,t}}{\partial \omega_{i,t} \partial \phi_{i,t}}\right] \cdot \left(\pi'_{i,t}\hat{\Sigma}_t \cdot \pi_{i,t}\right)^{-1/2} \cdot \hat{\Sigma}_t \cdot \pi_{i,t}\hat{\mu}_{i,t}(\gamma_i) +$$

$$\left[\frac{\partial^2 u_{i,t}}{\partial \omega_{i,t} \partial \omega_{i,t}} + \lambda_{i,t} \cdot \frac{\partial^2 b^{*M}_{i,t}}{\partial \omega_{i,t} \partial \omega_{i,t}}\right] \cdot \left(\pi'_{i,t}\hat{\Sigma}_t \cdot \pi_{i,t}\right)^{-1/2} \cdot \hat{\Sigma}_t \cdot \pi_{i,t}\pi'_{i,t} \cdot \hat{\Sigma}_t +$$

$$\left\{\frac{\partial u_{i,t}}{\partial \omega_{i,t}} + \lambda_{i,t} \cdot \frac{\partial b^{*M}_{i,t}}{\partial \omega_{i,t}}\right\} \cdot \left\{\left(\pi'_{i,t}\hat{\Sigma}_t \cdot \pi_{i,t}\right)^{-1/2} \cdot \hat{\Sigma}_t - \left(\pi'_{i,t}\hat{\Sigma}_t \cdot \pi_{i,t}\right)^{-3/2} \cdot \hat{\Sigma}_t \cdot \pi_{i,t} \cdot \pi'_{i,t} \cdot \hat{\Sigma}_t\right\}$$

and,

$$h^2_{i,t} = \left[\frac{\partial^2 u_{i,t}}{\partial \phi_{i,t} \partial \phi_{i,t}} + \lambda_{i,t} \cdot \frac{\partial^2 b^{*M}_{i,t}}{\partial \phi_{i,t} \partial \phi_{i,t}}\right] \cdot \pi_{i,t} \cdot \hat{\mu}'_{i,t}(\gamma) +$$

$$\left[\frac{\partial^2 u_{i,t}}{\partial \phi_{i,t} \partial \omega_{i,t}} + \lambda_{i,t} \cdot \frac{\partial^2 b^{*M}_{i,t}}{\partial \phi_{i,t} \partial \omega_{i,t}}\right] \cdot \left(\hat{\pi}'_{i,t}\hat{\Sigma}_t \cdot \hat{\pi}_{i,t}\right)^{1/2} +$$

$$\left\{\frac{\partial u_{i,t}}{\partial \phi_{i,t}} + \lambda_{i,t} \cdot \frac{\partial b^{*M}_{i,t}}{\partial \phi_{i,t}}\right\}$$

Depending upon the parametric form of the returns-generating process adopted, the following partial derivative of the utility function can be calculated:

$$\frac{\partial \hat{\mu}_{i,t}}{\partial \gamma_i} = G_{i,t}^2 = \begin{bmatrix} 1 & x_{i,1,t} \cdots x_{i,K,t} & r_{i,1,t-1} & x_{i,1,t} \cdot r_{i,1,t-1} \cdots x_{i,1,t} \cdot r_{i,1,t-1} \\ 1 & x_{i,1,t} \cdots x_{i,K,t} & r_{i,2,t-1} & x_{i,1,t} \cdot r_{i,2,t-1} \cdots x_{i,K,t} \cdot r_{i,2,t-1} \\ \cdot & & \cdots & \cdots \\ 1 & x_{i,1,t} \cdots x_{i,K,t} & r_{i,A,t-1} & x_{i,1,t} \cdot r_{i,A,t-1} \cdots x_{i,K,t} \cdot r_{i,A,t-1} \\ \cdot & & \cdots & \cdots \\ \cdot & \cdots & r_{i,A,t-L} & x_{i,1,t} \cdot r_{i,A,t-L} \cdots x_{i,K,t-L} \cdot r_{i,A,t-L} \end{bmatrix}$$

This in turn, permits us to define the requisite $A \times P + (K + 1) \cdot (L + 1) \cdot N$ matrix, $R_{i,t}^2 = [P_{i,t}^2 0 \ldots h_{i,t}^2 \cdot G_{i,t}^2 \ldots 0]$, where the $h_{i,t}^2 \cdot G_{i,t}^2$ consists the ith position after $P_{i,t}^2$, and each of the zero matrices, 0, are of the same order. Needless to say, the basic algorithm remains the same, if an alternate returns-generating process were adopted by the investigator, then the structure of the matrix $G_{i,t}^2$, would differ.

Again, notice here that in the case of interior or boundary non-corner solutions, one may employ the simplifying results in Equations 47 and 48; whereas, with boundary corner solutions using the circular approximants, Equations 53 and 54 may be employed. However, as compared to our analysis in Appendix B, the main difference is that, rather than treating $\hat{\mu}_{i,t}$ as a given constant, we now regard it as a parametric function of γ_i.

NOTES

1. Nielsen (1987) has stressed that in the mean–variance portfolio-selection model, the induced preferences for asset holdings are not necessarily monotone; that is, more of a portfolio is not necessarily better even if the portfolio has positive expected return. In particular, for diversification purposes, the portfolio selection problem predicts that an investor typically wants only a limited number of shares of an asset, and beyond that the increase in mean return from acquired additional shares of the asset is not sufficient to compensate for the increased risk.

2. This is the case even though a stochastic returns-generating process has been advanced, since the inputs to the portfolio selection problem require the expectation of the anticipated rates of return and the associated covariance matrix—both of which are deterministic.

3. For a further technical discussion, see Ingersoll (1987), Huang and Litzenberger (1988), and Duffie (1988, 1992).

4. Kroll, Levy, and Markowitz (1984) have demonstrated that mean-variance analysis is often a sufficient normal approximation to the more exact "direct utility maximization". We further assume that the utility function is well behaved and concave. In particular, the utility be strictly increasing in expected rate of return of the portfolio (ϕ), and nonincreasing in its variance and the indifference curves in risk-return space are a convex set. This will ensure that the first-order conditions for interior maximum will be necessary and sufficient.

5. Dybvig and Ross (1982) have shown that under certain conditions the efficient frontier will not be a convex set and Dybvig (1984) has demonstrated that the efficient frontier can have kinks. Throughout this paper we assume that the efficient frontier is a convex set although, as shown in Section

IV and Appendix A, the Lagrange interpolation polynomial approximations are general enough to handle all discontinuities, and the efficient frontier will always be concave.

6.   In order to conform to the notation employed for the heterogeneous returns-generating process, the subscript i is retained here even though the process is the same for each investor.

7.   In certain applications, there may be dimensional restrictions which preclude the joint estimation of the $A \cdot (L + 1)$ parameters. In such cases, for each asset, the $(L + 1)$ parameters, $\{\alpha_{l,a}\}$, associated with Equation 8 may be estimated consistently using the OLS residuals. As is well known, such a procedure only sacrifices the efficiency of the VAR estimators.

8.   The number of parameters that have to be estimated in this homogeneous autoregressive case can be contrasted to the single index model of Sharpe (1963) where $3A + 2$ parameters need to be estimated.

9.   We adopt the customary terminology of "expected" rates of return when referring to the asymptotically normal, asymptotically unbiased, and consistent estimates, $\{\hat{\alpha}_{l,a}\}$, of the $\{\alpha_{l,a}\}$ obtained under a VAR specification.

10.   The availability of a set of investor characteristics is a *sine qua non* for developing a heterogeneous returns-generating process. In cases where such data are not available, the only option may be to use the homogeneous returns-generating process. However, in such cases, one may still determine the structural parameters of the investors' utility function, as well those in the homogeneous returns-generating process, *ex post*.

11.   Here, it is appropriate to inquire about the problems of dimensionality. In particular, in the heterogeneous case, there are N investors, A assets, K investor characteristics, and L lagged period histories of asset returns to be considered. However, in the present context, particularly since the period of observation on asset returns may be daily, and computerized records on individual/institutional investors are typically kept over a significant number of periods, T is likely to be large in much of empirical work. Thus, the principal dimensionality issue arises from the fact that the number of potential risky assets actually under consideration may also be large. However, if in reality, investors focus upon the behavior of a limited number of stocks, etc., which may vary from one investor to another, as is quite likely to be the case, then the "curse of dimensionality" may be avoided.

12.   It is customary in empirical applications of the Markowitz model to first formulate a returns-generating process for asset returns, and then to estimate its parameters on the basis of the preceding historical time-series data. The remaining parameters in the investors' utility function must be specified, *ex ante*, by the investor to compute the optimal portfolio. The goal in this section is, therefore, to discuss the econometric methods associated with *ex ante* calibration of the "taste parameter" within the utility function of a Markowitz model based upon actual portfolio decisions of investors.

13.   The next section considers the more demanding task of jointly calibrating both the "taste parameters" and the parameters of the returns-generating process.

14.   Let Φ be an arbitrary square matrix of order $A \times A$. We employ the symbol, Φ^+, to denote a suitable inverse of Φ which can be calculated using either Cholesky decomposition, Crout decomposition, or Moore–Penrose pseudo-inverse.

15.   McGuire, Farley, Lucas, and Winston (1968), Barten (1969), and Powell (1969) have demonstrated that the GLS/ML estimates are invariant with respect to which assets are deleted from s standard budget-share or demand system.

16.   In the case of "backtracking", line-search procedures using a quasi-Newton algorithm, Dennis and Schnabel (1983, p. 129) recommend imposition of a minimum step-size as part of the algorithm's convergence test. As they note: "This criterion prevents the line-search from looping forever if $(-[H]^{n+} \cdot [g]^n)$ is not a descent direction. [This sometimes occurs at the final iteration $(n + 1)$ of minimizing algorithms, owing to finite-precision errors, especially if the gradient is calculated by finite differences.] (emphasis and notation added)." In such cases, provided the remaining conditions are also satisfied, the algorithm is said to converge in the preceding iteration, n.

17.   The work of Elton, Gruber, and Padberg (1976), Kwan (1984), Alexander and Resnick (1985), and Cheun and Kwan (1988) provide other relevant criteria for optimal portfolio selection.

18. Here, it is important to stress that it is *only* necessary to approximate the unknown efficient boundary function, $b_{i,t}^M(\phi_{i,t}, \omega_{i,t}) = 0$, in the neighborhood of the expected rate of return, $\phi_{i,t}^{*M}$, associated with the prevailing portfolio, $\pi_{i,t}^{*M}$.

19. A portfolio is of the same *type* as another if both contain the same assets in positive amounts, though the non-zero proportions in each may differ.

20. A recent example for an algorithm for optimal portfolio selection is in Lewis (1988). This paper uses Markowitz's (1956) critical line approach to determine optimal portfolio weights when the utility function is dependent upon the mean and the variance, but can only be used when the constraints are linear. Our methodology, however, is general enough to accommodate any institutional restriction, linear or nonlinear. Furthermore, the algorithm simultaneously determines the parameter values which best fit the portfolio selection model to *actual* investor portfolios and the *optimal* values of the investor portfolios.

ACKNOWLEDGMENT

M.J. Hartley is Professor of Economics at the Department of Economics and Finance, College of Business Administration, University of New Orleans, New Orleans, LA; and G.S. Bakshi is Associate Professor of Finance at the Robert H. Smith School of Business, University of Maryland, College Park, MD.

REFERENCES

Alexander, G. (1976). The derivation of the efficient sets. *Journal of Finance and Quantitative Analysis* *11*, 817–830.

Alexander, G. (1977). An algorithm for deriving the capital market line. *Management Science*, *23*, 1183–1186.

Alexander, G., & Francis, J. (1986). *Portfolio analysis*. Englewood Cliffs, NJ: Prentice Hall.

Alexander, G., & Resnick, B. (1985). More on estimation risk and simple rules for optimal portfolio selection. *Journal of Finance*, *40*, 125–133.

Bakshi, G., & Chen, Z. (1994). Baby boom, population aging, and capital markets. *Journal of Business*, *67*, 165–202.

Bakshi, G., & Chen, Z. (1996). The spirit of capitalism and stock market prices. *American Economic Review*, *86*, 133–157.

Barten, A. (1969). Maximum-likelihood estimation of a complete system of demand equations. *European Econometric Review*, *1*, 7–73.

Bellman, A., & Roth, R. (1983). *Quasilinearization and the identification problem*. Singapore: World Scientific Press.

Black, F. (1972). Capital market equilibrium with restricted borrowing. *Journal of Business*, *45*, 444–455.

Brennan, M. (1971). Capital market equilibrium with divergent borrowing and lending rates. *Journal of Financial and Quantitative Analysis*, *6*, 407–418.

Cheung, S., & Kwan, C. (1988). A note on simple criteria for optimal portfolio selection. *Journal of Finance*, *53*, 241–245.

Dennis, J., & Schnabel, R. (1983). *Numerical methods for unconstrained optimization and nonlinear equations*. Englewood Cliffs, NJ: Prentice-Hall.

Duffie, D. (1988). *Security markets stochastic models*. San Diego: Academic Press.

Duffie, D. (1992). *Dynamic asset pricing theory*. Princeton, NJ: Princeton University Press.

Duffie, D., & Singleton, K. (1993). Simulated moments estimation of Markov models of asset prices. *Econometrica*, *61*, 929–952.

Dumas, B., & Luciano, E. (1991). An exact solution to a dynamic portfolio choice problem under transaction costs. *Journal of Finance, 56*, 577–595.

Dyl, E. (1975). Negative betas: the attraction of selling short. *Journal of Portfolio Management, 1*, 74–76.

Dybvig, P. (1984). Short sale restrictions and kinks on the mean variance frontier. *Journal of Finance, 39*, 239–244.

Dybvig, P. (1988). Distributional analysis of portfolio choice. *Journal of Business, 61*, 369–394.

Dybvig, P., & Ross, S. (1982). Portfolio efficiency sets. *Econometrica, 50*, 1525–1546.

Elton, E., & Gruber, M. (1991). *Modern portfolio theory and investment analysis*. New York: John Wiley.

Elton, E., Gruber, M., & Padberg, M. (1976). Simple criteria for optimal portfolio selection. *Journal of Finance, 31*, 1341–1357.

Ferson, W. (1994). Theory and empirical testing of asset pricing models. In R. Jarrow, W. Ziemba, & V. Maksimovic (Eds.), *The finance handbook* (Chap. 6). North-Holland.

Green, R. (1986). Positively weighted portfolios on the minimum-variance frontier. *Journal of Finance, 41*, 1051–1068.

Hansen, L. (1982). Large sample properties of generalized method of moments estimators. *Econometrica, 45*, 1029–1179.

Hansen, L., & Singleton, K. (1982). Generalized instrument variable estimation of nonlinear rational expectations models. *Econometrica, 50*, 1269–1286.

Hardle, W. (1990). *Smoothing-techniques with implementation*. Berlin: Springer-Verlag.

Hartley, H.O. (1961). The modified Gauss-Newton methods for fitting nonlinear regression functions by least squares. *Technometrics, 3*, 269–280.

Hartley, M. (1986). Calibration of macroeconomic models with incomplete data. *Computers and mathematics with applications: an international journal series A*. Bellman Memorial Issue 6 (pp. 769–776).

Hartley, M. (1988). Neoclassical econometrics: The kernel. *Journal of Mathematical Analysis and Applications, 2*, 313–328.

Hartley, M. (1994). A systems approach to the calibration of deterministic nonlinear simultaneous equation models with incomplete data. *Applied Stochastic Models and Data Analysis*. Forthcoming.

Harvey, C. (1991). The world price of covariance risk. *Journal of Finance, 46*, 111–157.

Hausman, J., & Wise, D. (1978). A conditional probit model for qualitative choice: discrete decisions recognizing interdependence and heterogeneous preferences. *Econometrica, 46*, 403–426.

Huang, C.-F., & Litzenberger, R. (1988). *Foundations for financial economics*. Englewood Cliffs, NJ: Prentice Hall.

Kroll, Y., Levy, H., & Markowitz, H. (1984). Mean-variance versus direct utility maximization. *Journal of Finance, 39*, 47–62.

Isaacson, E., & Keller, H. (1966). *Analysis of numerical methods*. New York: John Wiley.

Ingersoll, J. (1987). *The theory of financial decision making*. Rowman & Littlefield.

Lewis, A. (1988). A simple algorithm for portfolio selection problem. *Journal of Finance, 53*, 71–82.

Maddala, G. (1983). *Limited dependent and qualitative variables in econometrics*. Cambridge: Cambridge University Press.

Markowitz, H. (1952). Portfolio selection. *Journal of Finance, 7*, 77–91.

Markowitz, H. (1956). The optimization of a quadratic function subject to linear constraints. *Naval Research Logistics Quarterly, 3*, 111–133.

Markowitz, H. (1959). *Portfolio selection: efficient diversification of investments*. New York: John Wiley.

Markowitz, H. (1987). *Mean variance analysis in portfolio choice and capital markets*. Oxford: Basil Blackwell.

McFadden, D. (1989). A method of simulated moments for estimation of discrete response models without numerical integration. *Econometrica, 57*, 995–1026.

Merton, R. (1972). An analytical derivation of the efficient frontier. *Journal of Financial and Quantitative Analysis, 7*, 1850–1872.

Merton, R. (1973). An intertemporal capital asset pricing model. *Econometrica, 41*, 867–888.

Merton, R. (1980). On estimating the expected rate of return on the market: an exploratory investigation. *Journal of Financial Economics, 8*, 323–361.

McGuire, T., Farley, J., Lucas, R., & Winston, R. (1968). Estimation and inference for linear models in which subsets of the dependent variables are constrained. *Journal of the American Statistical Association, 63*, 1201–1213.

Nielsen, L. (1987). Portfolio selection in the mean-variance world: a note. *Journal of Finance, 47*, 1371–1471.

Quandt, R. (1983). Computational problems and methods. *Handbook of econometrics* (Vol. I). Amsterdam: North-Holland.

Rao, C. (1973). *Linear statistical inference and its applications*. New York: John Wiley.

Roll, R. (1977). A critique of asset pricing theory tests—Part 1: On past and potential testability of the theory. *Journal of Financial Economics, 4*, 129–176.

Ross, S. (1976). The arbitrage theory of capital asset pricing. *Journal of Economic Theory, 13*, 341–360.

Ross, S. (1977). The capital asset pricing model (CAPM), short sale restrictions and related issues. *Journal of Finance, 32*, 177–183.

Sharpe, W. (1963). A simplified model for portfolio analysis. *Management Science, 9*, 277–293.

Sharpe, W. (1991). Capital asset prices with and without negative holdings. *Journal of Finance, 46*, 489–509.

Tobin, J. (1958). Liquidity preference as behavior towards risk. *Review of Economic Studies, 26*, 65–86.

Tobin, J. (1965). The theory of portfolio selection. In F. Hahn & F. Brechling (Eds.), *The theory of interest rates*. London: MaxMillan.

THE IMPACT OF OFFERING SIZE ON THE INITIAL AND AFTERMARKET PERFORMANCE OF IPOs

Karen M. Hogan and Gerard T. Olson

ABSTRACT

IPOs of common stock attract a great deal of investor attention due to the possibility of large returns available to those investors who purchase the stock on the day of offer. Using methodology employed by Aggarwal and Rivoli (1990) and Ritter (1991), we analyzed 1,640 IPOs for the time period 1986–1995 to determine the size effect on the initial and aftermarket performance of IPOs. The results show that the amount of underpricing varies inversely with the size of the offering. Investors who buy at the offering price and purchase firms in the smallest quintile earn on average 0.11 per dollar more than the largest quintile when looking at the initial 14 days of trading. Extending the results to 365 trading days shows the smallest firms earning on average 0.17 per dollar more than the largest quintile firms. Moreover, the smallest firms continue to provide investors who buy at the offering price an average 12% return up to 1 year. These results are consistent with the argument that investment bankers underprice IPOs in thinner trading markets more than those that will be trading in more active markets. When initial day returns are excluded, the results show no significant returns for the smallest two quintiles up to 14 days of trading but significant

Advances in Investment Analysis and Portfolio Management, Volume 7, pages 91–103.
Copyright © 2000 by JAI Press Inc.
All rights of reproduction in any form reserved.
ISBN: 0-7623-0658-0

negative returns for the two largest quintiles. Extending the results to 365 trading days we find that both quintile 2 and quintile 5 table significant negative abnormal returns. The presence of significantly negative returns when the initial offer price is excluded can possibly lend support to the existence of fads.

I. INTRODUCTION

IPOs of common stock attract a great deal of investor attention due to the possibility of large returns available to those who purchase on the day of offer. There are two anomalies concerning the pricing of IPOs. First, investors earn significant returns during early trading. For specific examples refer to Chalk and Peavy (1987), Miller and Reilly (1987), Aggarwal and Rivoli (1990), Ibbotson, Sindelar, and Ritter (1991), and Rudd (1993). Second, investors purchasing after the first day of trading lose money on their investments in the long run. For specific examples refer to Muscarella and Vetsuypens (1989), Aggarawal and Rivoli (1990), Ritter (1991), and Midgett and DeCarlo (1992).

Several explanations have been postulated for the abnormal returns exhibited by IPOs during initial trading. First, IPOs are underpriced by investment bankers. Baron (1982) describes underpricing as a consequence of the principal-agent relationship between the issuing firm and its investment banker. Rock (1986) describes underpricing as a method to attract uninformed investors. Beatty and Ritter (1986) contend that investment bankers will underprice the issue to ensure that it will be completely sold. Tinic (1988) argues that underpricing is a form of insurance for the investment banker against investor lawsuits and less investor interest in future offerings. One would expect that if IPOs are underpriced by investment bankers, the thinner trading markets associated with small IPOs would result in more underpricing than large IPOs. A finding that small IPOs provide investors with greater initial returns than large IPOs would provide empirical support for the underpricing by investment bankers theory.

The second explanation for the abnormal returns exhibited by IPOs during initial trading centers on the strategic goals of the issuing firm. Allen and Faulhaber (1989) assume that the issuing firm has the best information concerning the future prospects of the firm. Underpricing can be viewed as a signal to investors of the good firm's expectation of superior performance in the future. However, a study by Jegadeesh, Weinstein, and Welch (1993) indicates that the return on the date of the IPO does not play a unique role in predicting future seasoned equity offers. Their results imply issuers do not have to rely on costly underpricing as a market signal. Since there is generally less information dispersed about smaller IPOs, one would expect that these firms would need to provide a larger signal than larger IPOs. An empirical finding that small IPOs have larger returns than large IPOs would be consistent with the signaling theory.

A third explanation for the abnormal returns exhibited during initial trading focuses on the behavior of investors in IPOs. Shiller (1981), Debont and Thaler (1985), Camerer (1989), and Aggarwal and Rivoli (1990) contend that abnormal returns are the result of overvaluation of investors in early trading due to investment fads. A fad investment is defined as a temporary overvaluation caused by the overoptimism of investors.

An initial finding that IPOs experience negative returns after early trading would provide empirical support for the fad theory. Moreover, it can be argued that fad investments will be more common in larger IPOs where there are more investors and more information available. A finding that large IPOs have larger negative returns than small IPOs after early trading would render additional empirical support for the fad theory.

The second anomaly related to the pricing of IPOs is concerned with their long-run or aftermarket performance. Although IPOs generally make excellent investments if investors can purchase at the offering price and hold the stock for 1 day, long-run returns are not as positive. Muscarella and Vetsuypens (1989), Aggarwal and Rivoli (1990), and Ritter (1991) found that investors in IPOs earned negative returns after the first day of trading. By segmenting the sample, it can be determined whether the aftermarket performance of IPOs is related to the size of the offering.

Using methodology employed by Aggarwal and Rivoli (1990) and Ritter (1991), this paper will analyze 1,640 IPOs to determine the size effect on the initial and aftermarket performance of IPOs. Both the Aggarwal and Rivoli (1990) and Ritter (1991) studies analyzed data from the late 1970s to mid-1980s. This study will analyze a more current data set spanning 1986 to 1995 to determine if the return patterns found in the previous studies can be generalized to other time periods. Moreover, segmenting the sample according to offering size can provide a stronger test of the underpricing, signaling, and fad theories of IPO performance.

II. DATA AND METHODOLOGY

The sample for the study is obtained from Securities Data Corporation's World Wide New Issues database. The data covers a sample of 1,640 IPOs occurring from January 1986 through July 1995. Two sets of abnormal returns for the IPOs are calculated, one assuming purchase at the offering price, and the other assuming purchase at the end of the first day of trading. The initial returns and aftermarket returns for each stock are calculated. In this paper we define the initial or short-run performance to be 14 days or less and the aftermarket performance from 28 days to 365 days. The returns for each stock are compared to returns on the NASDAQ stock exchange over the same time period.

The return for security i purchased on the day of offer (day 0) and sold on day t is defined as:

$$r_{it} = \frac{P_{it} - P_{i0}}{P_{i0}}$$

where P_{it} = the closing price of stock i at the end of t days of trading after the initial offer, and P_{i0} = the initial offering price of stock i.

The return on the market index during the same time period is defined as:

$$r_{mt} = \frac{I_t - I_0}{I_0}$$

where I_t = the value of the NASDAQ index at the end of t days of trading after the initial offer, and I_0 = the value of the NASDAQ index on the day of the offer.

The abnormal return for security i purchased on the day of offer and sold on day t is defined as:

$$ar_{it} = \left[r_{it} - r_{mt} \right] * 100$$

The average market adjusted return for a portfolio of n securities from buying at the initial offer date and selling t trading days later is defined as:

$$AR_t = \frac{1}{n} \sum_{i=1}^{n} ar_{it}$$

Wealth relatives are also calculated using the same method as Ritter (1991) and Aggarwal, Leal, and Hernandez (1993). A wealth relative (WR_t) is defined as:

$$WR_t = \frac{1 + \dfrac{1}{n} \sum_{i=1}^{n} r_{it}}{1 + \dfrac{1}{n} \sum_{i=1}^{n} r_{mt}}.$$

A wealth relative above 1 indicates IPOs outperforming the NASDAQ benchmark, a value below one indicates underperformance of the IPO, and a value of 1 indicates the IPOs performance matches that of the NASDAQ benchmark.

In order to evaluate IPO returns which do not include the initial offer price the above stock returns are recalculated beginning with day $t = 1$ instead of day $t = 0$. The returns on the market and the wealth relatives are also recalculated for the same period.

III. EMPIRICAL RESULTS

Panel A of Table 1 presents the aggregate mean-abnormal returns, standard errors, corresponding t statistics, and wealth relatives for buying the IPO on the date of offer and selling t days later. The first day average market-adjusted return is 7.9% with an associated t statistic of 20.83. The average market-adjusted return remains

Table 1.   Market Adjusted Performance of 1,640 IPOs Up to One Year for
the period 1986 to 1995

Days	AR_t	Standard Error	t-Statistic	Wealth Relative
Panel A: Mean Abnormal Return from Offer Price				
1	7.90	0.38	20.83*	1.08
2	7.85	0.38	20.41*	1.08
3	7.73	0.39	19.97*	1.08
4	7.67	0.40	19.10*	1.08
7	7.68	0.43	18.06*	1.08
14	7.05	0.47	15.00*	1.07
28	7.70	0.55	13.95*	1.08
60	8.39	0.75	11.14*	1.08
90	9.13	0.97	9.41*	1.09
180	8.49	1.29	6.58*	1.08
365	4.10	1.89	2.17**	1.04
Panel B: Mean Abnormal Return Less Day 1 Return				
2	–0.03	0.09	–0.30	1.00
3	–0.11	0.12	–0.96	1.00
4	–0.19	0.14	–1.38	1.00
7	–0.23	0.16	–1.45	1.00
14	–0.93	0.21	–4.49*	0.99
28	–0.45	0.31	–1.47	1.00
60	–0.08	0.50	–0.15	1.00
90	0.36	0.67	0.54	1.00
180	–0.44	1.00	–0.44	1.00
365	–5.11	1.51	–3.39*	0.95

Notes: *Indicates significance at the 1% level.
**Indicates significance at the 5% level.
***Indicates significance at the 10% level.

relatively stable in aftermarket trading slightly increasing until 180 days from issue
and decreasing thereafter. Wealth relatives decrease from 1.08 on day 1 to 1.04 at
the end of one year. Investors who are lucky enough to purchase at the offering price
earned a 4% excess return over the market after 1 year of trading. The results are
significant at the 1% level up to 180 days and at the 5% level for 365 days.

The aggregate mean-abnormal returns from investing in the stock at the end of
day 1 and selling t days later are shown in Panel B of Table 1. Excluding the returns
earned during the first day of trading, investors suffer a loss in their wealth position.
The mean-abnormal return at the end of day 14 is –0.93% and –5.11% for day 365.
Both are significant at the 1% level. Investors who purchase at the end of day 1

Table 2. Summary Statistics of 1,640 IPOs for the Period 1986–1995
Sorted by Size of Offering

	Quintile 1	Quintile 2	Quintile 3	Quintile 4	Quintile 5
Mean Size of Offering	4,286,662	10,331,136	23,676,297	52,153,414	263,079,661
Median Size of Offering	4,498,750	10,000,000	23,450,000	49,411,248	176,500,000
Standard Development of Size	1,221,341	2,930,330	5,021,772	13,657,410	266,660,003
Range: Low	350,000	6,187,500	16,000,000	33,000,000	83,066,662
High	6,150,700	16,000,000	32,900,000	82,960,000	2,000,000,000
Percent of Issues with Negative Day 1 Returns	16.46%	18.60%	18.60%	15.85%	10.37%

retain $0.95 for every dollar invested in the IPOs by the end of the first year of trading. The results for the entire sample are consistent with prior research of Muscarella and Vetsuypens (1989), Aggarwal and Rivoli (1990), and Ritter (1991) who found positive excess initial returns including the day of offer, but a decline in wealth for both initial and aftermarket trading when the offer day is excluded.

It is possible that the aggregate results are masking differences in performance as a result of the size of the firm undertaking the IPO. In order to test the effects of size on the returns earned by investors, the sample is grouped into quintiles from smallest to largest according to the size of the offering. Table 2 presents summary statistics for each of the quintiles. Mean size of the offering ranges from $4.29 million for the smallest quintile to $263.08 million for the largest quintile. The percent of the IPOs with a negative return during the first day of trading is 16.46% for quintile 1, 18.60% for quintile 2, 18.60% for quintile 3, 15.85% for quintile 4, and 10.37% for quintile 5.

Table 3 reports mean abnormal returns, standard errors, *t* statistics, and wealth relatives for each of the quintiles up to the initial 14 days after the offering date for the sample period. The amount of underpricing varies inversely with the size of the offering. The first day average market adjusted return is 13.51% for quintile 1, 8.27% for quintile 2, 7.98% for quintile 3, 6.85% for quintile 4, and 2.88% for quintile 5. All quintile 1 through 5 *t* statistics are significant at the 1% level for each day 1 through 14. Wealth relatives range from 1.14 for quintile 1 to 1.03 for quintile 5 at the end of 14 days of trading. Investors who purchase at the offering price earned $0.11 more per dollar invested by owning the smallest quintile IPOs rather than the largest ones after 14 days of trading. The results are consistent with the notion that investment bankers underprice IPOs in thinner trading markets more than those that will be trading in more active markets. The results are also consistent with the signaling theory of Allen and Faulhaber (1989). Since there is generally

Table 3. Market Adjusted Performance of IPOs from Offer Price Up to 14 Days of Trading Sorted by Size of Offering

	AR_t	Standard Error	t-Statistic	Wealth Relative
Quintile 1				
1 Day	13.51	1.11	12.17*	1.14
2 Days	13.19	1.10	11.94*	1.13
3 Days	13.01	1.11	11.68*	1.13
4 Days	13.12	1.17	11.21*	1.13
7 Days	13.66	1.30	10.51*	1.14
14 Days	13.20	1.41	9.35*	1.13
Quintile 2				
1 Day	8.27	0.80	10.35*	1.08
2 Days	8.36	0.81	10.31*	1.08
3 Days	8.39	0.82	10.25*	1.08
4 Days	8.26	0.86	9.60*	1.08
7 Days	8.18	0.88	9.26*	1.08
14 Days	7.56	0.98	7.72*	1.08
Quintile 3				
1 Day	7.98	0.76	10.43*	1.08
2 Days	8.11	0.84	9.63*	1.08
3 Days	7.94	0.85	9.35*	1.08
4 Days	7.81	0.90	8.71*	1.08
7 Days	7.59	0.93	8.15*	1.08
14 Days	7.29	1.06	6.86*	1.07
Quintile 4				
1 Day	6.85	0.82	8.34*	1.07
2 Days	6.68	0.80	8.37*	1.07
3 Days	6.31	0.77	8.16*	1.06
4 Days	6.03	0.78	7.74*	1.06
7 Days	5.94	0.81	7.35*	1.06
14 Days	4.94	0.90	5.46*	1.05
Quintile 5				
1 Day	2.88	0.54	5.29*	1.03
2 Days	2.90	0.56	5.17*	1.03
3 Days	3.01	0.60	4.99*	1.03
4 Days	3.12	0.60	5.24*	1.03
7 Days	3.03	0.59	5.10*	1.03
14 Days	2.28	0.67	3.43*	1.02

Notes: *Indicates significance at the 1% level.
**Indicates significance at the 5% level.
***Indicates significance at the 10% level.

less information available about smaller IPOs, one would expect that these firms would need to provide a larger signal than larger IPOs.

Table 4 presents the mean abnormal returns, standard errors, t statistics, and wealth relatives for each of the quintiles from the end of day 1 up to 14 days of trading. Excluding the returns earned during the first day of trading, investors suffer

Table 4. Market Adjusted Performance of IPOs from the End of Day 1 Up to 14 Days of Trading Sorted by Size of Offering

	AR_t	Standard Error	t-Statistic	Wealth Relative
Quintile 1				
2 Days	−0.22	0.22	−1.01	1.00
3 Days	−0.34	0.30	−1.13	1.00
4 Days	−0.28	0.38	−0.73	1.00
7 Days	0.02	0.41	0.05	1.00
14 Days	−0.54	0.50	−1.08	0.99
Quintile 2				
2 Days	0.16	0.30	0.53	1.00
3 Days	0.21	0.35	0.59	1.00
4 Days	0.05	0.40	0.13	1.00
7 Days	−0.01	0.45	−0.02	1.00
14 Days	−0.68	0.57	−1.18	0.99
Quintile 3				
2 Days	0.02	0.18	0.12	1.00
3 Days	−0.12	0.24	−0.52	1.00
4 Days	−0.30	0.28	−1.04	1.00
7 Days	−0.51	0.34	−1.46	0.99
14 Days	−0.93	0.48	−1.92***	0.99
Quintile 4				
2 Days	−0.11	0.17	−0.63	1.00
3 Days	−0.40	0.23	−1.70***	1.00
4 Days	−0.65	0.27	−2.39**	0.99
7 Days	−0.76	0.30	−2.58*	0.99
14 Days	−1.81	0.42	−4.25*	0.98
Quintile 5				
2 Days	0.02	0.10	0.16	1.00
3 Days	0.09	0.15	0.64	1.00
4 Days	0.21	0.16	1.30	1.00
7 Days	0.12	0.18	0.66	1.00
14 Days	−0.69	0.27	−2.54**	0.99

Notes: *Indicates significance at the 1% level.
          **Indicates significance at the 5% level.
          ***Indicates significance at the 10% level.

a loss in their wealth position for each of the quintiles. Significant negative returns at the end of 14 trading days are present in the three largest quintiles. Quintile 4 shows the worst results with a return of −1.81%, while quintile 3 and 5 returns are −0.93% and −0.69%, respectively. It appears that all of the initial gains are made the first day and when returns for the first day are excluded the larger firms

Table 5. Market Adjusted Performance of IPOs from Offer Price Up to One Year of Trading Sorted by Size of Offering

	AR_t	Standard Error	t-Statistic	Wealth Relative
Quintile 1				
28 Days	13.75	1.64	8.41*	1.14
60 Days	13.55	2.15	6.30*	1.13
90 Days	15.95	3.14	5.08*	1.16
180 Days	18.73	4.22	4.44*	1.18
365 Days	12.98	5.77	2.25**	1.12
Quintile 2				
28 Days	8.09	1.17	6.92*	1.08
60 Days	8.50	1.64	5.18*	1.08
90 Days	8.07	1.88	4.30*	1.08
180 Days	3.90	2.34	1.67***	1.04
365 Days	−3.94	3.21	−1.23	0.96
Quintile 3				
28 Days	8.06	1.31	6.17*	1.08
60 Days	11.23	1.93	5.81*	1.11
90 Days	12.97	2.34	5.55*	1.13
180 Days	12.72	3.13	4.07*	1.12
365 Days	9.27	5.30	1.75***	1.08
Quintile 4				
28 Days	6.44	1.07	6.03*	1.06
60 Days	7.48	1.43	5.25*	1.07
90 Days	8.31	1.72	4.83*	1.08
180 Days	8.57	2.50	3.43*	1.08
365 Days	7.20	3.63	1.99**	1.06
Quintile 5				
28 Days	2.14	0.73	2.95*	1.02
60 Days	1.20	0.93	1.29	1.01
90 Days	0.36	1.18	0.30	1.00
180 Days	−1.46	1.29	−1.13	0.99
365 Days	−5.02	1.94	−2.59*	0.95

Notes: *Indicates significance at the 1% level.
　　　　**Indicates significance at the 5% level.
　　　　***Indicates significance at the 10% level.

experience worse performance than do the smaller firms. The finding that large IPOs have larger negative returns than small IPOs after early trading provides additional empirical support for the fad theory.

Table 5 shows long run aftermarket performance for each quintile from the date of offer to days 28, 60, 90, 180, and 365. Investing in the smallest IPOs while

Table 6. Market Adjusted Performance of IPOs from the End of Day 1 Up to One Year of Trading Sorted by Size of Offering

	AR_t	Standard Error	t-Statistic	Wealth Relative
Quintile 1				
28 Days	−0.38	0.72	−0.53	1.00
60 Days	−0.92	1.24	−0.74	0.99
90 Days	−0.92	2.06	0.45	1.01
180 Days	3.23	3.23	1.00	1.03
365 Days	−3.03	4.50	−0.67	0.97
Quintile 2				
28 Days	−0.12	0.85	−0.14	1.00
60 Days	0.05	1.28	0.04	1.00
90 Days	−0.41	1.52	−0.27	1.00
180 Days	−4.21	1.98	−2.13**	0.96
365 Days	−11.70	2.86	−4.09*	0.89
Quintile 3				
28 Days	−0.44	0.74	−0.60	1.00
60 Days	1.98	1.24	1.60	1.02
90 Days	3.27	1.56	2.09**	1.03
180 Days	2.86	2.37	1.21	1.03
365 Days	−1.38	3.95	−0.35	0.99
Quintile 4				
28 Days	−0.47	0.63	−0.75	1.00
60 Days	0.29	1.01	0.29	1.00
90 Days	0.78	1.24	0.63	1.01
180 Days	0.53	1.97	0.27	1.01
365 Days	−1.24	3.04	−0.41	0.99
Quintile 5				
28 Days	−0.83	0.41	−2.05**	0.99
60 Days	−1.78	0.64	−2.80*	0.98
90 Days	−2.74	0.87	−3.15*	0.97
180 Days	−4.60	1.04	−4.41*	0.96
365 Days	−8.20	1.80	−4.55*	0.93

Notes: *Indicates significance at the 1% level.
**Indicates significance at the 5% level.
***Indicates significance at the 10% level.

including initial day returns results in consistently higher returns than any other firm size. The mean abnormal return at 180 days from the offer date is significantly positive for the four smallest quintiles. At day 365 when the offer price is included three of the five quintiles show significant positive returns with quintile 1 the largest at 12.98%, quintile 3 at 9.27%, and 7.20% for quintile 4. Quintile 5 is the only quintile with a significantly negative day 365 return of –5.02%. Wealth relatives range from 1.12 for quintile 1 to 0.95 for quintile 5 at the end of 1 year of trading. Investors who purchase at the offering price earned 12% more than the market average by owning the smallest quintile IPOs but 5% less than the market average by owning the largest quintile after 1 year of trading. The results indicate that after 1 year of trading the initial investors in the smallest IPOs maintain the increase in their wealth position but investors in the largest IPOs suffer a decrease in their wealth.

Table 6 presents the mean abnormal aftermarket returns less the first day for each of the quintiles for days 28, 60, 90, 180, and 365. IPOs underperformed the market in two of the five quintiles. Quintile 5 is the only quintile with consistent negative returns ranging from –0.83% on day 28 to –8.20% on day 365. Investing in the largest quintile stocks would have resulted in an average return of only $0.93 per dollar invested in the market. IPOs in quintile 2 had the worst overall return of –11.70% by day 365. Investors buying stocks in quintile 2 day 1 after the offer on average ended up with only $0.89 per dollar invested in the market after 365 days. The results on day 365 for the other three quintiles are not significantly different than zero lending support to the idea that the aftermarket for IPOs in these size categories is efficient. However, with the significant negative returns shown in two of the five quintiles and for the entire sample at 365 days depicted in Panel B of Table 1 the existence of fads cannot be dismissed.

IV. CONCLUSIONS

This study analyzed 1,640 IPOs over the period 1986 to 1995 to determine the size effect on the initial and aftermarket performance of IPOs. The aggregate results when the initial offer price is included support previous studies by Aggarwal and Rivoli (1990) and Ritter (1991) that show investors at the offering price earn significant positive returns after adjusting for market movements. Analyzing for cross-sectional differences related to size demonstrates that the smallest group of firms outperforms all other firm sizes. The largest quintile firms underperform all other IPOs being issued during the sample period. The finding that small IPOs provide investors with greater initial returns than large IPOs provides empirical support for the underpricing by investment bankers theory. The results are also consistent with the notion that firms use underpricing as a means to signal their expectations of good performance in the future.

Not including the initial price the aggregate results show significantly negative excess returns for day 14 and day 365. The finding that IPOs experience negative returns after early trading provides empirical support for the fad theory. Quintile results show negative 1-year returns for two of the five quintiles with the largest quintile showing consistent negative returns beginning on day 14. Since it can be argued that fad investments will be more common in larger IPOs where there are more investors and more information available, the finding that large IPOs have larger negative returns than small IPOs after early trading renders additional empirical support for the fad theory. However, the results on day 365 for the other three quintiles are not significantly different than zero lending support to the idea that the aftermarket for IPOs in these size categories is efficient.

In summary, including initial-day returns, the results support the argument that investment bankers underprice IPOs in thinner trading markets more than those that will be trading in more active trading markets. However, the negative abnormal returns which occur for some quintiles when the security is purchased at the end of day 1 instead of day 0 calls into question the efficiency of the aftermarket for IPOs and possibly supports the presence of fads.

NOTES

1. For a detailed review of the IPO literature, see *Restructuring Corporate America*, Clark, Gerlach, and Olson: Dryden, 1996.
2. Since the t statistics assume normality and independence whereas the distribution of returns is positively skewed, caution should be used in interpretation.

REFERENCES

Aggarwal, R., Leal, R., & Hernandez, L. (1993). The aftermarket performance of initial public offerings in Latin America. *Financial Management*, 42–53.
Aggarwal, R., & Rivoli, P. (1990). Fads in the initial public offering market? *Financial Management*, 45–57.
Franklin, A., & Faulhaber, G. (1989). Signaling by underpricing in the IPO market. *Journal of Financial Economics, 23*, 303–323.
Baron, D. (1982). A model of the demand for investment banking advising and distribution services for new issues. *The Journal of Finance, 4*, 955–976.
Beatty, R.P., & Ritter, J.R. (1986). Investment banking, reputation, and the underpricing of initial public offerings. *Journal of Financial Economics, 15*, 213–232.
Camerer, C. (1989). Bubbles and fads in asset prices: A review of theory and evidence. *Journal of Economic Surveys*, 3–41.
Chalk, A.J., & Peavy, J.W. III. (1987). Initial public offerings: Daily returns, offering types and the price effect. *Financial Analysts Journal*, 65–69.
Clark, J., Gerlach, J., & Olson, G. (1996). *Restructuring corporate America*, Dryden.
Dawson, S.M. (1978–1984). Secondary stock market performance of initial public offers, Hong Kong, Singapore, and Malaysia. *Journal of Business Finance and Accounting, No. 1*, 65–76.
DeBont, W., & Thaler, R. (1985). Does the stock market overreact? *Journal of Finance*. 793–805.
Finn, F.J., & Higham, R. (1988). The performance of unseasoned new equity issues-cum-stock exchange listings in Australia. *Journal of Banking and Finance, 12*, 333–351.
Ibbotson, R.G., Sindelar, J., & Ritter, J. (1988). Initial public offerings. *Journal of Applied Corporate Finance*, 37–45.

Jegadeesh, N., Weinstein, M., & Welch, I. (1993). An empirical investigation of IPO returns and subsequent equity offerings. *Journal of Financial Economics*, 153–175.

Miller, R.E., & Reilly, F.K. (1987). An examination of mispricing, returns, and uncertainty for initial public offerings. *Financial Management*, 33–38.

Muscarella, C.J., & Vetsuypens, M.R. (1989). A simple test of baron's model of IPO underpricing. *Journal of Financial Economics, 24*, 125–135.

Ritter, J.R. (1984). Signaling and the valuation of unseasoned new issues: A comment. *The Journal of Finance, XXXIX, No.4*, 1231–1237.

_____, (1984). The "hot issue" market of 1980. *Journal of Business, 57, No. 2*, 215–240.

_____, (1991). The long run performance of initial public offerings. *The Journal of Finance, XLVI, No. 1*, 3– .

Rock, K. (1986). Why new issues are underpriced. *Journal of Financial Economics, 15*, 187–212.

Rudd, J.S. (1991). Another view of the underpricing of initial public offerings. *FRBNY Quarterly Review*, 83–85.

Shiller, R. (1981). Do stock prices move too much to be justified by subsequent changes in dividends? *American Economic Review*, 421–436.

Tinic, S.M. (1988). Anatomy of initial public offerings of common stock. *The Journal of Finance, XLIII, No. 4*, 789–822.

PORTFOLIO FORMATION METHODS:
LINEAR PROGRAMMING AS AN ALTERNATIVE TO RANKING

Robert A. Wood, Michael S. McCorry,
Bonnie F. Van Ness, and Robert A. Van Ness

ABSTRACT

In financial economics studies portfolio formation is used to reduce the noisy signals caused by individual securities' variations and hence, to focus on the systematic impact of the theory or event being examined. One frequently used technique of portfolio formation for ceteris paribus testing consists of "ranking" securities according a single variable value, e.g., average price or beta. We demonstrate how a linear programming technique can be used to form both divergent and matching portfolios and contrast the resulting portfolios with those formed via a simple ranking technique.

I. INTRODUCTION

In financial economic studies portfolio formation is frequently used to reduce the noisy signals caused by individual securities variations. Much of the noise caused

Advances in Investment Analysis and Portfolio Management, Volume 7, pages 105–115.
Copyright © 2000 by JAI Press Inc.
All rights of reproduction in any form reserved.
ISBN: 0-7623-0658-0

by a stock's idiosyncratic risk, bid–ask bounce, etc. can be neutralized by grouping stocks into portfolios.

Portfolio formation for empirical studies generally has one of two objectives. One is to construct portfolios that maximize the mean differences in a portfolio characteristic. The second objective entails selection of portfolios that have similar characteristics for matching or control purposes.

While several procedures are used for portfolio formation, a frequently used technique is a single-variable grouping method termed "ranking." In this procedure the stocks are ranked from highest to lowest according to the value of a single variable such as average price or beta. Then the stocks are grouped into portfolios using a predetermined percentage of the total number in the sample. For example, if the research methodology calls for four portfolios, then the securities in the sample are assigned to the portfolios according to their quartile ranking. The ranking technique is used to create maximum dispersion between the portfolios with respect to the ranking variable and the applicable methodology is then used to identify differences in behavioral characteristics between portfolios with high rankings and those with low rankings. A normal assumption is that other portfolio characteristics are equal. However, ranking implicitly ignores all portfolio values except that of the ranking variable. This can cause a major problem when one or more of the portfolio characteristics have a high degree of absolute correlation with the targeted single variable. If this correlation is not controlled for, then the inferences drawn from an empirical study may be biased.

Alternatively, a linear programming (LP) technique is used in academic studies to construct portfolios that maximize differences in portfolio attributes. Wood and McInish (1995) use an LP technique to create portfolios whose differences in order share is as great as possible while the composition of attributes which affect portfolio trading performance is nearly identical. The authors maximize the dispersion of order share—as measured by the Herfindahl Index—across portfolios while maintaining portfolios with equal financial leverage, dividend payout, and market-to-book ratios.

Frequently, rather than maximizing the differences between portfolios, a research design will call for control or matching portfolios. Several of some studies have successfully employed an LP portfolio formation model to select matching or control portfolios. Lau, McCorry, McInish, and Van Ness (1996) use the LP approach to construct a matching portfolio of NASDAQ stocks with which to contrast the characteristics of a portfolio of NASDAQ stocks which also trade on the Chicago Stock Exchange. Wood and McInish (1994) use the LP technique to form matching portfolios—one portfolio of stocks which is subject to NYSE Rule 390 and another portfolio of similar stocks which is not subject to the rule. Again, McInish and Wood (1994) use the LP technique to form matching portfolios—one comprising NASDAQ/NMS stocks and the other comprising exchange-traded securities—in order to examine the effect of location on stock price volatility.

The linear programming technique generates different portfolios than a single variable method for several reasons. First, an LP model can hold multiple constraints constant, thereby decreasing the likelihood of bias caused by correlation between the various portfolio characteristics.

Second, an advantage is that the LP portfolio selection procedure is able to maximize the differences in the mean level of a specific variable—e.g., average price—between extreme portfolios, but hold constant the difference between each consecutive portfolio. So, the difference in the level of the target variable between portfolios one and two is about the same as that between portfolios two and three, etc. This ability adds consistency to the application of the methodology and to the interpretation of results. When the traditional single-variable ranking method is used to create portfolios which maximize the differences in a target variable, the difference in the mean value of the variable between portfolios one and two may be quite large, while the difference in the variable level of portfolios three and four may be negligible.

Third, the LP portfolio construction method can hold multiple-variable moments constant. In some instances, merely holding the means of specific attributes equal for each portfolio can be inadequate since the equal-mean condition can be satisfied by selecting an extreme portfolio with very high and low attribute levels and the other extreme portfolio with all average level attributes. Holding the mean and variance (standard deviation) of these attributes approximately constant across the portfolios prevents this occurrence and yields portfolios that display similar distribution characteristics over multiple variables. Consequently, the portfolios resulting from the LP technique provide the basis for a true *ceteris paribus* test. The LP model can also be used to equalize higher moments of the portfolio attributes in each portfolio.

While linear programming has been used in financial market studies to facilitate portfolio formation, the advantages of this portfolio formation technique have not been clearly outlined. The objective of this paper is to illustrate the multivariate LP portfolio construction technique, compare it with a traditional single-variable grouping procedure, and thereby demonstrate the LP advantages.

This paper is constructed as follows: Section II describes the data and methodology; Section III compares the LP method of portfolio construction with the single-variable ranking method; Section IV examines an LP approach for forming matching or control portfolios; and Section V concludes the review.

II. DATA AND METHODOLOGY

Our sample consists of every stock trading on the NYSE during the 1993 calendar year. For each of the 980 stocks in our sample, we compute—using the ISSM database—or extract, from the Compustat database (designated with an *), the following nine financial variables for the 1993 calendar year:

1. ASSETS: Log of (the end-of-year total assets[*]).
2. PRICE: Average daily stock price.
3. BETA: Beta.
4. $VOLUME: Log of the average daily dollar trading volume.
5. LEVERAGE: Debt-to-assets[*].
6. HERFINDAHL: Herfindahl index of trading dispersion.
7. M/B: Market to book ratio[*].
8. PAYOUT: Average dividend payout ratio[*].
9. TRADES: Average number of trades per day.

To facilitate comparison, we construct sets of five portfolios using a single-variable ranking method and a multivariate LP approach. The formulation of the LP model used for selecting five portfolios which maximize the difference in portfolio average PRICE is as follows:

Maximize:

$$\Sigma_j f_{5j} PRICE_j - \Sigma_j f_{1j} PRICE_j, j = 1, \ldots, 980 \text{ firms} \tag{1}$$

Subject to:

$$\Sigma_j f_{i-kj} PRICE_j - \Sigma_j f_{i-k-1,j} PRICE_j = \Sigma_j f_{i-k-1,j} PRICE_j - \Sigma_j f_{i-k-2,j} PRICE_j,$$
$$i = 1, \ldots, 5 \text{ portfolios}, k = 3, 4, 5 \tag{1a}$$

$$S_j f_{ij} X_j = \Sigma X_j/5_j \pm \Delta \quad i = 1, \ldots 5 \text{ portfolios.} \tag{1b}-(1q)$$

X = ASSETS (Equation 1b), BETA (Equation 1c), $VOLUME (Equation 1d), LEVERAGE (Equation 1e), HERFINDAHL (Equation 1f), M/B (Equation 1g), PAYOUT (Equation 1h), TRADES (Equation 1i), squared deviation of ASSETS (Equation 1j), squared deviation of BETA (Equation 1k), squared deviation of $VOLUME (Equation 1l), squared deviation of LEVERAGE (Equation 1m), squared deviation of HERFINDAHL (Equation 1n), squared deviation of M/B (Equation 1o), squared deviation of PAYOUT (Equation 1p), squared deviation of TRADES (Equation 1q):

$$S_j f_{ij} = 980/5 \pm \Delta \tag{1r}$$

$$S_j f_{ij} = 1 \pm \Delta \quad j = 1, \ldots, 980 \text{ firms} \tag{1s}$$

where f_{ij} is the LP solution variable which represents the amount of the ith portfolio's funds invested in firm j, X represents, in turn, each of the remaining variables described above, and X^2 represents the squared values of these variables.

The Δ has a value of 0.1% of each of the right-hand side values, which allows the LP to attain feasibility. The functions of the constraints and the objective function will be explained next.

The objective function maximizes the difference in the level of PRICE between portfolio one and five, while constraint (1a) equalizes the difference in the mean level of PRICE between portfolios one and two, two, and three, etc. Equations 1b through 1i hold the first moments of the control variables equal, while Equations 1j through 1q hold the second moments equal. Constraint (Equation 1r) divides the 980 firms approximately evenly across the five portfolios, while constraint (Equation 1s) forces each firm into at least one portfolio. Note that firms may be split between portfolios, although this occurs infrequently—97.6% of the nonzero solutions values (f_i's) were 1.0.

Alternatively, we choose five portfolios using the "ranking" procedure. In this procedure the stocks are ranked from highest to lowest according to PRICE. The stocks are then grouped into portfolios according to their quintile ranking.

We compare the effectiveness of the LP and ranking methods in selecting the five portfolios which maximize the differences between mean sample values of a targeted portfolio characteristic. Table 1 displays the set of five portfolios constructed using the LP objective function of maximizing the differences in PRICE across portfolios. Table 2 shows the portfolios resulting from the ranking procedure where the dispersion in mean PRICE is maximized.

Table 1. Portfolios Formed Utilizing a Linear Programming Method to Maximize Differences Across Portfolios by PRICE[a]

Variable Name	Portfolio Number	Number in Portfolio	Mean	Standard Deviation
ASSETS	1	202	7.19618	1.70767
	2	214	7.20048	1.71643
	3	212	7.20651	1.71947
	4	216	7.22743	1.71683
	5	211	7.21167	1.71981
PRICE	1	202	24.86818	15.08430
	2	214	28.70214	22.25659
	3	212	34.76464	25.59498
	4	216	38.88933	29.44681
	5	211	42.54249	31.90845
BETA	1	202	1.02778	0.41137
	2	214	1.02751	0.41132
	3	212	1.02915	0.41248
	4	216	1.02818	0.41092
	5	211	1.02839	0.41527

(continued)

Table 1. Continued

Variable Name	Portfolio Number	Number in Portfolio	Mean	Standard Deviation
$VOLUME	1	202	15.17928	1.62272
	2	214	15.19719	1.65461
	3	212	15.20999	1.66327
	4	216	15.21748	1.62274
	5	211	15.19964	1.61554
LEVERAGE	1	202	26.79157	17.00741
	2	214	26.91869	17.03276
	3	212	26.80216	17.01524
	4	216	26.80816	16.97978
	5	211	26.78648	17.00426
HERFINDAHL	1	202	0.08185	0.05552
	2	214	0.07904	0.05601
	3	212	0.08142	0.05767
	4	216	0.07964	0.05501
	5	211	0.08047	0.05644
M/B	1	202	2.06027	1.42005
	2	214	2.06019	1.42563
	3	212	2.05983	1.42453
	4	216	2.05894	1.42359
	5	211	2.05984	1.42377
PAYOUT	1	202	49.88123	57.70554
	2	214	49.91298	57.60139
	3	212	49.95431	57.69883
	4	216	50.06299	57.56886
	5	211	50.05777	57.70848
TRADES	1	202	122.7273	196.8436
	2	214	123.0618	196.8764
	3	212	122.8948	196.5270
	4	216	122.9689	196.5223
	5	211	122.9690	196.5270

Note: [a]This table presents 5 portfolios formed using an LP model maximizing differences in PRICE, while holding other portfolio variables constant. Listed below are the number of stocks in each portfolio as well as the portfolio mean and standard deviation of the following financial variables: ASSETS, the log of the end-of-year total assets; PRICE, average daily stock price; BETA; $VOLUME, the log of the average daily dollar trading volume; LEVERAGE, debt-to-assets; HERFINDAHL, Herfindahl index of trading dispersion; M/B, market-to-book ratio; PAYOUT, average dividend payout ratio; and TRADES, average number of trades per day.

Table 2. Portfolios Formed Utilizing the Ranking Method to Maximize Differences Across Portfolios by PRICE[a]

Variable Name	Portfolio Number	Number in Portfolio	Mean	Standard Deviation
ASSETS	1	196	8.45808	1.51390
	2	196	7.66194	1.49857
	3	196	7.17107	1.61143
	4	196	6.68609	1.42723
	5	196	6.03394	1.44536
PRICE	1	196	63.69146	35.72167
	2	196	36.03688	8.41443
	3	196	26.54404	2.04577
	4	196	19.40006	2.25045
	5	196	11.61800	2.41156
BETA	1	196	1.02602	0.30520
	2	196	0.97908	0.40509
	3	196	1.00714	0.43383
	4	196	1.02958	0.47158
	5	196	1.09795	0.42534
$VOLUME	1	196	16.82020	1.30295
	2	196	15.77905	1.27664
	3	196	15.14594	1.35401
	4	196	14.55827	1.30200
	5	196	13.69891	1.35500
LEVERAGE	1	196	23.02964	16.44177
	2	196	25.82015	13.89128
	3	196	27.19474	17.09000
	4	196	28.63775	17.85407
	5	196	29.19775	18.63631
HERFINDAHL	1	196	0.05813	0.02769
	2	196	0.07782	0.05079
	3	196	0.08805	0.05903
	4	196	0.10369	0.07174
	5	196	0.11816	0.07362
M/B	1	196	2.69607	1.80929
	2	196	2.09739	1.24342
	3	196	2.05249	1.34997
	4	196	1.83857	1.19690
	5	196	1.61520	1.22437
PAYOUT	1	196	38.41678	28.29585
	2	196	45.60218	41.66013
	3	196	49.19575	50.02450
	4	196	55.08907	62.86853
	5	196	61.57090	85.40697

(continued)

Table 2. Continued

Variable Name	Portfolio Number	Number in Portfolio	Mean	Standard Deviation
TRADES	1	196	233.4225	280.2774
	2	196	143.4254	229.1349
	3	196	99.1517	130.8761
	4	196	79.5914	124.3996
	5	196	58.9772	103.3666

Notes: [a]This table presents 5 portfolios formed using a ranking method to maximize differences in PRICE. Listed below are the number of stocks in each portfolio as well as the portfolios mean and standard deviation of the following financial variables: ASSETS, the log of the end-of-year total assets; PRICE, average daily stock price; BETA; $VOLUME, the log of the average daily dollar trading volume; LEVERAGE, debt-to-assets; HERFINDAHL, Herfindahl index of trading dispersion; M/B, market-to-book ratio; PAYOUT, average dividend payout ratio; and TRADES, average number of trades per day.

Finally, we construct a set of five identical portfolios—matching or control portfolios. The objective of matching portfolios is the minimization of the differences in the portfolio attributes. Table 3 presents the mean and standard deviation of each of the nine financial variables listed above when the LP model is used to form five identical portfolios.

Table 3. Portfolios Formed Utilizing the Linear Programming Method to Achieve Equality Across All Portfolios[a]

Variable Name	Portfolio Number	Number in Portfolio	Mean	Standard Deviation
ASSETS	1	205	7.18877	1.77115
	2	212	7.20136	1.71714
	3	212	7.21235	1.69331
	4	216	7.20222	1.68128
	5	210	7.20397	1.70296
PRICE	1	205	31.46219	24.12422
	2	212	31.45809	24.19045
	3	212	31.47372	24.21588
	4	216	31.39524	24.25395
	5	210	31.46676	24.12299
BETA	1	205	1.02809	0.41076
	2	212	1.02793	0.41394
	3	212	1.02940	0.41223
	4	216	1.02795	0.41388
	5	210	1.02618	0.41866

(continued)

Table 3. Portfolios Formed Utilizing the Linear Programming Method to Achieve Equality Across All Portfolios[a]

Variable Name	Portfolio Number	Number in Portfolio	Mean	Standard Deviation
$VOLUME	1	205	15.17208	1.93827
	2	212	15.20047	1.69236
	3	212	15.22185	1.59460
	4	216	15.20047	1.61118
	5	210	15.20467	1.59938
LEVERAGE	1	205	26.77950	16.94445
	2	212	26.77600	17.00278
	3	212	26.81365	16.98757
	4	216	26.72270	17.08896
	5	210	26.78339	17.00184
HERFINDAHL	1	205	0.08279	0.05615
	2	212	0.09138	0.06021
	3	212	0.09040	0.06117
	4	216	0.08641	0.05473
	5	210	0.09624	0.06179
M/B	1	205	2.06021	1.42565
	2	212	2.05994	1.43015
	3	212	2.06255	1.42948
	4	216	2.05994	1.42897
	5	210	2.05640	1.43585
PAYOUT	1	205	49.88159	57.70583
	2	212	49.97494	57.58520
	3	212	50.04521	57.62842
	4	216	49.97494	57.61843
	5	210	49.98872	57.51942
TRADES	1	205	122.6841	196.8889
	2	212	122.9137	196.7278
	3	212	123.0865	196.5650
	4	216	122.8275	196.7815
	5	210	122.9475	196.7443

Notes: [a]This table presents 5 portfolios formed using an LP model minimizing differences in all variables. Listed below are the number of stocks in each portfolio as well as the portfolios mean and standard deviation of the following financial variables: ASSETS, the log of the end-of-year total assets; PRICE, average daily stock price; BETA; $VOLUME, the log of the average daily dollar trading volume; LEVERAGE, debt-to-assets; HERFINDAHL, Herfindahl index of trading dispersion; M/B, market-to-book ratio; PAYOUT, average dividend payout ratio; and TRADES, average number of trades per day.

III. COMPARATIVE RESULTS FOR DIVERGENT PORTFOLIOS

In *ceteris paribus* testing, isolation of a single variable is critical to the research methodology. In this section we compare the effectiveness of the single-variable ranking and LP portfolio formation techniques in creating sets of five portfolios which maximize the differences in mean PRICE across portfolios while holding other portfolio characteristics constant.

Table 1 displays the mean and standard deviations of key financial characteristics of the five portfolios resulting from the LP procedure. With the exception of PRICE, the resulting portfolio characteristics are nearly identical. The portfolio mean PRICE ranges from $24.87 to $42.54. Furthermore, the distance between portfolio mean PRICE is approximately equal and the standard deviations range from 62.5 to 77.5% of their respective mean values.

On the other hand, the portfolios formed using the traditional ranking procedure do not conform to the *ceteris paribus* assumptions. PRICE, the targeted variable characteristic—Table 2, ranges from $11.62 to $63.69 and the standard deviations range from 7.7 to 56.1% of their respective mean values. Further, the distance between the portfolio mean values of PRICE is highly variable—a difference of $27 between portfolios 1 and 2 versus a difference of $8 between portfolios 4 and 5. With the exception of BETA, the other mean portfolio which are theoretically held constant appear to systematically vary from portfolio to portfolio. Unless otherwise controlled for, these correlations can confound the research design.

IV. LP FOR IDENTICAL PORTFOLIOS

In direct contrast to research designs that require divergent portfolios are studies which rely on equivalent portfolios. It is readily apparent when examining Table 3 that the set of five portfolios constructed using the LP model holds both the portfolio mean values and standard deviations constant for all nine financial variables. If needed, the LP method has the ability to equalize higher moments. This set of five portfolios would work well for control or matching purposes.

V. CONCLUSIONS

Linear programming is an excellent tool for the financial researcher. Empirical studies that utilize a portfolio approach to reduce the effects of individual security variations (noise) may be enhanced by utilizing an LP model in the portfolio selection process.

We illustrate the differing portfolio selections that result from portfolio formation with the LP method of portfolio construction and the traditional single variable ranking method. The LP method can maximize the mean difference in a target variable and maintain equality in other specified variables for a true *ceteris paribus* research design. Further, for a matching or control situation, the LP procedure has the ability to hold multiple moments of all targeted characteristics equal across portfolios.

REFERENCES

Lau, S.T., McCorry, M.S., McInish, T.H., & Van Ness, R.A. (1996). Trading of NASDAQ stocks on the Chicago Stock Exchange. *The Journal of Financial Research, 19,* 579–584.

McInish, T.H., & Wood, R.A. (1986). Adjusting for beta bias: An assessment of alternate techniques: A note. *Journal of Finance, 41,* 277–286.

McInish, T.H., & Wood, R.A. (1995). Competition, fragmentation, and market quality. *The industrial organization and regulation of the securities industry* (pp. 63–92). The University of Chicago Press.

McInish, T.H., & Wood, R.A. (1994). Working Paper—University of Memphis, Volatility of NASDAQ/NMS and listed stocks.

Wood, R.A., & McInish, T.H. (1994). Working Paper—University of Memphis, The effect of NYSE rule 390 on spreads, premiums and volatility.

RISK DIVERSIFICATION THROUGH EXPERT USE

Christian Genest and Michel Gendron

ABSTRACT

This paper is concerned with the evaluation of the common risk diversification strategy that consists of allocating portions of an investor's assets to different fund managers or experts who claim to be better informed than others about the future value of the market return. While important gains in utility might accrue from an appropriate use of the latent dependencies in these experts' information sets, it is shown that the common diversification approach performs generally quite well under the realistic assumption that the experts' opinions are positively correlated. This is accomplished by comparing this risk-diversification practice to an optimal investment policy derived under full information, within the context of a standard normal returns–exponential utility market-timing model.

I. INTRODUCTION

A common risk spreading measure consists of selecting a number of fund managers or financial experts to whom parts of an investor's assets are entrusted in order to reach a desired level of risk diversification. In a differential information framework

Advances in Investment Analysis and Portfolio Management, Volume 7, pages 117–129.
Copyright © 2000 by JAI Press Inc.
All rights of reproduction in any form reserved.
ISBN: 0-7623-0658-0

where each expert claims to be better informed than others about the future value of the market return, this investment strategy may be considered suboptimal, because it fails to exploit the complementarities that typically exist between the experts' information sets. Since access to these information sources could clearly lead to superior investment strategies, one may wonder what is the loss of efficiency incurred when risk diversification is achieved by simply splitting the assets (equally or not) among the experts.

To answer this question, it is appropriate to compare the expected utility of this common portfolio delegation mechanism with that of an ideal investment strategy based on the entire information possessed by a given set of experts. This paper shows how this can be done using a multivariate version of the standard normal returns–exponential utility market-timing model. It is found that, except in extreme circumstances, a simple allocation of the wealth among the experts is not far from optimal under the realistic assumption that their private signals are positively correlated. This observation remains valid even when the investor's assets are split equally between the financial experts.

A description of the differential information framework used in this note is given in Section II, and the optimal investment policy under full information is identified in Section III. This ideal strategy is then compared with the common risk-diversification approach in Section IV, using the expected utility criterion. Section V briefly concludes this paper.

II. THE MODEL

The differential information framework used in this note is a straightforward generalization of the standard normal returns–exponential utility market-timing model exploited by Gendron and Genest (1990), among others, to evaluate the performance of a single fund manager facing investment constraints. In this one-period, partial-equilibrium model, the market return in excess of the risk-free rate is assumed *ex ante* to be normally distributed with mean μ and variance σ^2, denoted:

$$R_m \approx N(\mu, \sigma^2)$$

To portray the diversity of opinions, it is supposed that individual i in a set of $n \geq 2$ financial experts has the ability to observe a private signal Y_i which, given a realization $R_m = r_m$ of the market return, also follows a normal distribution with mean r_m and variance σ_i^2. Possible dependence between these signals is accounted for by the assumption that conditionally on r_m, the column vector $Y = (Y_1, \ldots, Y_n)'$ follows a multivariate normal distribution with covariance matrix Σ, namely:

$$Y|R_m = r_m \approx N(r_m e, \Sigma)$$

where e stands for an $n \times 1$ vector of ones.

Upon observing the signal $Y_i = y_i$, each expert uses Bayes' theorem to update a subjective distribution for R_m. A standard calculation shows that the posterior distribution for R_m is:

$$R_m|Y_i = y_i \approx N(\mu_i, \tau_i^2)$$

where $\mu_i = \tau_i^2(\mu/\sigma^2 + y_i/\sigma_i^2)$ and $1/\tau_i^2 = 1/\sigma^2 + 1/\sigma_i^2$. It is this posterior distribution which expert i would use to determine the proportion X_i of an investor's assets that one would invest in the market. This proportion is obtained by maximizing the investor's end-of-period utility of portfolio return:

$$R_p = X_i R_m$$

Assuming an exponential utility function with risk aversion parameter $\theta > 0$, the solution to the maximization problem:

$$X_i = \arg \max E(-e^{-\theta X_m R_m}|Y_i = y_i)$$

is unique and given by:

$$X_i = \frac{E(R_m|Y_i = y_i)}{\theta \, \mathrm{var}(R_m|Y_i = y_i)} = \frac{\mu}{\theta\sigma^2} + \frac{1}{\theta\sigma_i^2} y_i$$

which shows that for expert i, the investment policy is a linear function of one's private signal. In particular, this manager would shortsell the market if $X_i < 0$ and would borrow to invest if $X_i > 1$.

Now suppose that an investor hires $n \geq 2$ financial experts, each of whom is entrusted with a portion of the assets to be managed. Let $0 \leq w_i \leq 1$ represent the fraction of these funds allocated to manager $1 \leq i \leq n$, so that $w_1 + \cdots + w_n = 1$ by definition. Care should be exerted to distinguish w_i from the proportion X_i that manager i invests in the market on behalf of the assets' owner. While X_i may be negative or greater than 1 to reflect the fact that the manager may choose to shortshell or borrow to invest, the weight w_i is necessarily comprised between 0 and 1, as it merely represents the fraction of the investor's assets that this expert was entrusted with.

The market share resulting from this naive diversification strategy is given by:

$$X = \sum_{i=1}^{n} w_i X_i$$

It amounts to investing in the market a weighted linear average of the proportions X_i of assets chosen by the managers. While this investment policy stems from a portfolio delegation mechanism, it is akin to a linear combination of forecasts, a technique whose value has been demonstrated again and again in a variety of economic contexts; see Clemen (1989) for a review. The main difficulty associated with this procedure is the determination of the portion of funds which should be entrusted to each expert (Winkler and Clemen, 1992). An appealing rule would be to allocate the assets between managers according to their level of "expertise", in some sense of the word. In practice, absence of discriminating information in this regard would reasonably lead to equal weights. The issue of weight selection will be revisited in Section IV.

Incidentally, the investment strategy $\overline{X}$ could also be justified via an opinion pooling argument. Assuming that an investor could have access to the experts' posterior distributions $f_1, \ldots, f_n$ for R_m, the investor could then form his or her own opinion by taking a weighted geometric mean of these density functions. The resulting distribution:

$$f(r_m) = \prod_{i=1}^{n} f_i^{w_i}(r_m) / \int \prod_{i=1}^{n} f_i^{w_i}(r) dr$$

is referred to as a logarithmic opinion pool in the statistical literature (Genest and Zidek, 1986). In the special case where each of the f_i's is normal with mean μ_i and variance τ_i^2 as defined above, it is easy to see that f is itself normal with mean $\overline{\mu}$ and variance $\overline{\tau}^2$ satisfying:

$$\overline{\mu} = \overline{\tau}^2 \left(\sum_{i=1}^{n} w_i \mu_i / \tau_i^2 \right), \quad 1/\overline{\tau}^2 = \sum_{i=1}^{n} w_i / \tau_i^2$$

so that, given f, the proportion of assets that should be invested in the market is:

$$\overline{X} = \frac{\overline{\mu}}{\theta \overline{\tau}^2} = \sum_{i=1}^{n} w_i X_i$$

Weighted geometric averages of expert opinions are externally Bayesian in the sense of Madansky (1978). In short, this means that once f has been computed, an investor no longer needs to refer to the experts to update it when new, common knowledge evidence relevant to the market return becomes available. Because of the way in which f was obtained, its updating via Bayes' theorem would be equivalent to the weighted geometric average of the experts' updated distributions. This property is valuable to investors in that recourse to the experts is superfluous when new public information is released.

III. THE FULL-INFORMATION INVESTMENT STRATEGY

Suppose that an investor had direct access to the experts' private signals, $Y_i = y_i$, or that the investor could infer them from their posterior distributions. Further assume that the investor knew the dependence structure between these signals, as embodied in the conditional distribution of the column vector $Y = (Y_1, \ldots, Y_n)'$ given $R_m = r_m$. If the prior distribution of the market return is common knowledge, the investor would then have in hand all the data required to make a decision based on the posterior distribution of R_m given $Y = y$. The solution to the maximization problem:

$$X_{\text{full}} = \arg \max E(-e^{-\theta X_{\text{full}} R_m} | Y = y)$$

would then be optimal, based on the information sets of the experts consulted.

Given a value of the vector $Y = y$, the posterior distribution of R_m is normal with mean:

$$E(R_m | Y = y) = \mu + \sigma^2 e' \Psi^{-1}(y - \mu e)$$

and variance

$$\text{var}(R_m | Y = y) = \sigma^2(1 - \sigma^2 e' \Psi^{-1} e)$$

provided that $\Psi = \Sigma + \sigma^2 ee'$ has an inverse (when $n = 2$, e.g., such is the case unless $\rho = 1$ and $\sigma_1 = \sigma_2$). Using the fact that $\Psi^{-1} = \Sigma^{-1} - \sigma^2 \Sigma^{-1} ee' \Sigma^{-1}/(1 + \sigma^2 e' \Sigma^{-1} e)$ whenever Σ^{-1} exists, it follows that:

$$E(R_m | Y = y) = \frac{\mu + \sigma^2 e' \Sigma^{-1} y}{1 + \sigma^2 e' \Sigma^{-1} e}$$

and:

$$\text{var}(R_m | Y = y) = \frac{\sigma^2}{1 + \sigma^2 e' \Sigma^{-1} e}$$

so that:

$$X_{\text{full}} = \frac{\mu + \sigma^2 e' \Sigma^{-1} y}{\theta \sigma^2}$$

varies linearly with the signals, as is the case with $\overline{X}$. It is important to note, however, that the inverse of the correlation matrix Σ often contains *negative* elements.

To illustrate this remark, suppose that:

$$\Sigma = \begin{pmatrix} 1 & 2 \\ 2 & 10 \end{pmatrix}$$

a situation where the experts' signals are highly correlated but of wildly varying precision. In that case, it is easy to verify that the weights of y_1 and y_2 in X_{full} are respectively equal to 8/6 and $-1/6$, so that:

$$\theta X_{\text{full}} = \frac{\mu}{\sigma^2} + \frac{8}{6} y_1 - \frac{1}{6} y_2$$

Clearly, this strategy could not be replicated by any choice of weights w_1, w_2, in:

$$\theta\overline{X} = \frac{\mu}{\sigma^2} + w_1 y_1 + w_2 \frac{y_2}{10}$$

even negative ones! This is hardly surprising, of course, given that the investment policy X_{full} assumes direct access to the experts' private signals and complete knowledge of their dependence structure. In practice, however, such information is difficult to access and to process, if only because most financial experts are loath of formulating but their final investment recommendation. In fact, it could be argued that managers are usually unable to identify precisely their information basis, including what they believe to be private signals. While the investment strategy X_{full} is inoperative, it is a good standard against which to gage the loss of efficiency of the common investment policy $\overline{X}$. This question, which is central to this paper, is examined in the following section with particular attention to the special cases where experts' signals are independent or equicorrelated.

IV. EVALUATION OF THE COMMON RISK DIVERSIFICATION STRATEGY

Conditional on a set of experts, the highest possible level of expected utility that can be achieved is given by the strategy X_{full}, as the latter assumes access to these experts' signals and complete knowledge of their dependence structure. By opposition, investors who would bypass the experts altogether and who would act according to their prior beliefs would invest a proportion $X_{null} = \mu/(\theta\sigma^2)$ in the market. The difference in expected utility between the full- and the no-information strategies provides a natural gage against which to measure the relative value of the intermediate diversification strategy $\overline{X}$.

Let:

$$p = \frac{E(-e^{-\theta X_{full} R_m}) - E(-e^{-\theta \overline{X} R_m})}{E(-e^{-\theta X_{full} R_m}) - E(-e^{-\theta X_{null} R_m})}$$

represent the relative loss in expected utility that is incurred when $\overline{X}$ is used instead of X_{full}. Note that this ratio, which is comprised between 0 and 1, is invariant under affine transformations of the utility function. This is an essential requirement, because von Neumann–Morgenstern utility functions are only unique up to location and scale.

A simple calculation shows that:

$$E(-e^{-\theta X_{null} R_m}) = -e^{-\mu^2/2\sigma^2}$$

To compute the other expectations in p, it suffices to observe that both $\theta\overline{X}$ and θX_{full} can be expressed in the form $a'Y + b$ with $b = \mu/\sigma^2$ and an appropriate choice of $a = (a_1, \ldots, a_n)'$. Writing:

$$E\{-e^{-(a'Y+b)R_m}\} = E\{-e^{-bR_m}E(e^{-a'Yr_m}|R_m = r_m)\}$$

and using the fact that the conditional distribution of $a'Y$ given $R_m = r_m$ is normal with mean $r_m a'e$ and variance $a'\Sigma a$, it is plain that:

$$E(e^{-a'Yr_m}|R_m = r_m) = e^{-V(a)r_m^2}$$

with $V(a) = a'e - a'\Sigma a/2$, because the left-hand side is the moment generating function of the random variable $a'Y$ evaluated at the point $-r_m$. Simple integration then yields:

$$E\{-e^{-(a'Y+b)R_m}\} = E\{-e^{-V(a)R_m^2-bR_m}\} = \frac{-1}{\sqrt{1+2\sigma^2 V(a)}} e^{-\mu^2/2\sigma^2}$$

so long as $V(a) \geq -1/2\sigma^2$.

It is clear that $V(a)$ is a concave function whose maximum occurs when $a = \Sigma^{-1}e$, which corresponds to X_{full}, as expected. For investment strategy X with weight vector $w = (w_1, \ldots, w_n)'$, one has $a = \Delta^{-1}w$ with $\Delta = \text{diag}(\Sigma)$. One may thus write:

$$p = \frac{\sqrt{q}-1}{\sqrt{1+\sigma^2 e'\Sigma^{-1}e} - 1}$$

in terms of the ratio:

$$q = \frac{1+\sigma^2 e'\Sigma^{-1}e}{1+2\sigma^2(e'\Delta^{-1}w - w'\Delta^{-1}\Sigma\Delta^{-1}w/2)}$$

which is comprised between 1 and $1 + \sigma^2 e'\Sigma^{-1}e$.

The vector w^* that minimizes this expression yields the largest possible expected utility that can be achieved through an investment strategy of the form $\overline{X}$. The value of the corresponding strategy, $\overline{X}_{opt}$, is examined below as a function of Σ in two special cases of interest. Considering the large extent to which financial experts share the same information and methods of analysis, as highlighted for example by Figlewski and Urich (1983) in their investigation of composite predictions for the weekly change in the money supply, the following discussion focusses on positive dependence between the experts' signals.

A. Case 1: Two Experts

It can be assumed without loss of generality that $\sigma_1^2 \leq \sigma_2^2$. If ρ stands for the correlation between the signals Y_1 and Y_2 given $R_m = r_m$, the denominator of q reduces to:

$$1 + 2\sigma^2\left(\frac{w_1}{\sigma_1^2} + \frac{w_2}{\sigma_2^2}\right) - \sigma^2\left(\frac{w_1^2}{\sigma_1^2} + 2\frac{w_1 w_2 \rho}{\sigma_1\sigma_2} + \frac{w_2^2}{\sigma_2^2}\right)$$

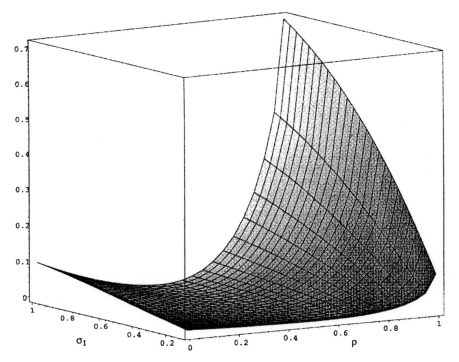

Figure 1. Plot of the Ratio p as a Function of $\rho \in [0,1]$ and $\sigma_1 \in [1/10,1]$ when $n = 2$ and $\sigma_2 = 2\sigma_1$. The Left Panel Portrays the Relative Loss in Efficiency Associated with the Investment Strategy $\bar{X}_{opt}$ which Uses Optimal Weights w^*. The Right Panel Displays the Relative Loss Associated with a Strategy $\bar{X}$ in which Equal Weights are Used for the Two Experts

so that the optimal weight for expert 1 is given by:

$$w_1^* = \frac{\sigma_2^2 - \rho\sigma_1\sigma_2}{\sigma_1^2 + \sigma_2^2 - 2\rho\sigma_1\sigma_2} \in [0,1]$$

when $\rho \leq \sigma_1/\sigma_2$ and equals one otherwise. Accordingly, all the weight is given to the better of the two experts when their signals are highly positively correlated. Note that when $\rho = 0$, the weights w_i^* are proportional to the precision $h_i = 1/\sigma_i^2$ of the signals, a reasonable prescription that is not necessarily optimal when there are more than two experts, however.

Graphs of the relative loss in expected utility associated with two different investment strategies of the form $\bar{X}$ are depicted in Figure 1 as a function of ρ and σ_1, under the assumptions that $\sigma_2 = 2\sigma_1$ and that the variance σ^2 of the market return

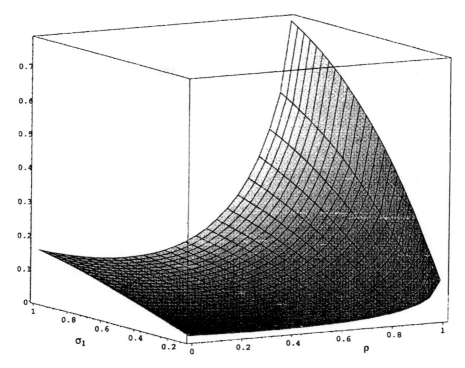

Figure 1. Continued

is 1. The left panel displays the value of p when optimal weights w^* are used in the formula for $\overline{X}$, while the right panel shows what happens when $w_1 = w_2 = 1/2$. One can see that the loss is minimal (typically smaller than 10%) in both cases, unless the experts' signals are *very* strongly correlated *and* have a variance that is at least as large as that of the market.

A comparison of the two panels of Figure 1 further shows that the use of optimal weights w^* is only marginally preferable to the simple-minded strategy $\overline{X}_{equal}$ in which equal weights are given to the two experts. To confirm this, the loss in expected utility incurred when $\overline{X}_{equal}$ is used instead of $\overline{X}_{opt}$ was compared with the maximum expected utility that can be achieved over the no-information strategy X_{null} by any strategy of the form $\overline{X}$. The resulting ratio:

$$r = \frac{E(-e^{-\theta X_{opt} R_m}) - E(-e^{-\theta \overline{X}_{equal} R_m})}{E(-e^{-\theta X_{opt} R_m}) - E(-e^{-\theta X_{null} R_m})}$$

is depicted in Figure 2 as a function of ρ and σ_1 under the same assumptions as before. As can be seen, the use of optimal weights as opposed to equal weights

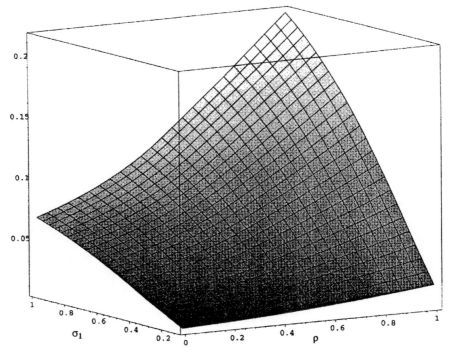

Figure 2. Plot of the Ratio r as a Function of $\rho \in [0,1]$ and $\sigma_1 \in [1/10,1]$ when $n = 2$ and $\sigma_2 = 2\sigma_1$

provides only marginal gains in expected utility (typically inferior to 10%) in realistic conditions of relative precision and dependence between the experts' signals with respect to the market.

These various observations remain true, in substance, for other values of the ratio σ_2/σ_1 and of the variance of the market return. For example, it is easy to check analytically that when $\rho = 0$ and $w_1 = w_2$, $p \le 1/4$ for *any* values of σ, σ_1, σ_2. Thus if the two experts are conditionally independent and given the same weight, irrespective of the precision of their signals, the loss associated with the use of $\overline{X}_{equal}$ cannot exceed 25% of any other investment strategy of the form $\overline{X}$.

B.   Case 2: Interchangeable Experts

Assume that conditional on the value of R_m, one has $\text{var}(Y_i) = \sigma_0^2$ and $\text{corr}(Y_i, Y_j) = \rho \ge -1/(n - 1)$ for all $1 \le i < j \le n$. Standard diversification arguments suggest that equal weights should then be given to each expert. It is easy to check that one has indeed $\overline{X}_{equal} = \overline{X}_{opt}$ (and hence $r = 0$) in this case. Substituting $w^* = e/n$ in the formula for q and using the fact that there exists an explicit expression for the inverse of an equicorrelation matrix, one may express p in the form:

$$p = P_{n,\rho} = \frac{\sqrt{A_{n,\rho}/B_{n,\rho}} - 1}{\sqrt{A_{n,\rho}} - 1}$$

where:

$$A_{n,\rho} = 1 + \frac{n}{1 + (n-1)\rho} \frac{\sigma^2}{\sigma_0^2}$$

and:

$$B_{n,p} = 1 + \frac{(2n-1) - (n-1)\rho}{n} \frac{\sigma^2}{\sigma_0^2}$$

A graphical representation of $p = P_{n,\rho}$ as a function of ρ is given in Figure 3 for various values of n. It was assumed for convenience that $\sigma/\sigma_0 = 1$ but the graph is

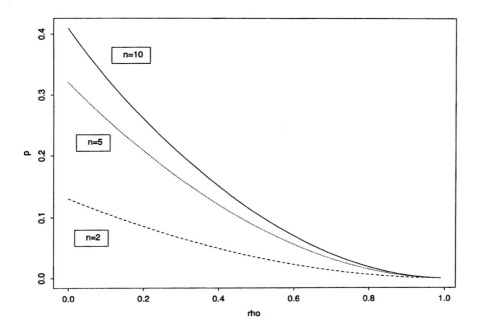

Figure 3. Plot of the Ratio $p_{n,\rho}$ as a Function of ρ for Three Different Values of n

similar for other values of this ratio. Although this is not easy to establish analytically, one can see that $p_{n,\rho}$ is decreasing in ρ for fixed n, as well as increasing in n for fixed ρ. It vanishes when $p = 1$ or $n = 1$ and tends to 1 when $\rho < 1$ and $n \to \infty$. It can also be shown that p is always smaller than $(n^2 - 2n + 1)/n^2$ when $\rho = 0$, and hence for any positive value of ρ in the present case. These results are conform to intuition. On one hand, the diversification strategy $\overline{X}_{\text{equal}}$ with weights $w^* = e/n$ is clearly optimal if $n = 1$ and hence must approach $\overline{X}_{\text{full}}$ when $n \geq 2$ exchangeable experts become indistinguishable as $\rho \to 1$. On the other hand, the strategy $\overline{X}_{\text{equal}}$ gradually becomes inefficient as the number of experts increases, because each signal brings in additional information that the standard diversification scheme cannot exploit.

V. DISCUSSION

The calculations presented in this paper illustrate that under realistic conditions of precision of the expert signals and dependence between them, common risk diversification strategies of the type $\overline{X}$ fare quite well, in terms of expected utility, when compared to the high standard provided by the unattainable, full-information strategy $\overline{X}_{\text{full}}$. Furthermore, it appears that there is comparatively little to lose in allocating one wealth's equally among experts rather than in an optimal fashion.

While the value of this simple-minded portfolio delegation strategy could be quite small as compared to the optimal when the number of experts is large, it should be borne in mind that the investment strategy $\overline{X}_{\text{opt}}$ could only be implemented if the investor had direct access to the private signals. This raises the issue of eliciting truthful information, as discussed by Bhattacharya and Pleiderer (1985) in a delegated portfolio management context, for example. This problem is complicated by the fact that in circumstances delineated by Admati and Pfleiderer (1990), fund managers may find it valuable to restrict the usage of their information, by adding noise in a direct sale or by pricing usage in their mutual funds.

By avoiding the issue of signal elicitation, the common risk diversification strategy $\overline{X}$ escapes most of these difficulties, as well as agency problems (for a recent treatment of the latter issue, see Dow and Gorton, 1997). Given a judicious choice of experts, it should thus perform quite well in absolute terms, under realistic conditions of dependence between the signals. The multivariate version of the standard normal returns–exponential utility market timing model employed here could actually be used to measure the effect of selecting different sets of experts on the global level of expected utility yielded by different investment strategies of the form $\overline{X}$. While the conclusions presented herein will be robust to small departures from the hypotheses of the model, it would also be of interest to test their validity for entirely different classes of utility functions and multivariate distributions between expert signals. This could be the object of future work.

ACKNOWLEDGMENTS

The authors are grateful to an anonymous referee for comments which led to substantial improvements in the paper's presentation. Partial funding in support of this work was provided by the Natural Sciences and Engineering Research Council of Canada, by the Social Sciences and Humanities Research Council of Canada, as well as by the Fonds pour la formation de chercheurs et l'aide à la recherche du Gouvernement du Québec.

REFERENCES

Admati, A.R., & Pfleiderer, P. (1990). Direct and indirect sale of information. *Econometrica, 58,* 901–928.

Bhattacharya, S., & Pfleiderer, P. (1985). Delegated portfolio management. *Journal of Economic Theory, 36,* 1–25.

Clemen, R.T. (1989). Combining forecasts: A review and annotated bibliography. *International Journal of Forecasting, 5,* 559–583.

Dow, J., & Gorton, G. (1997). Noise trading, delegated portfolio management, and economic welfare. *Journal of Political Economy, 105,* 1024–1050.

Figlewski, S., & Urich, T. (1983). Optimal aggregation of money supply forecasts: Accuracy, profitability and market efficiency. *The Journal of Finance, 28,* 695–710.

Gendron, M., & Genest, C. (1990). Performance measurement under asymmetric information and investment constraints. *The Journal of Finance, 45,* 1655–1661.

Genest, C., & Zidek, J.V. (1986). Combining probability distributions: A critique and an annotated bibliography (with discussion). *Statistical Science, 1,* 114–148.

Madansky, A. (1978). Externally Bayesian groups. Unpublished manuscript, University of Chicago Graduate School of Business.

Winkler, R.L., & Clemen, R.T. (1992). Sensitivity of weights in combining forecasts. *Operations Research, 43,* 609–614.

A NOTE ON THE LENGTH EFFECT OF FUTURES HEDGING

Donald Lien and Yiu Kuen Tse

ABSTRACT

We point out in this paper that under certain model specifications, the theoretical optimal hedge ratios are stable under aggregation. That is, the same theoretical optimal hedge ratio is applicable irrespective of the hedging horizon. In general, to estimate the optimal hedge ratio it is natural to use a statistical model in which the sampling interval coincides with the hedging horizon. This approach is appropriate for models that are not stable under aggregation. When the stable-under-aggregation property holds, it may be desirable to use a shorter sampling interval for a more effective use of the sample data. For example, the hedge ratio estimated from 1-day return data may outperform the hedge ratio estimated from 5-day return data in terms of out-of-sample hedging effectiveness, even though the hedging horizon is 5 days. The conjecture is illustrated with the Nikkei Stock Average (NSA) 225 data.

I. INTRODUCTION

In this paper we consider the estimation of the optimal hedge ratio when the duration of the hedging period changes. By optimal hedge ratio, we refer to the minimum

Advances in Investment Analysis and Portfolio Management, Volume 7, pages 131–143.
Copyright © 2000 by JAI Press Inc.
All rights of reproduction in any form reserved.
ISBN: 0-7623-0658-0

variance hedge ratio.[1] This problem has long been discussed in the literature. For example, in proposing a measure for hedging effectiveness, Ederington (1979) constructed hedge ratios for different hedging horizons and compared their effectiveness. Figlewski (1984) commented on the Ederington measure and provided some similar calculations. The problem was extensively examined in Malliaris and Urrutia (1991). All the above papers, however, constructed the hedge ratios using the regression method. Chou, Denis, and Lee (1996) reevaluated the issue adopting the vector autoregression (VAR) and the error correction (EC) models. Analytical results for the EC models were provided by Geppert (1995).

Several conclusions can be drawn from the above studies. First, the optimal hedge ratio changes as the length of the hedging period changes. In general, the hedge ratio tends to increase when the hedging horizon increases. Second, the within-sample hedging effectiveness increases as the hedging horizon increases. Justifications of these results are as follows: (1) as the hedging horizon increases, the trading noises are smoothed out; (2) arbitrage relationship brings the spot and futures prices closer to each other, resulting in a larger hedge ratio; and (3) as the hedging duration increases, the spot-price series become noisier. Note that the hedging effectiveness is calculated by subtracting the ratio of the risk of the hedged portfolio to the spot-price risk from one. Thus, a bigger spot-price risk tends to enhance the hedging effectiveness.

In empirical applications the hedge ratios must be estimated based on some statistical models. As the hedge ratios are determined by the second moments of the spot and futures prices only, we may conclude that different statistical models give rise to different hedge ratios to the extent that they produce different estimated second moments. Obviously, the differences in the estimates of the second moments with respect to different hedging horizons have impacts on the estimated hedge ratios. This conclusion echoes the proposal by Findley (1983) and others that different models should be employed to forecast the multiperiod first moments. Figlewski (1997) made a similar suggestion for volatility forecasting

We point out in this paper that under certain model specifications, the theoretical optimal hedge ratios are stable under aggregation. That is, the same theoretical optimal hedge ratio is applicable irrespective of the hedging horizon. In general, to estimate the optimal hedge ratio it is natural to use a statistical model in which the sampling interval coincides with the hedging horizon. However, if the stable-under-aggregation property holds, it may be desirable to use a shorter sampling interval for a more effective use of the sample data. Thus, the choice of the sampling interval depends upon the trade-off between accepting possibly some model specification errors (when the hedge ratios are in fact not stable under aggregation) versus improving the estimation efficiency through more effective use of the sample data. It is possible that, in terms of out-of-sample hedging effectiveness, the hedge ratio estimated from 1-day return data outperforms the hedge ratio estimated from 5-day return data, even when the hedging horizon is 5 days. This possibility is demonstrated with the Nikkei Stock Average (NSA) 225 data.

II. OPTIMAL HEDGE RATIOS

Consider a one-period hedging model with a hedging horizon of n (days). The current time is t and the end of the hedging period is $t + n$. At time t, a hedger is endowed with a nontradable spot position that is to be liquidated at time $t + n$. To reduce the risk exposure, the hedger sells x futures contracts. Let p_j and f_j denote, respectively, the spot and futures prices at time j, for $j = t$ or $t + n$. The payoff π from the spot and futures transactions is given by $\pi = (p_{t+n} - p_t) + x(f_t - f_{t+n})$.

Assume the hedger attempts to minimize the risk (as measured by the variance) based upon the information available at time t, the optimal futures position, denoted by $x^*(n)$, is given by:

$$x^*(n) = \text{cov}\,(p_{t+n} - p_t, f_{t+n} - f_t|I_t)/\text{var}\,(f_{t+n} - f_t \mid I_t)$$

$$= \text{cov}(\Delta_n p_{t+n}, \Delta_n f_{t+n}|I_t)/\text{var}(\Delta_n f_{t+n}|I_t) \tag{1}$$

where I_t denotes the information set at time t, $\text{cov}(.,.)$ is the (conditional) covariance operator, and $\text{var}(\cdot)$ is the (conditional) variance operator. Also, Δ_n is the price-difference operator such that $\Delta_n p_j = p_j - p_{j-n}$ and $\Delta_n f_j = f_j - f_{j-n}$. In this paper the price variables are measured in logarithmic scale, so that $\Delta_n p_j$ and $\Delta_n f_j$ represent the n-day spot and futures returns, respectively. Thus, the optimal hedge ratio is determined by the second moments of the logarithmic price differences corresponding to the specific hedging horizon. The remaining task is to estimate these second moments.

In the literature there are many statistical models for spot and futures prices. Regardless of the selected statistical model, the researcher must decide what sampling interval to use for the estimation when the hedging horizon n is greater than 1. The direct approach is to consider models for $\Delta_n p_{t+n}$ and $\Delta_n f_{t+n}$ so that the hedging horizon is the same as the sampling interval. The second moments required in Equation 1 could then be directly calculated, from which the hedge ratio can be obtained. Alternatively, we can use statistical models for $\Delta_1 p_j$ and $\Delta_1 f_j$. It is noted that:

$$\text{cov}(\Delta_n p_{t+n}, \Delta_n f_{t+n}|I_t) = \text{cov}\left(\sum_{j=t+1}^{t+n} \Delta_1 p_j, \sum_{j=t+1}^{t+n} \Delta_1 f_j | I_t\right) \tag{2}$$

$$\text{var}(\Delta_n f_{t+n}|I_t) = \text{var}\left(\sum_{j=t+1}^{t+n} \Delta_1 f_j|I_t\right) \tag{3}$$

Thus, $x^*(n)$ can be calculated from the second moments of $\Delta_1 p_j$ and $\Delta_1 f_j$. In fact, statistical models for $\Delta_k p_j$ and $\Delta_k f_j$ can be applied to generate an estimate of $x^*(n)$ as long as n is a multiple of k. Therefore, to determine the optimal hedge ratio for a 10-day hedge, we can model 1-day, 2-day, 5-day, or 10-day spot and futures returns. Chou, Denis, and Lee (1996) applied the regression method to the NSA data from January 1, 1989 to December 31, 1993. They used sampling intervals that coincide with the hedging horizons and found that the hedge ratio is 0.7429, 0.9352, and 1.0085 when the hedging horizon is 1 day, 1 week, and 5 weeks, respectively. Thus, the estimated hedge ratio increases with the duration of the hedging period.

III. STATISTICAL MODELS AND SAMPLING INTERVALS

To avoid serial correlation in the residuals, we shall only consider non-overlapping return data for the purpose of estimating the hedge ratios. Suppose a data set with T daily return observations is available. Then the hedge ratio of an n-day hedge may be determined from a sample of n-day returns with size T/n, which is assumed to be an integer. This is the direct approach, for which the sampling interval is equal to the hedging horizon. As we shall see below, there are circumstances in which the theoretical optimal hedge ratio is stable under aggregation.

When the stable-under-aggregation property holds the hedge ratio for n-day hedge should be calculated from the 1-day return data, due to the more effective use of the sample data. However, considerations for possible model misspecifications argue in favor of the direct approach. This is because if the model is misspecified, the use of a sampling interval that coincides with the hedging horizon is likely to mitigate the misspecifications.

We now consider and compare the following specifications: regression, VAR, and EC models. First, we consider the regression method. For the 1-day hedge, the regression model specifies the following:

$$\Delta_1 p_j = \alpha_1 + \beta_1 \Delta_1 f_j + \varepsilon_{1j} \tag{4}$$

The theoretical optimal 1-day hedge ratio is β_1, which can be estimated efficiently by the ordinary least-squares (OLS) estimate $\hat{\beta}_1$. Similarly, for the n-day hedge, the following regression model applies:

$$\Delta_n p_j = \alpha_n + \beta_n \Delta_n f_j + \varepsilon_{nj} \tag{5}$$

Thus, the theoretical optimal hedge ratio is β_n, which can be efficiently estimated by the OLS estimate $\hat{\beta}_n$. Ederington (1979), Figlewski (1984), Malliaris and Urrutia (1991), and Chou, Denis, and Lee (1996) all found that $\hat{\beta}_n$ differs from $\hat{\beta}_1$. Thus, the estimated hedge ratio varies with the duration of the hedging period.

On the other hand, in aggregating Equation 4 we obtain the following equation:

$$\Delta_n p_j = n\alpha_1 + \beta_1 \Delta_n f_j + \sum_{k=j-n+1}^{j} \varepsilon_{1k} \tag{6}$$

From Equations 5 and 6, we conclude that the regression model satisfies the stability-under-aggregation property, that is, the theoretical optimal hedge ratios are the same for different hedging horizons. In particular, if Equation 4 is correctly specified the theoretical optimal hedge ratio is always β_1 regardless of the length of the hedging period. When it is found that $\hat{\beta}_n$ differs significantly from $\hat{\beta}_1$, this may be an indication of the presence of specification errors in the regression model.

VAR model is another popular method for determining the hedge ratio. For 1-day hedge the model is specified as follows:

$$\Delta_1 p_j = \alpha_{1p} + \sum_{k=1}^{m} \beta_{1pk} \Delta_1 p_{j-k} + \sum_{t=1}^{m} \gamma_{1pi} \Delta_1 f_{j-i} + \varepsilon_{1pj} \tag{7}$$

$$\Delta_1 f_j = \alpha_{1f} + \sum_{k=1}^{m} \beta_{1fk} \Delta_1 p_{j-k} + \sum_{t=1}^{m} \gamma_{1fi} \Delta_1 f_{j-i} + \varepsilon_{1fj} \tag{8}$$

The above two equations represent a VAR model of order m. Usually, m is chosen to ensure that $\{\varepsilon_{1pj}\}$ and $\{\varepsilon_{1fj}\}$ are both white noises. For the n-day hedge, the corresponding VAR model is:

$$\Delta_n p_j = \alpha_{np} + \sum_{k=1}^{m} \beta_{npk} \Delta_n p_{j-kn} + \sum_{i=1}^{m} \gamma_{npi} \Delta_n f_{j-in} + \varepsilon_{npj} \tag{9}$$

$$\Delta_n f_j = \alpha_{nf} + \sum_{k=1}^{m} \beta_{nfk} \Delta_n p_{j-kn} + \sum_{i=1}^{m} \gamma_{nfi} \Delta_n f_{j-in} + \varepsilon_{nfj} \tag{10}$$

By aggregating Equations 7 and 8 over j, we obtain Equations 9 and 10, respectively, with the parameter vector $(\alpha_{nj}, \beta_{njk}, \gamma_{nji})$ being replaced by $(n\alpha_{1j}, \beta_{1jk}, \gamma_{1ji})$, for $j = p, f$.

From Equations 7 and 8, the optimal 1-day hedge ratio is given by $x^*(1) = \text{cov}(\varepsilon_{1pj}, \varepsilon_{1fj})/\text{var}(\varepsilon_{1fj})$. Assuming that the error terms of the VAR model are white noises, Equations 2 and 3 imply that the n-day hedge ratio $x^*(n)$ is equal to $x^*(1)$ for every n. Thus, the stability property holds for the VAR models as well. Hence, similar to the case of the regression method, the stability property weighs in favor of using a shorter sampling interval to increase the effective sample size, unless concern for model misspecifications suggests otherwise.

Many studies have shown that, although the spot and futures prices are nonstationary, the two series move closely together so that in the long run the difference between them is stationary. In other words, the basis as defined by $z_j = f_j - p_j$ is stationary. In econometric terminology, the two series are said to be cointegrated. When a cointegration relationship exists between two series, the Engle–Granger representation theorem states that a corresponding EC model exists for the two series. In our case, the EC model expresses $\Delta_n p_j$ and $\Delta_n f_j$ as linear functions of the lagged differences of the spot and futures prices as well as the lagged basis. For the 1-day hedge, we consider the following equations:

$$\Delta_1 p_j = \alpha_{1p} + \sum_{k=1}^{m} \beta_{1pk}\Delta_1 p_{j-k} + \sum_{i=1}^{m} \gamma_{1pi}\Delta_1 f_{j-i} + \delta_{1p}(f_{j-1} - p_{j-1}) + \varepsilon_{1pj} \tag{11}$$

$$\Delta_1 f_j = \alpha_{1f} + \sum_{k=1}^{m} \beta_{1fk}\Delta_1 p_{j-k} + \sum_{i=1}^{m} \gamma_1 fi\Delta_1 f_{j-i} + \delta_{1f}(f_{j-1} - p_{j-1}) + \varepsilon_{1fj} \tag{12}$$

Using n-day returns, the EC model for the n-day hedge is as follows:

$$\Delta_n p_j = \alpha_{np} + \sum_{k=1}^{m} \beta_{npk}\Delta_n p_{j-kn} + \sum_{i=1}^{m'} \gamma_{npi}\Delta_n f_{j-in} + \delta_{np}(f_{j-n} - p_{j-n}) + \varepsilon_{npj} \tag{13}$$

$$\Delta_n f_j = \alpha_{nf} + \sum_{k=1}^{m} \beta_{nfk}\Delta_n p_{j-kn} + \sum_{i=1}^{m'} \gamma_{nfi}\Delta_n f_{j-in} + \delta_{nf}(f_{j-n} - p_{j-n}) + \varepsilon_{nfj} \tag{14}$$

Unlike the regression and the VAR models the stability-under-aggregation property does not hold for the EC model. Consequently, the theoretical optimal hedge ratio varies with the length of the hedging period when calculated from the EC model based upon 1-day returns using Equations 2 and 3. Thus, $x^*(n) \neq x^*(1)$ whenever $n \neq 1$. We demonstrate this property in the Appendix for a simplified version of the 1-day return model. On the other hand, the optimal hedge ratio derived from the n-day return model in Equations 13 and 14 will also differ from $x^*(1)$ and $x^*(n)$ calculated from the 1-day returns in Equations 2 and 3. Thus, for the EC models misspecification errors become the dominant factor, and we expect the hedge ratio calculated from n-day returns to perform better in out-of-sample comparisons than that calculated from 1-day returns.

IV.   AN EMPIRICAL EXAMPLE

We consider the NSA 225 spot index and futures price. Our data set consists of 2,100 daily return observations of the spot index and the futures price, covering the period from January 1989 through August 1997. The futures contract is traded on the Singapore International Monetary Exchange (SIMEX). Daily closing values of the spot index and settlement price of the futures contracts are used. For the futures prices, we use the nearest regular contracts and roll over to the next contract around the tenth of the contract month. The regular contract months are March, June,

September, and December. All contracts expire on the third Wednesday of the contract month.

Our main concern is to examine the post-sample hedging effectiveness of various estimated hedge ratios with respect to the choice of the sampling interval. The results should throw light upon the choice of the sampling interval given the hedging horizon and the selected statistical model. As such, we shall not attempt to test directly the validity of the stability-under-aggregation property of various statistical models. Obviously, as far as empirical applications are concerned, the hedging effectiveness is the dominant question.

We use the first 1,700 daily observations as the initial estimation sample. Thus, when the sampling (return) interval is k, the initial estimation sample size is $1,700/k$. For a hedging horizon of n, the next $40/n$ non-overlapping post-sample hedged portfolios over n-day horizons are examined for their returns. The hedge ratios are then reestimated by rolling over the estimation sample. In each rollover we maintain $1,700/k$ observations by dropping (augmenting) $40/k$ k-day return observations in (at) the beginning (end). Thus, altogether the hedge ratios are reestimated 10 times for a total of $400/n$ post-sample portfolio comparisons. We take the values of k and n to be 1, 2, 5, and 10, and consider combinations of k and n as long as $k \le n$.

For the regression method, the hedge ratios are estimated from Equation 5 using OLS. For the VAR model, we estimate Equations 9 and 10 individually using OLS. As the regressors of Equations 9 and 10 are the same, the OLS estimates are asymptotically equivalent to the maximum likelihood estimates (MLE). We calculate the required variance and covariance from the estimated residuals of the two equations. The optimal value of m is determined based on minimizing the Schwarz criterion. For $k = 1, 2, 5,$ and 10, the optimal values of m are, respectively, 6, 3, 2, and 1.

For the EC modeling, the augmented Dickey–Fuller test verifies that the spot and futures price series are integrated of order one (that is, each series has one unit root). Also, the basis series is found to be stationary. Thus, the spot and futures prices are cointegrated. We fit a bivariate EC model in which the residuals across the two equations are assumed to have a constant variance–covariance matrix. The parameters are then estimated jointly using MLE. The following model is adopted (after fitting lower order models and eliminating insignificant parameters):

$$\Delta_k p_j = \alpha_{kp} + \delta_{kp}(f_{j-k} - p_{j-k}) + \varepsilon_{kpj} \tag{15}$$

$$\Delta_k f_j = \alpha_{kf} + \beta_{kf1}\Delta_k f_{j-k} + \varepsilon_{kfj} \tag{16}$$

We assume $(\varepsilon_{kpj}, \varepsilon_{kfj})$ to be normal with zero mean and a constant variance matrix.

It is noted that the above equations are used for all values of k considered, although in some cases not all estimated parameters are statistically significant. Nonetheless, the cointegration tests show that an EC model exists for all k-day

Table 1. Optimal Hedge Ratios (Using the First 1700 Observations)

	Sampling Interval (days)			
Model	1	2	5	10
OLS	0.9185	0.9557	0.9847	0.9640
VAR	0.9184	0.9559	0.9781	0.9683
EC	0.8468	0.9056	0.9500	0.9562

return models. For a 1-day return model, however, all estimated parameters in Equations 15 and 16 are statistically significant.

Table 1 presents the optimal hedge ratios for different statistical models and different sampling intervals using the first 1,700 observations. The results indicate the optimal hedge ratios derived from OLS and VAR models are very similar. Regardless of the sampling interval, the EC hedge ratio is always smaller than the other two. There is a general tendency for the hedge ratio to increase with increasing sampling interval length.[2] Table 2 provides summary statistics of the optimal hedge ratios estimated from rollover samples. The average hedge ratios from different models and different sample intervals exhibit the same relationships as those displayed in Table 1. The 1-day OLS hedge ratio has the smallest standard deviation (0.0016) while the 1-day EC hedge ratio has the largest standard deviation (0.0043). The 5-day EC hedge ratio also has a small standard deviation (0.0018).

In the post-sample comparison we examine the mean and variance of the returns of the hedged portfolios. The results are summarized in Tables 3 through 5. Table 3 shows that, for the 5-day hedging horizon the hedge ratio obtained from 2-day

Table 2. Summary Statistics of Optimal Hedge Ratios

Model	Sampling Interval (days)	Mean	Standard Deviation	Minimum	Maximum
OLS	1	0.9200	0.0016	0.9183	0.9226
	2	0.9559	0.0028	0.9512	0.9589
	5	0.9834	0.0025	0.9789	0.9859
	10	0.9664	0.0023	0.9636	0.9697
VAR	1	0.9201	0.0021	0.9176	0.9234
	2	0.9552	0.0022	0.9513	0.9582
	5	0.9753	0.0028	0.9703	0.9781
	10	0.9702	0.0021	0.9682	0.9734
EC	1	0.8523	0.0043	0.8468	0.8603
	2	0.9084	0.0023	0.9056	0.9122
	5	0.9518	0.0018	0.9500	0.9554
	10	0.9578	0.0028	0.9551	0.9625

Table 3. Out-of-Sample Hedging Performance: Regression Method[a]

Hedging Duration (days)	Sampling Interval (days)	Portfolio Mean	Portfolio Variance
1	1	0.001367	0.112971
2	1	0.002751	0.116247
2	2	0.004894	0.111487
5	1	0.006878	0.187610
5	2	0.012236	0.177799
5	5	0.016024	0.180194
10	1	0.013756	0.220230
10	2	0.024472	0.170512
10	5	0.032047	0.155859
10	10	0.028202	0.165794

Note: [a]This table summarizes the mean and variance of the hedged portfolio returns (in percentage) of various hedging horizons n based on the hedge ratios estimated from different sampling (return) intervals k. The initial estimation sample size is $1700/k$ return observations. When the hedging horizon is n, the results are based on a total of $400/n$ hedged portfolios.

returns achieves the minimum risk (as measured by the variance). For the 10-day hedging horizon the hedge ratio calculated from the 5-day returns has the best out-of-sample performance. As the duration of the hedging period increases, the relative performance of the 1-day hedge ratio decreases. The cost of specification errors outweighs the benefits of the larger sample size. However, matching the duration of the hedging period with the sampling interval does not provide the best

Table 4. Out-of-Sample Hedging Performance: VAR Method[a]

Hedging Duration (days)	Sampling Interval (days)	Portfolio Mean	Portfolio Variance
1	1	0.001376	0.113141
2	1	0.002752	0.116417
2	2	0.004835	0.111584
5	1	0.006879	0.187993
5	2	0.012089	0.178151
5	5	0.014936	0.178680
10	1	0.013759	0.221435
10	2	0.024177	0.171873
10	5	0.029872	0.158164
10	10	0.029498	0.163544

Note: [a]This table summarizes the mean and variance of the hedged portfolio returns (in percentage) of various hedging horizons n based on the hedge ratios estimated from different sampling (return) intervals k. The initial estimation sample size is $1700/k$ return observations. When the hedging horizon is n, the results are based on a total of $400/n$ hedged portfolios.

Table 5. Out-of-Sample Hedging Performance: EC Model[a]

Hedging Duration (days)	Sampling Interval (days)	Portfolio Mean	Portfolio Variance
1	1	–0.000671	0.119528
2	1	–0.001342	0.140884
2	2	0.002016	0.118853
5	1	–0.003354	0.241014
5	2	0.005040	0.192901
5	5	0.011478	0.178891
10	1	–0.006708	0.395061
10	2	0.010079	0.241017
10	5	0.022955	0.176669
10	10	0.025801	0.173322

Note: [a]This table summarizes the mean and variance of the hedged portfolio returns (in percentage) of various hedging horizons n based on the hedge ratios estimated from different sampling (return) intervals k. The initial estimation sample size is $1700/k$ return observations. When the hedging horizon is n, the results are based on a total of $400/n$ hedged portfolios.

performance. As shown in Table 4, the same conclusions apply to the results for the VAR model.

The EC model, however, presents quite different conclusions (see Table 5). Herein, the hedge ratio calculated from n-day returns always provides the best performance when the length of the hedging period is n days. Moreover, the hedging performance declined drastically when the return interval does not match with the hedging horizon. For example, the variance of the 10-day hedged portfolio is 0.1733 if the hedge ratio is estimated from 10-day returns. It becomes, however, 0.3951 when the hedge ratio is estimated from 1-day return, which represents an increase of 128%. For the regression and the VAR methods, the increase is about 33%.

V. CONCLUDING REMARKS

In summary, the empirical results support our arguments that the choice of the sampling interval in the estimation of the hedge ratio depends upon the stability property of the hedge ratio under aggregation for the particular statistical model adopted. Because the stability-under-aggregation property holds for both the regression and vector autoregression (VAR) models, the optimal hedge ratio estimated from these models using 1-day returns may outperform the optimal hedge ratio estimated using n-day returns even if the hedging horizon is n-day. This result is illustrated using the Nikkei Stock Exchange (NSA) 225 spot and futures markets. For the error correction (EC) models, the stability property does not hold and we find that the hedge ratio calculated from n-day returns provides the best performance when the duration of the hedging period is also n days.

The three models considered in this review generate constant hedge ratios over time. Recent studies indicate that, in some cases, time-varying hedge strategies may be more appropriate. A popular approach for time-varying hedge is to model the data using a bivariate generalized autoregressive conditional heteroskedasticity (GARCH) model. While Kroner and Sultan (1993) found GARCH strategy to be useful, in a systematic study of 10 commodities and securities Lien, Tse, and Tsui (1998) found that the conventional ordinary least-squares (OLS) hedge ratio outperforms the GARCH ratio in out-of-sample comparisons.

Obviously, the GARCH models do not satisfy the stability property. Consequently, we expect that time-varying hedge ratios estimated from n-day returns to outperform the hedge ratios estimated from other return intervals when the duration of the hedging period is n days. Whether this conjecture can be substantiated is a topic for future research.

ACKNOWLEDGMENTS

The authors wish to acknowledge helpful comments and suggestions from two anonymous referees and the editor, Cheng Few Lee. The research of the first author is, in part, supported by a faculty research grant from the University of Kansas.

APPENDIX

Here we consider a simplified EC model to illustrate the calculation of the optimal hedge ratio for the n-day hedge from a 1-day return model. Suppose that:

$$\Delta p_t = \alpha z_{t-1} + \varepsilon_{pt} \tag{A1}$$

$$\Delta f_t = -\beta z_{t-1} + \varepsilon_{ft} \tag{A2}$$

where $z_{t-1} = f_{t-1} - p_{t-1}$. By subtracting Equation A2 from Equation A1, we obtain $z_t = (1-\alpha - \beta)z_{t-1} + (\varepsilon_{ft} - \varepsilon_{pt})$. Consequently:

$$z_t = \sum_{k=0}^{\infty} (1 - \alpha - \beta)^k (\varepsilon_{f,t-k} - \varepsilon_{p,t-k}) \tag{A3}$$

Let σ_{ij} denote $\text{cov}(\varepsilon_{it}, \varepsilon_{jt})$, for $i, j = p$ or f. From Equations A1 through A3, we have, assuming presample residuals are fixed:

$$\text{cov}(\Delta_1 p_{t+n}, \Delta_1 f_{t+n} | I_t) = \sigma_{pf} - \alpha\beta \text{var}(z_{t+n-1} | I_t)$$

$$= \sigma_{pf} - \alpha\beta(\sigma_{pp} + \sigma_{ff} - 2\sigma_{pf})[1 - (1 - \alpha - \beta)^{n-1}](\alpha + \beta)^{-1} \tag{A4}$$

Similarly:

$$\text{var}(\Delta_1 f_{t+n} | I_t) = \sigma_{ff} + \beta^2(\sigma_{pp} + \sigma_{ff} - 2\sigma_{pf})[1 - \alpha - \beta)^{n-1}](\alpha + \beta)^{-1} \tag{A5}$$

Let $\sigma = \sigma_{pp} + \sigma_{ff} - 2\sigma_{pf}$. Upon substituting the above two expressions into Equations 2 through 3, we obtain the following:

$$\text{cov}(\Delta_n p_{t+n}, \Delta_n f_{t+n}|I_t) = \sigma_{pf} - \alpha\beta\sigma[1 - n(\alpha + \beta) - (1 - \alpha - \beta)^n](\alpha + \beta)^{-2} \quad (A6)$$

$$\text{var}(\Delta_n f_{t+n}|I_t) = \sigma_{ff} + \beta^2\sigma[1 - n(\alpha + \beta) - (1 - \alpha - \beta)^n](\alpha + \beta)^{-2} \quad (A7)$$

Thus, the theoretical optimal hedge ratio depends upon α, β, σ_{pp}, σ_{ff}, σ_{pf} and n, and the stability-under-aggregation property does not hold.

NOTES

1.   Cheung, Kwan, and Yip (1990), Kolb and Okunev (1992, 1993), Lien and Luo (1993), and Lien and Shaffer (1998) discussed the minimum extended Gini hedge ratio. de Jong, de Roon, and Veld (1997) and Lien and Tse (1998a, 1998b) discussed the minimum lower partial moment hedge ratio. Nonetheless, the minimum variance hedge ratio remains the most popular one.

2.   Bootstrap methods can be applied to test the equality of hedge ratios estimated from different sampling intervals. We do not perform the tests in this note as the issues are not directly related to our purposes.

REFERENCES

Cheung, C.S., Kwan, C.C.Y., & Yip, P.C.Y. (1990). The hedging effectiveness of options and futures: A mean-Gini approach. *Journal of Futures Markets, 10,* 61–73.

Chou, W.L., Denis, K.K.F., & Lee, C.F. (1996). Hedging with the Nikkei index futures: The conventional versus the error correction model. *Quarterly Review of Economics and Finance, 36,* 495–505.

de Jong, A., de Roon, F., & Veld, C. (1997). Out-of-sample hedging effectiveness of currency futures for alternative models and hedging strategies. *Journal of Futures Markets, 17,* 817–837.

Ederington, L. (1979). The hedging performance of the new futures markets. *Journal of Finance, 34,* 157–170.

Figlewski, S. (1984). Hedging performance and basis risk in stock index futures. *Journal of Finance, 39,* 657–669.

Figlewski, S. (1985). Hedging with stock index futures: Theory and applications in a new market. *Journal of Futures Markets, 5,* 183–199.

Figlewski, S. (1997). Forecasting volatility. *Financial Markets, Institutions & Instruments, 6,* 2–88.

Findley, D.F. (1983). On the use of multiple models for multi-period forecasting. In: *Proceedings of American Statistical Association Meeting, Business and Economics Sections,* p. 528–531.

Geppert, J.M. (1995). A statistical model for the relationship between futures contract hedging effectiveness and investment horizon length. *Journal of Futures Markets, 15,* 507–536.

Kolb, R.W., & Okunev, J. (1992). An empirical evaluation of the extended mean-gini coefficient for futures hedging. *Journal of Futures Markets, 12,* 177–186.

Kolb, R.W., & Okunev, J. (1993). Utility maximizing hedge ratios in the extended mean-Gini framework. *Journal of Futures Markets, 13,* 597–609.

Kroner, K.F., & Sultan, J. (1993). Time varying distribution and dynamic hedging with foreign currency futures. *Journal of Financial and Quantitative Analysis, 28,* 535–551.

Lien, D., & Luo, X. (1993). Estimating extended mean-Gini coefficient for futures hedging. *Journal of Futures Markets, 13,* 665–676.

Lien, D., & Shaffer, D. (1998). A note on estimating the minimum extended Gini hedge ratio. *Journal of Futures Markets*, forthcoming.

Lien, D., & Tse, Y.K. (1998a). Hedging time-varying downside risk. *Journal of Futures Markets, 18*, 705–722.

Lien, D., & Tse, Y.K. (1998b). Hedging downside risk with futures contracts. *Applied Financial Economics*, forthcoming.

Lien, D., Tse, Y.K., & Tsui, A.K.C. (1998). *Evaluating the hedging performance of GARCH strategies.* Mimeo.

Malliaris, A.G., & Urrutia, J.L. (1991). The impacts of the lengths of estimation periods and hedging horizons on the effectiveness of a hedge: Evidence from foreign currency futures. *Journal of Futures Markets, 11*, 271–289.

ASYMMETRIC-NESTED GARCH MODELS, TRADING VOLUME, AND RETURN VOLATILITY:
AN EMPIRICAL STUDY OF THE TAIWAN STOCK MARKET

Li-Ju Tsai and Yin-Hua Yeh

ABSTRACT

The ability to forecast stock market volatility has been proved to be an important issue in forming portfolio and asset valuation. Thus, selecting an appropriate econometric model in estimating volatility merits dedicated theoretical investigation. In this study we attempt to determine a better functional form to describe the asymmetry of Taiwan stock volatility, by modifying Hentschel's (1995) nested generalized autoregressive conditional heteroskedasticity (GARCH) models. Our approach is quite different from most of the empirical studies that arbitrarily treat some of the parameters in the conditional variance equation as known a priori. Furthermore, under the free parameterization of the GARCH model, the empirical results suggest that our modified version by including trading volume, compared with Hentschel's model, can better explain the returns and volatility of the Taiwan stock market. The trading volume has

Advances in Investment Analysis and Portfolio Management, Volume 7, pages 145–161.
Copyright © 2000 by JAI Press Inc.
All rights of reproduction in any form reserved.
ISBN: 0-7623-0658-0

significantly positive effects on stock return and volatility, and the impact of negative shock on volatility is higher than that of positive shock, only when the shocks are not very large. This fictitious symmetry in affecting volatility, when the shock is large, might be ascribed to the 7% price limit on the Taiwan stock market.

I. INTRODUCTION

With the deregulation and liberalization of capital markets, the sizes (in terms of the number of listed companies, market capitalization, and value of share trading) of emerging Asian markets have grown rapidly in recent years. In addition, higher return volatility is another particular characteristic of emerging markets in Asia. Among these emerging Asian markets, Taiwan's stock market, with tremendous trading value and volatile return, provides invaluable opportunities for research. For the value of share trading, Taiwan's stock market is far higher than other emerging Asian markets. The average annual trading value of Taiwan's stock market was about 505.8 billion U.S. dollars from the years 1987 to 1997, whereas those of the stock markets in South Korea, Hong Kong, Thailand, and Singapore were 138.6, 121, 42.5, and 40.6 billion U.S. dollars, respectively, during the same period.[1]

Bekaert and Harvey (1997) noted that the unconditional return volatility of Taiwan's stock market is highest among the emerging Asian markets. Hence, it is vital to get a better understanding of the return volatility in these emerging markets in order to determine the costs of capital, evaluate direct foreign investment, and allocate assets in accordance with concern for the international portfolio. This paper investigates the return volatility of Taiwan's stock market by adopting a more appropriate econometric model, the asymmetric GARCH family model. The purpose of this paper is therefore to provide useful insights into the return volatility of the Taiwan stock market.

A. Asymmetric GARCH Models

In the stream of return volatility research, the ARCH model introduced by Engle (1982) is a milestone because it captures some of the empirical regularity of equity returns, such as volatility clustering and thick-tailed returns. Subsequently, Bollerslev (1986) presented a generalized ARCH (GARCH) model, which is a parsimonious parameterization of the conditional variance. Also, Engle, Lilien, and Robins (1987) provided the ARCH-M (ARCH-in mean) model to describe that changing conditional variances may directly affect the expected return on a portfolio. Numerous empirical results evidenced the success of the GARCH class of models.[2]

Furthermore, the prior empirical work of Black (1976), Christie (1982), and Schwert (1990) supported the view that changes in stock prices are negatively correlated with changes in stock volatility. The following research used the GARCH class of models to investigate the asymmetric impact of news on volatility: Nelson's

(1991) exponential GARCH (EGARCH) model, the nonlinear-asymmetric GARCH (N-A GARCH) model of Engle and Ng (1993), the GJR GARCH model of Glosten, Jagannathan, and Runkle (1993), and the threshold GARCH (TGARCH) model of Zakoian (1991). The major finding of these works was that negative shocks (bad news) introduce more volatility than positive shocks (good news). Possible explanations are the "financial leverage effect" and "volatility feedback effect" as suggested by Black (1976) and Campell and Hentschel (1992). In the leverage effect, when bad news hits the market, stock prices tumble. The debt–equity ratio (measured in market value terms) rises as a consequence. The financial risk of a company increases, causing higher volatility in its stock return. Furthermore, in the volatility feedback effect, large pieces of good news tend to be followed by other large pieces of news (i.e., volatility is persistent). A given piece of news increases future expected volatility, which in turn increases the required rate of return on stocks and lowers the stock prices, dampening the positive impact of the good news. On the other hand, the increased expected volatility caused by a large piece of bad news will also increase the required rate of return and lower the stock price, which amplifies the negative impact of bad news.

Recently, Hentschel (1995) developed a parametric family of GARCH models that nests these most popular symmetrical and asymmetric GARCH models, thereby highlighting the relationship between the models and their treatment of asymmetry. The nesting clearly shows the connection between the existing models, and permits new standard nested tests to determine the relative quality of each of the models' fits. The above popular GARCH models, including EGARCH, GJR, N-A GARCH, and TGARCH, are supposed to somewhat arbitrarily assume a particular diffusion process for the conditional variance. Since little is known about the relative quality of fit of the various GARCH models, the choice of the diffusion limit has thus far been guided more by convenience than pragmatism. The tests based on Hentschel's model should serve as a useful guide in choosing among the possible diffusion processes for the variance.

B. Trading Volume and Return Volatility

The relationship between trading volume and return volatility is important for at least three reasons. First, French and Roll (1986) provided the "trading noise hypothesis" inferring that trading itself can speed up the flow of information and introduce noise into stock returns. From this they predicted a positive relationship between trading volume and price volatility.

Second, some researches based on examination of the effect of trading volume on price change and volatility questioned whether trading volume itself has any information content. For example, Admati and Pfleiderer (1988) extended Kyle's model (1985) to explain the effect of trading volume on return volatility. They argued that the discretionary liquidity traders, who trade for liquidity purposes but have some discretion over the timing of their trades, prefer to trade when the market is "thick." Informed traders also want to trade when the market is thick. Therefore, when there is an increased level of discretionary liquidity trading, more informed traders will be trading. An increase in the number of informed traders' means "more competition" among these traders, which will cause prices to be more informative. The theory therefore suggests that higher trading volume will lead to higher return volatility (Chan and Chan, 1993; Liu, 1996).

Third, based on the studies on dispersion of beliefs, trading volume, and price volatility, Morse (1980) proposed that as the difference between investors regarding the assessment of the price of assets becomes larger, their trading motivations and the trading volume would be larger. Therefore, during the price-adjustment process, an increasing in trading volume will induce a positive return autocorrelation series, and will in turn expand the volatility of the stock return. Shalen (1993) examined a two-period noisy national expectation model of a futures market and showed that the dispersion of past and current beliefs help to explain the positive correlation between the variance in price changes (based on his particular measure of price volatility) and trading volume. In addition, Foster and Viswanathan (1995) presented a speculative trading model that predicted conditional heteroskedasticity in trading volume and the variance in price changes.

Therefore, this paper combines the Hentschel's nested family of asymmetric GARCH models with the trading volume and return volatility relationship to build empirical models for better insights into the volatility of Taiwan's stock market. Moreover, we compared our model with Hentschel's model to see if the inclusion of trading volume could better explain the returns and volatility of the Taiwan stock market. The reasons for examining Taiwan's stock market are twofold. First, compared the world major stock markets such as that of the United States, Taiwan's stock market is smaller in size and has fewer institutional investors trading in the market. Therefore, it is less sophisticated in terms of investors. In other words, the percentage of noise traders and discretionary liquidity traders within the total number of investors in Taiwan's stock market is relative high, therefore a positive relationship between trading volume and return volatility will be close to the projection of the above theories. Second, as stated above, it is now well known that the return volatility of emerging stock markets is higher than that of developed stock markets. Taiwan's stock market is representative of the emerging Asian markets. Our empirical results support the view that there is a strong positive relationship between trading volume and return volatility. The asymmetric effects on volatility are significant for small shocks but not for large shocks.

The remainder of this paper is organized as follows: Section II discusses the models that form the basis for our empirical analysis; Section III describes our data, the empirical estimation results, and hypothesis testing; Section IV compares our revised trading volume model with Hentschel's model, and tests the robustness of our model; and Section V concludes the paper.

II. EMPIRICAL MODELS

First, we introduce Hentschel's GARCH model as a building block of our empirical model. Hentschel's model includes Equations 1 to 4:

$$r_{t+1} = \mu + \gamma\sigma_t^2 + \eta_{t+1} \quad \eta_{t+1} \mid \psi_t \sim N(0, \sigma_t^2) \tag{1}$$

where r_{t+1} = the rate of the market portfolio; μ is a constant; σ_t^2 is the conditional variance; $\gamma\sigma_t^2$ is a time-varying risk premium; ψ_t is the information set containing all relevant variables up to time t; and η_{t+1} is a heteroskedastic error term. It can be decomposed as:

$$\eta_{t+1} = \sigma_t\varepsilon_{t+1} \quad \varepsilon_{t+1} \sim N(0,1) \tag{2}$$

Let σ_t evolve according to:

$$\frac{\sigma_t^\lambda - 1}{\lambda} = \omega + \alpha\sigma_{t-1}^\lambda f^\nu(\varepsilon_t) + \beta\frac{\sigma_{t-1}^\lambda - 1}{\lambda} \tag{3}$$

where:

$$f(\varepsilon_t) = \mid \varepsilon_t - b \mid - c(\varepsilon_t - b) \tag{4}$$

In general, Equation 3 is a law of motion for the Box–Cox (1964) transformation of the conditional standard deviation, and the parameter λ determines the shape of the transformation. For $\lambda > 1$ the transformation of σ_t is convex, while for $\lambda < 1$ it is concave. The parameter ν serves to transform the (potentially shifted and rotated) absolute value function $f(\cdot)$.

Hentschel refers to parameter b and c in Equation 4 as the "shift" and "rotation" parameters, respectively. A positive value for b causes a rightward shift of the news impact curve. A positive value for c corresponds to a clockwise rotation. These two cases match the stylized facts of stock return volatility. For negative shocks, volatility rises more than for equally large, but positive, shocks. However, these two types of asymmetry are distinct. The asymmetry caused by the shift is most pronounced for small shocks. But it becomes a negligible part of the total response for extremely large shocks. On the contrary, the asymmetric effect caused by the rotation remains a constant relative size to the total response. Moreover, a zero shock results in the smallest increase of conditional variance. In brief, shift is the dominant source of asymmetry for small shocks, while rotation is more important for large shocks.[3]

Equation 3 nests all popular GARCH models. The special cases are obtained by appropriately restricting the parameters λ, ν, b, and c to some specific values. For example, with the conditions of $\lambda = 0$, $\nu = 1$, $b = 0$, and free c, the EGARCH model is suggested. If $\lambda = 1$, $\nu = 1$, $b = 0$ and $\mid c \mid \leqq 1$, the TGARCH model is recommended. The conditions of $\lambda = \nu = 2$, $b = 0$, and free c imply GJR GARCH model.

Table 1. Nested Asymmetric GARCH Models[a]

λ	ν	b	c	Models
0	1	0	free estimated	EGARCH
1	1	0	$|c| \leq 1$	TGARCH
2	2	0	free estimated	GJR GARCH
2	2	free estimated	0	Nonlinear-asymmetric GARCH (Engle and Ng, 1993)

Notes: [a]This table documents the Hentschel's (1995) nested asymmetric GARCH models. With specific restriction on the four parameters λ, ν, b, and c (the first four columns), model specifications (column 5) are identified through the conditional variance equations $\sigma_t^\lambda - 1/\lambda = \omega + \alpha\sigma_{t-1}^\lambda \times f^\nu(\varepsilon_t) + \beta\sigma_{t-1}^\lambda - 1/\lambda$ (Equation 3), and $f(\varepsilon_t) = |\varepsilon_t - b| - c(\varepsilon_t - b)$ (Equation 4). In all members of GARCH family, a transformation of the conditonal satandard deviation, σ_t, is determined by the transformation function of the inniovations, $f(\varepsilon_t)$, and lagged transformed conditional standard deviations σ_{t-1}.

If $\lambda = \nu = 2$, free b, and $c = 0$, a nonlinear-asymmetric model is supported. The conditions for parameters setting and model specifications are summarized in Table 1.

Hentschel's test, based on daily U.S. stock returns, rejects all of the standard models in favor of the more general parameterization of Equation 3 in which the estimate of λ is 1.5. These results suggest that we shouldn't arbitrarily restrict the values of λ, ν, b, and c.

Since there are several researches, such as Epps and Epps (1976), Gallant et al. (1992), and Campbell et al. (1993), finding that the relationship between trading volume and price changing is strong, we included a lag-one trading volume to the conditional mean equation. Because the prior researches of Morse (1980), French and Roll (1986), Admati and Pfleiderer (1988), Lamoureux and Lastrapes (1990), and Shalen (1993) suggest that there is correlation between trading volume and the volatility of stock returns, we include trading volume in the conditional variance equation. Meanwhile, the setup of a dependent variable y_t of ARCH model is usually assumed to be generated by the following conditional mean equation, $y_t = x_t'\beta + u_t$, where x_t denotes a vector of predetermined explanatory variables, which could include lagged values of y (Hamilton, 1994, Time series analysis, Chap. 21). Therefore, our information set Ψ_t contains lag-one trading volumes and past returns up to time t. Corresponding to this information set, the conditional mean Equation 1 and conditional variance Equation 3 should be revised as follows:

$$r_{t+1} = \mu + \phi(L)r_t + \theta Q_t + \gamma\sigma_t^2 + \eta_{t+1} \tag{1}'$$

$$\frac{\sigma_t^\lambda - 1}{\lambda} = \omega + \alpha\sigma_{t-1}^\lambda f^\nu(\varepsilon_t) + \beta\frac{\sigma_{t-1}^\lambda - 1}{\lambda} + aQ_t^\nu \tag{3}'$$

where $\phi(L)$ is lag polynomial, Q_t is the trading volume at time t.[4]

To get appropriate estimates of the alternative GARCH type models, the innovation in Equation 1', η_{t+1} needs to be serially noncorrelated. We will employ the Schwarz criterion (SC) to select the optimal lag of Equation 1' in the next section.

III. EMPIRICAL RESULTS

Our empirical model was designed to estimate and test the hypotheses of the revised model: Equations 1', 2, 3' and 4. The empirical data was collected from the *Taiwan Economic Journal*. The data spanned the period from January 1, 1991 to September 24, 1996. The data included the daily return rates from the Taiwan weighted stock index[5] (TAIEX). Daily trading volumes were normalized using the total outstanding shares in the market. The number of observations was 1,644. The basic statistics for the Taiwan daily stock returns are shown in Table 2. The Kurtosis, Ljung–Box Q (5) and Lagrange multiplier test for ARCH effect [ARCH(5)] statistics reveal that the Taiwan daily stock returns are serially correlated, heteroskedastic, and leptokurtic. This indicates that it is appropriate to employ the AR-GARCH family of models to explain the data.

In comparison with some popular asymmetric GARCH models, we also estimated the GJR GARCH model of Glosten, Jagannathan, and Runkle (1993), Nelson's (1991) EGARCH model, the N-A GARCH model of Engle and Ng (1993), and TGARCH (Zakoian 1991) model. The conditional means equation remains the same as Equation 1'. The conditional variance equations are as follows:

$$\text{GJR: } \sigma_t^2 = \omega' + \alpha\sigma_{t-1}^2\left[(1 + c^2)\varepsilon_t^2 - c\,|\,\varepsilon_t\,|\,\varepsilon_t\right] + \beta\sigma_{t-1}^2 + aQ_t^2 \qquad (5)$$

$$\text{EGARCH: } \ln\sigma_t^2 = \omega'' + \alpha\,[|\varepsilon_t| - E\,|\,\varepsilon_t\,| - c\varepsilon_t] + \beta\ln\sigma_{t-1}^2 + aQ_t \qquad (6)$$

$$\text{N-A GARCH: } \sigma_t^2 = \omega''' + \alpha\sigma_{t-1}^2(\varepsilon_t - b)^2 + \beta\sigma_{t-1}^2 + aQ_t^2 \qquad (7)$$

Table 2. Summary Statistics for Daily Stock Return

This table reports the statistics of daily rates of return of Taiwan weighted stock index (TAIEX). LBQ (5) stands for the Ljung-Box Q statistic for 5 lags. ARCH (5) stands for the Lagrange Multiplier test of ARCH effect with 5 lags proposed by Engle(1982). The LBQ (5) and ARCH (5) statistics follow χ^2 distribution with degree of freedom of five.

Mean (%)	0.046	*P*-value of (mean = 0)	0.258
Standard Deviation (%)	1.662		
Skewness	–0.069	*P*-value of (skewness = 0)	0.249
Kurtosis	5.643	*P*-value of (Kurtosis = 3)	0.000
LBQ (5)	14.502	*P*-value of no correlation	0.013
ARCH (5)	210.873	*P*-value of no ARCH	0.000

$$\text{TGARCH: } \sigma_t = \omega'''' + \alpha\sigma_{t-1}(|\varepsilon_t| - c\varepsilon_t) + \beta\sigma_{t-1} + aQ_t^2 \tag{8}$$

Table 3 exhibits estimates of the parameters for the above four models and Hentschel's model. All of the parameters were estimated using maximize likelihood estimation (MLE) under the assumption of an i.i.d. standard normal distribution for the innovations. The ML estimates of alternative models are obtained using the statistical software package RATS v 4.0. The SIMPLEX algorithm is used to refine

Table 3. Estimates of Mean and Variance Equation Parameters[a]

Model	GJR GARCH	EGARCH	N-AGARCH	TGARCH	Hentschel's GARCH
μ	−0.153 (0.067)**	−0.169 (0.067)**	−0.150 (0.069)**	−0.164 (0.065)**	−0.170 (0.072)**
ϕ_1	0.049 (0.029)*	0.042 (0.028)	0.042 (0.029)	0.042 (0.027)	0.050 (0.029)*
θ	0.093 (0.063)	0.113 (0.057)*	0.095 (0.062)	0.099 (0.051)*	0.124 (0.067)*
γ	0.037 (0.031)	0.028 (0.028)	0.033 (0.030)	0.030 (0.029)	0.032 (0.032)
λ	[2]	[0]	[2]	[1]	2.319 (1.227)*
ν	[2]	[1]	[2]	[1]	2.624 (0.637)**
ω	0.136 (0.027)**	−0.110 (0.014)**	0.047 (0.031)	0.083 (0.017)**	−0.021 (0.013)
α	0.081 (0.014)**	0.202 (0.022)**	0.093 (0.013)**	0.103 (0.012)**	0.023 (0.012)*
β	0.821 (0.023)**	0.917 (0.014)**	0.818 (0.023)**	0.845 (0.019)**	0.794 (0.064)**
b	[0]	[0]	1.02 (0.160)**	[0]	0.806 (0.351)**
c	0.389 (0.092)**	0.481 (0.081)**	[0]	0.052 (0.087)	−0.034 (0.196)
a	0.054 (0.014)**	0.018 (0.004)**	0.057 (0.013)**	0.038 (0.009)**	0.018 (0.008)**

Notes: [a]The table presents the estimates of parameters for the GARCH family given by:

mean equation: $r_{t+1} = \mu + \phi_1 r_t + \theta Q_t + \gamma\sigma_t^2 + \eta_{t+1}$ (Equation 1'),

variance equation: $\sigma_t^\lambda - 1/\lambda = \omega + \alpha\sigma_{t-1}^\lambda \times f^\nu(\varepsilon_1) + \beta\sigma_{t-1}^{\lambda-1}/\lambda + aQ_t^\nu$ (Equation 3')

$f(\varepsilon_t) = |\varepsilon_t - b| - c(\varepsilon_t - b)$ (Equation 4)

In the first four models, the parameters λ, ν, b, and c are restricted to the stated values in [ ]. All the parameters are estimated by maximize likelihood estimation (MLE) under the assumption of an i.i.d. standard normal distribution for the innovations, $\varepsilon_t \sim N(0,1)$. The ML estimates of alternative models are obtained using the statistical software package RATS v 4.0. The SIMPLEX algorithm is used to refine the initial values of the parameters. After a few iterations, the algorithm is switched to the BHHH method to obtain the final estimates. The covariance matrix is estimated by the inverse of minus Hessian matrix. The numbers in parentheses are asymptotic standard errors. The notations * and ** indicate significant at 10% and 5% significance levels, respectively.

the initial values of the parameters. After a few iterations, the algorithm is switched to the BHHH method to obtain the final estimates. The covariance matrix is estimated by the inverse of minus Hessian matrix. The optimal lag of $\phi(L)$, selected by Schwarz criterion, in Equation 1' is lag one.

Before doing the empirical analysis, we need to check the positively and stationary conditions for our estimates. The sufficient conditions of positively in Hentschel's GARCH model are: $\tilde{\omega} = \lambda\omega - \beta + 1 > 0$, $\alpha \geq 0$, $\beta \geq 0$, $a \geq 0$ and $|c| \leq 1$ for $\nu \notin \{2, 4, 6, \ldots\}$. The parameter estimates in Table 3 satisfy all of these conditions ($\tilde{\omega} = -0.021 * 2.139 - 0.794 + 1 = 0.161 > 0$). The sufficient conditions of covariance stationary are: $\text{var}(\varepsilon_t) < \infty$, $\tilde{\omega} > 0$, and $E[(\alpha\lambda f^{\nu}(\varepsilon_t) + \beta)^{2/\lambda}] < 1$. The first condition is satisfied by construction. The second condition has been verified in the positivity condition. We checked the third condition by computing the sample mean of $[(\alpha\lambda f^{\nu}(\hat{\varepsilon}_t) + \beta)^{2/\lambda}]$ after estimation and its value is 0.911. Table 3 shows that the estimates of the mean equation parameters are similar across all models.[6]

In Table 3, the parameter a is positive and significant at a 5% significance level in all models. This result strongly supports the theoretical suggestion (Morse, 1980, the dispersion of beliefs hypothesis; French and Roll, 1986, the trading noise hypothesis; Admati and Pfleiderer, 1988, the discretionary liquidity trader hypothesis) that higher trading volume will lead to higher return volatility. Compared with the world's major stock markets, such as that of the United States, Taiwan's stock market is smaller in size and has fewer institutional investors trading in the market. Therefore, it is less sophisticated in terms of investors. In other words, the percentage of noise traders and discretionary liquidity traders out of the total number of investors in Taiwan's stock market is relatively high. Therefore, the positive relationship between trading volume and return volatility will be close to the projections from the above theories. On the other hand, Shen and Wang (1998) suggested that the price limit would increase the positive series autocorrelation on the stock return. The daily price limit in the Taiwan stock market will induce an increasing correlation between trading volume and return volatility.

The trading volume coefficients in the conditional mean equation (θ) of EGARCH, TGARCH and the revised model are significantly different from zero, which means that the trading volume would affect not only the volatility but also the expected return. All asymmetric parameters (b and c) are significant in Table 3, except for c in Hentschel's model. This implies that negative shocks result in a higher volatility than equally large positive shocks, which is consistent with the "financial leverage effect" and "volatility feedback effect." Different models represent different types of asymmetry. The GJR GARCH, EGARCH, and TGARCH models only allow for rotation parameter c to describe the asymmetric effects. However, the N-A GARCH model only allows for the shift parameter to capture the asymmetric effects. Only Hentschel's model allows for both types of asymmetry. Therefore, we employed a more complete set of likelihood ratio test statistics to further understand the asymmetric effects.

Table 4. Likelihood Ratio Tests for Asymmetry in Volatility[a]

Maintained Hypothesis	H_0	H_A		
		$c = 0$, b free	$b = 0$, c free	b and c free
$\lambda = \nu = 2$	$b = c = 0$	28.41 (<0.001)	24.56 (<0.001)	28.44 (<0.001)
	$c = 0$, b free			0.030 (0.86)
	$b = 0$, c free			3.88 (0.049)
$\lambda = 1$, $\nu = 1$	$b = c = 0$	3.66 (0.056)	27.33 (<0.001)	35.08 (<0.001)
	$c = 0$, b free			31.41 (<0.001)
	$b = 0$, c free			7.74 (0.005)
$\lambda = 0$, $\nu = 1$	$b = c = 0$	27.78 (<0.001)	29.23 (<0.001)	33.79 (<0.001)
	$c = 0$, b free			6.003 (0.014)
	$b = 0$, c free			4.55 (0.033)
$\lambda = \nu$	$b = c = 0$	27.55 (<0.001)	22.62 (<0.001)	27.840 (<0.001)
	$c = 0$, b free			0.282 (0.595)
	$b = 0$, c free			5.22 (0.022)
λ, ν free	$b = c = 0$	26.75 (<0.001)	23.59 (<0.001)	26.91 (<0.001)
	$c = 0$, b free			0.158 (0.691)
	$b = 0$, c free			165.72 (<0.001)

Notes: [a]This table is aimed at verifying whether asymmetry is an important feature of daily Taiwan stock market returns. The likelihood ratios test restrictions in the family of models is given by:

means equation: $r_{t+1} = \mu + \phi_1 r_t + \theta Q_t + \gamma \sigma_t^2 + \eta_{t+1}$ (Equation 1'),

variance equation: $\sigma_t^\lambda - 1/\lambda = \omega + \alpha \sigma_{t-1}^\lambda \times f^\nu(\varepsilon_t) + \beta \sigma_{t-1}^{\lambda-1}/\lambda + a Q_t^\nu$ (Equation 3')

$f(\varepsilon_t) = |\varepsilon_t - b| - c(\varepsilon_t - b)$ (Equation 4)

The first column lists the restrictions on λ and ν that from the maintained hypothesis for each panel. The second column shows the three of four possible types of asymmetry, which form the null hypothesis for each model. The asymmetry could be caused by a shift of the news impact curve, shown in the third column, or by a rotation of the news impact curve, shown in the fourth column, or by both a shift and a rotation, shown in the fifth column. The likelihood ratio statistics follow χ^2 distribution with degree of freedom of one or two. All models were estimated by maximum likelihood estimation under the assumption that $\varepsilon_t \sim N(0,1)$.

The results in Table 4 verify that asymmetry is an important feature of the Taiwan stock market's daily returns. The first column, in Table 4, lists the restrictions on λ and ν from the maintained hypothesis for each panel. The second column shows the three possible types of asymmetry ($b = c = 0$; $c = 0$, b free; $b = 0$, c free) which form the null hypothesis for each model. If there were no asymmetry, then b and c would equal zero, as indicated in the first row of each panel. This possibility can be tested against the three alternative hypotheses listed in the last three columns of the table. The asymmetry could be caused by a shift in the news impact curve, shown in the third column ($c = 0$, b free). Or by a rotation of the news impact curve, shown in the fourth column ($b = 0$, c free); or by both a shift and a rotation, shown in the fifth column (b and c free). The likelihood ratio statistics follow χ^2 distribution with a degree of freedom of one or two. The test results in the first row of each panel reject the possibility of a symmetric news impact curve in favor of any type of asymmetry.

Furthermore, several of the asymmetric models that have been proposed can be rejected in favor of the alternative that the asymmetry takes an additional form from the one specified by the model. For example, row three ($b = 0$, c free) of the first panel ($\lambda = \nu = 2$) mildly rejects the GJR model with a rotated news impact curve in favor of a model with a rotated and shifted news impact curve. Since the test in row two of the first panel does not reject the hypothesis that only the news impact curve shifts ($c = 0$, b free), the shift alone appears to be sufficient to capture the observed asymmetry within this class of models ($\lambda = \nu = 2$). On the other hand, row three of the third panel shows that the standard EGARCH of Nelson (1991) can be rejected in favor of an exponential GARCH model, in which both a shift and a rotation of the news impact curve are present. Finally, panels four ($\lambda = \nu$) and five (λ, ν free) strongly reject the rotated asymmetry pattern in favor of a shifted pattern.

From the above it would seem that we can conclude that the shifted asymmetry pattern is important in the Taiwan stock market. But the rotated asymmetry pattern is still inconclusive. This depends upon the values of λ and ν in the maintained hypothesis. Therefore, we need to further test the hypothesis of functional form. In Table 5, we apply the likelihood ratio test to see which kind of functional form is appropriate for the Taiwan stock market. Since Hentschel's model nests the other models, we use it as an unrestricted model in the likelihood ratio test for comparison with the other restricted models. The results in Table 5 show that we cannot reject the class of model: $\lambda = \nu = 2$, $c = 0$. This implies that asymmetric effects exist in the Taiwan stock market only when shocks are not very large. However, the dominant source of asymmetry for large shocks, parameter c, is not important for the volatility of the Taiwan stock market. The results in Table 5 conform to those of Table 4.

It has been previously argued that asymmetry is primarily a feature of the volatility response to large shocks. The results presented here contradict the previous assumption; i.e., only small shocks cause the asymmetry that affects volatility. As discussed earlier, for small shocks, asymmetry is primarily driven by

Table 5. Likelihood Ratio Tests of Functional Form[a]

Restricted Model	Unrestricted Model: λ, ν, b, and c are Free		
	Restriction	χ^2	P-Value
GJR GARCH	$\lambda = \nu = 2, b = 0$	$\chi^2 (3) = 7.910$	0.047
EGARCH	$\lambda = 0, \nu = 1, b = 0$	$\chi^2 (3) = 11.084$	0.011
N-A GARCH	$\lambda = \nu = 2, c = 0$	$\chi^2 (3) = 1.662$	0.645
TGARCH	$\lambda = \nu = 1, b = 0$	$\chi^2 (3) = 27.618$	(<0.001)

Note: [a]This table reports the results of likelihood ratio tests of each functional form to find out the most appropriate one to apply in Taiwan stock market. Since Hentschel's model nests the other models, we use it as an unrestricted model in the likelihood ratio tests for comparing with other restricted models. The likelihood ratio statistics follow χ^2 distribution with degrees of freedom of three. All models were estimated by maximum likelihood estimation under the assumption that $\varepsilon_t \sim N(0,1)$.

parameter b, while the asymmetry due to parameter c dominates for large shocks. In most of the models presented, parameter b is at least as important as parameter c, suggesting that small shocks make significant asymmetric contributions to volatility.

IV. MODELS COMPARISON AND DIAGNOSTIC TEST

The unrestricted model, Equations 1' and 3', in our paper is modified from Hentschel's model. We included the return of one lag (r_t) and trading volumes (Q_t) in the conditional mean, and Q_t^ν in the conditional variance. In order to justify these added variables in Equations 1' and 3', we set the coefficients of the added parameters to be zero, i.e., $\phi_1 = 0$ (ϕ_1 is the coefficient of r_t in the conditional mean equation), $\theta = 0$ (θ is the coefficient of Q_t in the conditional mean equation), and $a = 0$ (a is the coefficient of Q_t^ν in conditional variance equation), and considered the possible combinations as restricted models in Table 6 (first column). The second column shows the likelihood ratio tests of the restrictions, which follow χ^2 distribution with a degree of freedom of one to three. The results of the likelihood ratio tests show that all of the restricted models are rejected at a 5% level of significance. Moreover, the likelihood ratio test shows that compared with our model, the original Hentschel's model reported in the last row of Table 6 was also rejected. This verifies that the trading volumes can help to explain the conditional mean and conditional variance of Taiwan stock returns.

To further consider the role of ϕ_1, θ, and a, we investigated the i.i.d. condition of the standardized residuals $\hat{\eta}_{t+1}/\hat{\sigma}_t (= \hat{\varepsilon}_{t+1})$ both in the unrestricted and restricted models. The Ljung–Box Q (LBQ) statistic for 5 lags in Table 6 shows that adding both lag one stock return and trading volume to the conditional mean will help the residuals ($\hat{\varepsilon}_{t+1}$) to be serially noncorrelated, but adding Q_t^ν in the conditional variance does not help much. Since the residuals with the model set at $\phi_1 = 0$ and/or

Table 6. The Likelihood Ratio Tests of Different Combinations of Restricted Models with Added Variables: The Combination of $\phi_1 = 0$, $\theta = 0$, and $a = 0$[a]

Restriction Tests	Likelihood Ratio	LBQ (5)	ARCH (5)
Unrestricted model		6.604(0.252)	5.231(0.388)
$\phi_1 = 0$	6.370(0.012)	10.681(0.058)	5.637(0.343)
$\theta = 0$	5.906(0.015)	9.742(0.083)	5.542(0.353)
$\phi_1 = \theta = 0$	10.890(0.004)	18.384(0.003)	5.843(0.322)
$a = 0$	13.825(0.000)	6.446(0.265)	8.507(0.130)
$\phi_1 = a = 0$	17.568(0.000)	9.101(0.105)	9.107(0.108)
$\theta = a = 0$	19.029(0.000)	9.977(0.076)	8.989(0.109)
$\phi_1 = \theta = a = 0$	22.786(0.000)	14.656(0.012)	9.140(0.103)

Notes: [a]The unrestricted model, Equations 1' and 3', in our paper is modified from Hentschel's (1995). We include the return of one lag (r_{t-1}) and trading volumes (Q_t) in the condition mean, and Q_t^v in the conditional variance. In order to justify these added variables in Equations 1' and 3', we set the coefficients of added parameters to be zero, i.e., $\phi_1 = 0$ (ϕ_1 is the coefficient of r_t in conditional mean equation), $\theta = 0$ (θ is the coefficient of Q_t in conditional mean equation), and $a = 0$ (a is the coefficient of Q_t^v in conditional variance equation), and consider the possible combinations as restricted models (first column). The second column shows the likelihood ratio statistics of the restrictions, which follow χ^2 distribution with degree of freedom of one to three. Furthermore, we investigate the i.i.d. condition of the residuals $\hat{\eta}_{t+1}/\hat{\sigma}_t (= \hat{\varepsilon}_{t+1})$ both in the unrestricted and restricted models. LBQ (5) is the Ljung–Box statistic for 5 lags of $\hat{\varepsilon}_{t+1}$. ARCH (5) stands for the Lagrange multiplier test for ARCH effect with 5 lags. The LBQ (5) and ARCH (5) statistics follow χ^2 distribution with degree of freedom of five. The numbers in parentheses are asymptotic probability values. All parameter estimates were obtained by maximum likelihood estimation under the assumption that ε_t follows standard normal distribution, $\varepsilon_t \sim N(0,1)$.

$\theta = 0$ are still serially correlated with significant LBQ (5) statistics at a 10% significance level. However, the residuals with the model set at $a = 0$ are still serial uncorrelated with insignificant LBQ (5) statistics at 10% of significant level. On the contrary, The Lagrange multiplier test for ARCH effect with 5 lags [ARCH (5)] proposed by Engle (1982) in Table 6 shows that adding Q_t^v in conditional variance will help to alleviate ARCH effect in residuals ($\hat{\varepsilon}_{t+1}$). Since the residuals with the model set at $a = 0$ still has the ARCH effect with marginally significant ARCH (5) statistics at a 10% significance level. However, adding lag one stock return and/or trading volume to the conditional mean does not help as much as Q_t^v in the conditional variance since the residuals with the models set at $\phi_1 = 0$ and/or $\theta = 0$ does not have the ARCH effect with insignificant ARCH (5) statistics at a 10% significance level.

The first row of our empirical model in Table 6, supports that the i.i.d. condition of the residuals ($\hat{\varepsilon}_{t+1}$) holds in the unrestricted model. The last row in Table 6 reports the original Hentschel's model ($\phi_1 = \theta = a = 0$) and the result shows that their residuals in testing the Taiwan stock market are still serially correlated and with ARCH effect. Hence, our modified model, including the trading volume in Hentschel's model could help to alleviate the serial correlation of the residuals and to ameliorate the ARCH effect.

Table 7. Bias Test of Unrestricted and Restricted Models[a]

Models	Sign Bias	Negative Bias	Positive Bias	Joint Test
Equations 1' and 3'	−0.032	0.102	−0.028	2.528
Restricted model:	(−0.229)	(1.779)*	(−0.449)	[0.470]
	−0.071	0.094	−0.040	2.624
($\lambda = \nu = 2$, $c = 0$)	(−0.511)	(1.629)	(−0.649)	[0.453]

Notes: [a]The sign bias, negative size bias, positive size bias, and joint tests are those suggested by Engle and Ng (1993). We regress the squared standardized residuals $[(\hat{\eta}_{t+1}/\hat{\sigma}_t)^2]$ on three variables: (1) the indicator variable of sign bias test (S_t^-) which takes one if the residuals are negative and zero otherwise; (2) the product of the indicator variable (S_t^-) and the residual; and (3) the product of the residual and another indicator variable (S_t^+, which equals to $1 - S_t^-$). The numbers in parentheses are t-statistic. The numbers in [ ] are asymptotic probability values. The notations * and ** indicate significant at 10% and 5% significance levels, respectively.

Finally, we examined whether there are still some asymmetric patterns in the squared standardized residuals, $[(\hat{\eta}_{t+1}/\hat{\sigma}_t)^2]$, from the estimated Equations 1' and 3' to perform the diagnostic checking. We simultaneously used the sign bias test, the negative size bias test, and the positive size bias test proposed by Engle and Ng (1993). The sign bias test examines whether positive and negative innovations affect future volatility differently from the model prediction. The negative size bias test shows whether larger negative innovations are correlated with larger biases in predicted volatility. The positive size bias test focuses on the different impacts that large and small positive return shocks may have on volatility, which are not predicted by the volatility model. We regressed the squared standardized residual based on three variables: (1) the indicator variable of sign bias test (S_t^-) which takes one if the residual is negative and zero otherwise, (2) the product of the indicator variable (S_t^-) and the residual, and (3) the product of the residual and another indicator variable (S_t^+, which equals to $1 - S_t^-$). Since we cannot reject $\lambda = \nu = 2$, $c = 0$ we investigated the bias tests of both the unrestricted model (Equation 1' and 3') and the restricted model ($\lambda = \nu = 2$, $c = 0$). The results are reported in Table 7. The sign bias, positive size bias and joint tests were not significant in the unrestricted model. The negative size bias test was significant at a 10% significance level, but not significant at a 5% significance level in the unrestricted model. The restricted model passed all of these tests. The result supports $\lambda = \nu = 2$, $c = 0$ again. The result in which c was not significant is the same as the conclusion of Hentschel (1995). The difference between our result and Hentschel's is that we cannot reject $\lambda = \nu = 2$.

V. CONCLUSION

This study examined the behavior of Taiwan stock price volatility with focuses on the asymmetric effects and the relationship with trading volume. By extending

Hentschel's (1995) GARCH model to incorporate the trading volume in the empirical model, and testing the hypotheses of the nested GARCH models, this study produced the following results.

First, compared with Hentschel's model, our revision including the trading volume, is better in terms of explaining the daily return and volatility of Taiwan stock market. Second, the trading volume has significantly positive effects on stock return volatility. This result implies that high price-volatility is often coupled with heavy trading volume in a stock market. This is consistent with the empirical regularities. Third, negative shocks increase volatility more than equally large positive shocks, only when the shocks are not very large. If the shocks are very large, the asymmetric effects are not pronounced on volatility. Therefore when a market has a very large shock, we should not overestimate the asymmetric effects when investors adjust their portfolio.

The asymmetric patterns in shocks contradict previous findings. We doubt whether the 7% price limit circuit breaker on the Taiwan stock market could account for the phenomenon. Presumably, a piece of bad news would accompany a price fall, which might compound a slump in stock prices since a greater risk premium would be incurred by investors from the extra volatility (the price impact of volatility). However, the price impact of good news might be neutralized because a positive price effect counteracts the negative volatility impact. Following this argument, when the shock is small, an asymmetry in price impact might materialize. However, regardless the nature of news (good or bad), when the shock is large enough to cause the price impact of news absolutely dominates that of volatility. Therefore, a constantly enforced price limit may lead to a fictitious symmetry in the impulse when the shock is large.

Our results cannot reject the N-A GARCH model for the Taiwan stock market during the period from January 1, 1991 to September 24, 1996. We still do not suggest arbitrarily restricting the parameters of the starting model to any other period of data, as the N-A GARCH model does, since the structure of stock markets may change. Therefore Hentschel's model provides us with a general form to select an appropriate model for any data set.

ACKNOWLEDGMENTS

We would like to thank the helpful comments of Professor Pei-Gi Shu (Fu-Jen Catholic University), the discussant Professor Chung-Hua Shen (National Cheng-Chi University) and the seminar participants at the Fifth Conference on the Theories and Practices of Security and Financial Markets, Kaohsiung, Taiwan.

NOTES

1. The trading value of Taiwan stock market is 9,810 and 7,880 billion U.S. dollars both in 1989 and 1990, respectively. At the same time, the trading value of London stock market is 4,240 and 3,950

billion U.S. dollars. In 1997, the trading value of Taiwan stock market skyrocketed to 13,100 billion U.S. dollars as compared with 8,945 billion U.S. dollars of that of Tokyo stock market.

2.   See the survey by Bera and Higgins (1993) and Bollerslev, Chou, and Kroner (1992).

3.   As shown in Figure 1(d) of Hentschel (1995), by appropriately shifting and rotating the news impact curve, it is possible to have asymmetry for small shocks, a roughly symmetric response for moderate shocks, and asymmetry for very large shocks. The asymmetry for the large shocks, however, is the opposite of the asymmetry for the small shocks. This is true because the shift is the dominant source of asymmetry for small shocks, while the rotation is more important for large shocks.

4.   Since σ^2 is not a linear function of Q_t, it will not cause the collinearity problem between σ^2 and Q_t in Equation 1'.

5.   The cash dividend and stock dividends have been adjusted in preparing the Taiwan weighted stock. Hence we have incorporated the impact of dividends in our test.

6.   We also used the data from excess returns instead of returns to estimate Hentschel's model. The estimates for Equations 1' and 3' are:

$$\mu = -0.183(0.072)^{**}, \phi_1 = 0.050(0.029)^*, \theta = 0.125(0.067)^*, \gamma = 0.031(0.032), \lambda = 2.104(1.218)^*,$$
$$\nu = 2.616(0.638)^{**}, \omega = -0.021(0.013), \alpha = 0.023(0.012)^*, \beta = 0.797(0.063)^{**}, b = 0.802(0.353)^{**},$$
$$c = -0.030(0.197), a = 0.018(0.008)^{**}.$$

The numbers in parentheses are asymptotic standard errors. The notations * and ** indicate significance at 10 and 5% significance levels, respectively. The parameters and standard errors are similar to the results in Table 3. Therefore, the choice of return or excess return will not change our conclusions.

REFERENCES

Admati, A., & Pfleiderer, P. (1988). A theory of intraday patterns: Volume and price variability. *Review of Financial Studies 1*, 13–40.

Bekaert, G., & Harvey, C.R. (1997). Emerging equity market volatility. *Journal of Financial Economics, 43*, 29–77.

Bera, A.K., & Higgins, M.L. (1993). A survey of ARCH models: Properties, estimation and testing. *Journal of Economic Surveys, 7*, 305–366.

Black, F. (1976). Studies of stock price volatility changes. *Proceedings from the American Statistical Association, Business and Economics Statistics Section*, pp. 177–181.

Bollerslev, T. (1986). Generalized autoregressive conditional heteroskedasticity. *Journal of Econometrics, 31*, 307–327.

Bollerslev, T., Chou, R.Y., & Kroner, K.F. (1992). ARCH modeling in finance: A review of the theory and empirical evidence. *Journal of Econometrics, 52*, 5–59.

Box, G.E.P., & Cox, D.R. (1964). An analysis of transformations. *Journal of the Royal Statistical Society, 26*, 211–243.

Campbell, J., Grossman, S., & Wang, J. (1993). Trading volume and serial correlation in stock returns. *Quarterly Journal of Economics, 108*, 905–939.

Campbell, J.Y., & Hentschel, L. (1992). No news is good news: An asymmetric model of changing volatility in stock returns. *Journal of Financial Economics, 31*, 281–318.

Chan, K., & Chan, Y.C. (1993). Price volatility in the Hong Kong stock market: A test of the information and trading noise hypothesis. *Pacific-Basin Finance Journal*, 189–201.

Chou, R.Y. (1988). Volatility persistence and stock valuations: Some empirical evidence using GARCH. *Journal of Applied Econometrics, 3*, 281–318.

Christie, A.A. (1982). The stochastic behavior of common stock variances: Value, leverage, and interest rate effects. *Journal of Financial Economics, 10*, 407–432.

Engle, R.F. (1982). Autoregressive conditional heteroskedasticity with estimates of the variance of U.K. inflation. *Econometrica, 50*, 987–1008.

Engle, R.F., Lilien, D.M., & Robins, R.P. (1987). Estimating time varying risk premia in the term structure: The ARCH-M model. *Econometrica, 55*, 391–407.

Engle, R.F., & Ng, V.K. (1993). Measuring and testing the impact of news on volatility. *Journal of Finance, 48*, 1749–1778.

Epps, T., & Epps, M. (1976). The stochastic dependence of security price changes and transaction volumes: Implications for the mixture of distributions hypothesis. *Econometrica, 44*, 305–321.

Foster, F.D., & Viswanathan, S. (1995). Can speculative trading explain the volume-volatility relation? *Journal of Business Economic and Statistics, 13*, 379–396.

French, K.R., & Roll, R. (1986). Stock return variance: The arrival of information and the reaction of traders. *Journal of Financial Economics, 17*, 5–26.

Gallant, R., Rossi, P., & Tauchen, G. (1992). Stock prices and volume. *Review of Financial Studies, 5*, 199–242.

Glosten, L.R., Jagannathan, R., & Runkle, D. (1993). On the relation between the expected value and the volatility of the nominal excess return on stocks. *Journal of Finance, 48*, 1779–1801.

Hamilton, J.D. (1994). *Time series analysis*. Princeton, NJ: Princeton University Press.

Hentschel, L. (1995). All in the family nesting symmetric and asymmetric GARCH models. *Journal of Financial Economics, 39*, 71–104.

Kyle, A. (1985). Continuous auctions and insider trading. *Econometrica, 53*, 1315,1355.

Lamoureux, C.G., & Lastrapes, W.D. (1990). Heteroskedasticity in stock return data: Volume versus GARCH effects. *Journal of Finance*, 221–229.

Liu, Y.A. (1996). The impact of trading volume on stock returns and volatility: An examination of Taiwan and Hong Kong data. *Journal of Management Science, 13*, 91–106.

Morgan, I.G. (1976). Stock prices and heteroscedasticity. *Journal of Business, 49*, 496–508.

Morse, D. (1981). Price and trading volume reaction surrounding earnings announcements: A closer examination. *Journal of Accounting Research, 19*, 374–383.

Nelson, D.B. (1991). Conditional heteroskedasticity in asset returns: A new approach. *Econometrica, 59*, 347–370.

Schwert, G.W. (1990). Stock volatility and the crash of 1987. *Review of Financial Studies, 3*, 77–102.

Shalen, C.T. (1993). Volume, volatility, and the dispersion of beliefs. *The Review of Financial Studies, 6*, 405–434.

Shen, C.H., & Wang, L.R. (1998). Daily serial correlation, trading volume and price limits: evidence from the Taiwan stock market. *Pacific-Basin Finance Journal, 6*, 251–273.

Tauchen, G.E., & Pitts, M. (1983). The price variability-volume relationship on speculative markets. *Econometrica, 51, No. 2*, 485–505.

Zakoian, J.M. (1991). Threshold heteteroskedastic models. D. P. INSEE.

OPTIMAL MARKET TIMING STRATEGIES FOR ARMA(1,1) RETURN PROCESSES

Wei Li and Kin Lam

ABSTRACT

In this paper, we consider optimal market timing strategies under transaction costs. We assume that the asset's return follows an ARMA(1,1) model and use long-term investment growth as the objective of a market timing strategy which entails the shifting of funds between a risky asset and a riskless asset. By the use of stochastic dynamic programming techniques, we derive the optimal trading strategies for finite investment horizon, and analyze its limiting behavior. For finite horizon, the optimal decision in each step depends on two control variables. When investment horizon tends to infinity, we prove that the optimal strategy converges to a stationary policy, which also depends on two control variables. An integral equation of the two control variables is given. Numerical solutions and average returns associated with the limiting stationary strategy are also presented. Numerical results confirm that the no-transaction region increases as the transaction cost increases. Finally, the limiting stationary strategy is simulated using data in the Hang Seng Index Futures market in Hong Kong. The out-of-sample performance of the limiting stationary strategy is found to be comparable to that of a buy-and-hold strategy.

Advances in Investment Analysis and Portfolio Management, Volume 7, pages 163–190.
Copyright © 2000 by JAI Press Inc.
All rights of reproduction in any form reserved.
ISBN: 0-7623-0658-0

I. INTRODUCTION

Market timing is one of the two main components in the investment management process. As remarked by Jagannathan and Korajczyk (1986), "It is common practices to divide portfolio performance into two main components, security selection and market timing." The principal job of a market timer is to time when to enter into and when to get out of the market.

Market timing strategies are often used as a test of the predictability of stock returns (see Merton, 1981; Merton and Henriksson, 1981; Kon, 1983; Chang and Lewellen, 1984; Henriksson, 1984; Admati et al., 1986; Jagannathan and Korajczyk, 1986; Cumby and Modest, 1987; Ferson and Schadt, 1996). There is ample evidence that some market timing strategies can outperform the market (see e.g., Wagner, Shellans, and Paul, 1992; Hulbert, 1993). Shilling (1992) says that market timing is better than a buy-and-hold strategy. Larsen and Wozniak (1995) find that, "Market timing can work in the real world." Wagner (1997) states, "Why market timing works." In this paper, we assume that stock returns are predictable and follow a known stochastic model. We then derive the corresponding optimal market timing strategy in the presence of transaction costs. Specifically, if the return process of the risky asset follows an autoregressive moving average model ARMA(1,1), the optimal market timing strategy consists of the following decisions: (1) to switch from the risky to the riskless asset when tomorrow's predicted return in the risky asset is less than a constant, and (2) to switch from the riskless to the risky asset if tomorrow's predicted return is larger than a constant. The constants would depend on the autocorrelation of the return process as well as on c, the transaction cost.

Market timing is one form of active asset allocation management, which entails the shifting of funds between asset classes. Active asset allocation involves the adjustment of the percentage of funds invested in various assets. The classical approach is to derive a strategy which adjusts the portfolio through time to maximize the expected utility of consumption or terminal wealth (see e.g., Merton, 1969, 1971; Samuelson, 1969). Under this approach, the optimal strategy under transaction costs has been investigated by Constantinides (1979, 1986), Davis and Norman (1990), Dumas and Luciano (1991), among others. However, these results are based on the assumption that the price movements of the risky asset follows a Wiener–Brownian motion process.

Market timers take a different view towards the market. They believe that they have the ability to time the market, and try to be in the market in good periods and out of the market in bad periods. Since they do not believe in the random walk model, they would like to know the answer to the following question: If prices move according to a stochastic model other than the random walk, what is then the optimal trading strategy? This is exactly the question which we would like to address in this paper.

This paper is organized as follows. In Section II, we identify a suitable objective function for market timers and formulate the market timing decision as a stochastic dynamic programming problem. Section III gives a solution to this dynamic programming problem and obtains the optimal market timing strategy under finite investment horizon. Section IV deals with the limiting behavior of the optimal strategy for finite horizon, and establishes convergence as the time horizon tends to infinity. This section gives an integral equation for the two control variables of the limiting strategy, and derives its expected reward per step. Section V presents the numerical values of these control variables for the limiting strategy under realistic parameter values. The effect of transaction costs on market timing strategies is analyzed in this section. Section VI simulates the limiting strategy in the Hang Seng Index Futures market. Its performance is compared with the performance with the simple strategy and the buy-and-hold strategy. A conclusion can be found in Section VII.

II. OPTIMAL MARKET TIMING STRATEGY UNDER KNOWN DEPENDENCY PATTERN

A. Market Timing Strategies

A market timer is conventionally defined as a person who shifts completely his funds between a risky and a riskless asset, i.e., the funds are entirely invested either in risky or a riskless asset and there is no need to adjust the percentage of funds in the assets. If the investor finds an opportunity to enter the market, he will buy the stock with all the money he possesses.[1] If he is negative about the market, he will withdraw all the money from the market and invest in the riskless asset. Thus, the market timer's decision ultimately comes down to whether to be in or out of equities, therefore, 100% in or out of the equity market, which is different from that of the asset allocators. The asset allocators adjust the percentage of the risky asset to maximize their utility.

B. Growth-Optimal Criteria for Market Timers

It is the objective of a market timer to beat the market. They try to achieve this objective by shifting funds in and out of the stock market. By leaving the stock market and investing in a riskless asset from time to time, they are actually experiencing less risk than those investors adopting the buy-and-hold strategy. However, market timers leave the stock market not for the purpose of reducing risk, but for the purpose of enhancing returns. In this sense, market timers are quite risk-neutral. Thus, it is appropriate to assume that the performance measure for market timers is the expected average continuously compounded return. It is well known that this criteria of maximizing the expected terminal logarithmic (log-wealth) wealth will result in an investment strategy which guarantees that wealth will grow optimally (see e.g., Cox and Huang, 1989).

As remarked by Hakansson and Ziemba (1995), "The central feature of the growth-optimal strategy, also known as the geometric mean and the Kelly criterion, is the logarithmic shape of the objective function." We also mention here that the use of geometric mean as a performance measure of a market timing strategy is quite common, as in the test of the market timing ability of the Dow Theory in Brown, Goetzmann, and Kumar (1998).

C. A Market Timer's Optimization Problem

As reviewed in the previous section, market timers will choose to maximize their expected log-wealth at the end of an investment period. In order to obtain optimal strategies for market timers, it is essential to express the terminal wealth in terms of the investment decision variables. We now make the following assumptions:

1. The investor is self-financing, neither consumes nor deposits new cash into the portfolio during the trading periods, but reinvests his portfolio each period.
2. Investment decisions are made in discrete points in time ($t = 1, 2, \ldots$). The time interval can be "1 minute," "1 day," "1 month," or any fixed length of time. For simplicity, we just refer to the time interval as "1 day" hereafter.
3. The investor has an investment horizon of T days.
4. There are only two assets, one risky and one riskless. The riskless asset has a constant return throughout the investment period.
5. There are no dividends on the risky asset.
6. No shortselling or borrowing is allowed.
7. The transaction cost on the risky asset is c times the value traded, and there is no transaction cost for trading the riskless asset.

Trading decisions are made at the end of each day. The decision variable at the end of day $t - 1$ is denoted by d_t. It takes the value of "1" or "0," according to whether the investor is entirely in the risky or in the riskless asset. If the decision variable d_{t+1} differs from d_t, trading transaction has to be made, otherwise no transaction is necessary. Let w_t be the wealth at the end of day t before the trading decision, N_t be the number of shares hold before transaction, $N_{t'}$ be the number of shares after transaction, n_t be number of units of wealth invested in the riskless asset before transaction, and $n_{t'}$ be the number of units of wealth invested in the riskless asset after transaction. Then $w_t = (N_t p_t)^{d_t}(n_t p_t^0)^{1-d_t}$, where p_t is the stochastic price of the risky asset, and p_t^0 is the deterministic price of the riskless asset.

Let us consider the wealth w_{t+1} at day $t + 1$. When there is no transaction cost, it is easy to see that:

$$w_{t+1} = w_t \left(\frac{p_{t+1}}{p_t}\right)^{d_{t+1}} \left(\frac{p^0_{t+1}}{p^0_t}\right)^{1-d_{t+1}}$$

and the final wealth is:

$$w_T = w_0 \prod_{t=1}^{T} \left(\frac{p_t}{p_{t-1}}\right)^{d_t} \left(\frac{p^0_t}{p^0_{t-1}}\right)^{1-d_t}$$

where w_0 is the initial wealth.

If there are transaction costs, there are four cases as in Pesaran and Timmermann (1995):

I. $d_t = 1, d_{t+1} = 1$ (continuation in holding the risky asset):

$$N_{t'} = N_t = w_t/p_t$$

$$w_{t+1} = N_t p_{t+1} = w_t \frac{p_{t+1}}{p_t}$$

II. $d_t = 1, d_{t+1} = 0$ (switch from risky to riskless asset)

$$n_{t'} = w_t(1-c)/p^0_t$$

$$w_{t+1} = n_t p^0_{t+1} = w_t \frac{p^0_{t+1}}{p^0_t}(1-c)$$

III. $d_t = 0, d_{t+1} = 1$ (switch from riskless to risky asset)

$$N_{t'} = w_t(1-c)/p_t$$

$$w_{t+1} = N_t p_{t+1} = w_t \frac{p_{t+1}}{p_t}(1-c)$$

IV. $d_t = 0, d_{t+1} = 0$ (continuation in holding the riskless asset)

$$n_{t'} = n_t = w^0_t/p^0_t$$

$$w_{t+1} = n_t p^0_{t+1} = w_t \frac{p^0_{t+1}}{p^0_t}$$

Summarizing the above four cases, we have the following wealth dynamic:

$$w_{t+1} = w_t \left(\frac{p_{t+1}}{p_t}\right)^{d_{t+1}} \left(\frac{p^0_{t+1}}{p^0_t}\right)^{1-d_{t+1}} (1-c)^{|d_{t+1}-d_t|}$$

Hence the terminal wealth is given by:

$$w_T = w_0 \prod_{t=1}^{T} \left(\frac{p_t}{p_{t-1}}\right)^{d_t} \left(\frac{p_t^0}{p_{t-1}^0}\right)^{1-d_t} (1 - c)^{|d_t - d_{t-1}|}$$

The continuous compounded return in the whole period is given by:

$$\ln(w_T/w_0) = \sum_{t=1}^{T} [d_t r_t + (1 - d_t)r_t^0 - c'|d_t - d_{t-1}|]$$

where $r_t = \ln(p_t/p_{t-1})$ and $r = \ln(p_t^0/p_{t-1}^0)$ are the continuous compounded return for the risky asset and riskless asset respectively and $c' = -\ln(1 - c) \approx c$. For the sake of simplicity, we will use c instead of c' from now on.

According to the growth-optimal criterion, the objective of a market timer is to find a decision rule consisting of $d_1, d_2, \ldots, d_T$ to maximize the expected value of $\ln(w_T/w_0)$, i.e.:

$$\max_{d_t=0,1} E \sum_{t=1}^{T} [(r_t - r)d_t - c|d_t - d_{t-1}|] \tag{1}$$

Here d_0 equals 0 (or 1) if the initial wealth is invested in the riskless (or risky) asset.

D.   The Case of Short-Selling

Although the problem formulated above assumes no short-selling, the methodology can also be used to cover in the case when short-selling is allowed. The results are similar. Without short-selling, d_t is either 0 or 1. When short-selling is allowed, we assume that the investor is aggressive, therefore, if there is an indication of leaving the market in the case of no short-selling, he/she will short the risky asset, instead of holding the riskless asset. Therefore, the decision d_t takes values as either 1 or −1 when short-selling is allowed (see e.g., Levich and Thomas, 1993). Taylor (1988, 1992) tested the portfolio performance in the futures market under the allowance of short-selling by the use of a performance measure similar to what we use here.

E.   Price Dependence

It is obvious that the decision of when to enter into and when to get out of the market should depend on the pattern, if there is any, of the price movement of the underlying risky asset. Under different models of price movements, the optimal decisions should be different. Let p_t $(t = 1, 2, \ldots)$ be the stochastic price process of the risky asset at time t, and $r_t = \ln(p_t) - \ln(p_{t-1})$ be the continuously compounded return for an investor holding the risky asset at time t.

One type of model that has been suggested for the return process is the autoregressive moving average model (ARMA). De Bondt and Thaler (1985), Fama and French (1988), Poterba and Summers (1988), and Chopra, Lakonishock, and Ritter (1992) found correlation in returns of individual stocks and various portfolios over 3- to 10-year periods. Hodrick and Srivastava (1987), Taylor (1986, 1992), and Mark (1988) found positive autocorrelation among exchange rate returns. Conrad and Kaul (1990) reported first-order autocorrelation of 0.2 for a value-weighted portfolio of the largest companies during the period 1962–1985. Virtanen and Yli-Olli (1987) identified a nice ARMA model by fitting the index of the Finland stock market. For a discussion of their findings see Lam (1990). Amihud and Mendelson (1987), after testing market efficiency by the use of ARMA(1,1) models, remarked: "There are numerous violations of the random-walk form of the market efficiency hypothesis, primarily at the opening, with many of the open-to-open return series being well-explained by the ARMA(1,1) model." Also, the Fads model, a particular type of mean-reversion models (Summers, 1986; Fama and French, 1988; Poterba and Summers, 1988) and the linear-price trend model in Taylor (1986, 1992) are also ARMA(1,1) in nature.

Under an ARMA(1,1) model, the return r_t has the following representation:

$$r_t - \mu = \phi(r_{t-1} - \mu) + \theta\varepsilon_{t-1} + \varepsilon_t \tag{2}$$

where μ, ϕ ($|\phi| < 1$) and θ are constants, ε_t are i.i.d $N(0, \sigma^2)$ white noises. We also assume that μ, ϕ, θ, and σ are known to the investor since these parameters can be estimated from historical return data. Of course, the estimated parameters may not be the same parameters that govern the price dynamics in a future period. However, empirical results in Section VI show that the optimal rules on historical data also work well in the period one-step ahead. This shows that while ARMA(1,1) parameters may vary over time, the performance of the optimal strategy is rather robust to parameter changes.

F. Optimal Market Timing Strategy under Transaction Costs

In the absence of transaction costs, the optimal trading rule is trivial and is·given as follows: if the expected excess return $[E(r_t - r)]$ in the next period is positive, hold the risky asset; otherwise hold the riskless asset. This simple trading rule is used by many researchers in the testing of the predictability of stock returns, such as Breen, Glosten, and Jagannathan (1990), Leitch and Tanner (1991), Pesaran and Timmermann (1994, 1995), Knez and Ready (1996), Lander, Orphanides, and Douvogiannis (1997), and Lee (1997). This trading rule is referred to as the *simple trading rule* in this paper. When transaction cost is not negligible, this simple trading rule is no longer optimal and the optimization problem (Equation 1) becomes non-trivial. *Even if the expected excess return in the next period is negative, it may*

be worthwhile to hold onto the risky asset because, in subsequent periods, the
expected return can turn out to be positive again, and transaction costs may be
saved if we do not switch away from the risky asset too readily.

The problem of finding an optimal market timing strategy in the presence of
transaction costs now reduces to solving the following stochastic dynamic programming problem. Given an ARMA(1,1) return process r_t, we have to find, for a finite
investment horizon T, optimal decision rule consisting of $d_1, \cdots, d_T$ so that the
expected value of Equation 1 is maximized. To solve these stochastic dynamic
programming problems, we assume the constant risk-free rate r to be zero. No
generality is lost because if r is not equal to zero, we can redefine $r_t - r$ as r_t and
reduce the problem to one in which $r = 0$.

III. OPTIMAL DECISIONS FOR FINITE TIME HORIZON

A. State Space Representation of ARMA(1,1)

The state space representation of an ARMA(1,1) model (Equation 2) is given by
the following state equation and observation equation:

state equation

$$\mathbf{x}_{t+1} = A\mathbf{x}_t + \xi_{t+1}$$

observation equation

$$r_t = \mu + b^T \mathbf{x}_t$$

where

$$\mathbf{x}_t = \begin{pmatrix} r_t - \mu \\ \varepsilon_t \end{pmatrix}, \quad \xi_t = \begin{pmatrix} \varepsilon_t \\ \varepsilon_t \end{pmatrix}, \quad A = \begin{pmatrix} \phi & \theta \\ 0 & 0 \end{pmatrix}, \quad b = \begin{pmatrix} 1 \\ 0 \end{pmatrix}$$

B. Bellman Equation

Let $V_t(\mathbf{x}_{t-1}, d_{t-1})$ denote the maximum expected return that can be derived from
day t to T. Then the optimality equation, or Bellman equation, can be written as:

$$V_t(\mathbf{x}_{t-1}, d_{t-1}) = \max_{d_t=0,1} E[r_t d_t - |d_t - d_{t-1}|c + V_{t+1}(\mathbf{x}_t, d_t)] \tag{3}$$

where E stands for expectation. Because the investment process terminates at the
end of T periods, we can assume $V_{T+1}(\mathbf{x}_T, d_T) = 0$, and $V_t(\mathbf{x}_{t-1}, d_{t-1})$ can be solved
recursively. By the state space representation, Equation 3 can be rewritten as:

$$V_t(\mathbf{x}_{t-1}, d_{t-1}) = \max[-|d_{t-1}|c + EV_{t+1}(\mathbf{x}_t, 0),$$

$$b^T A \mathbf{x}_{t-1} + \mu - |1 - d_{t-1}|c + EV_{t+1}(\mathbf{x}_t, 1)]$$

Defining $s_t(\mathbf{x}_{t-1}) = V_t(\mathbf{x}_{t-1}, 1) - V_t(\mathbf{x}_{t-1}, 0)$, we have:

$$V_t(\mathbf{x}_{t-1}, d_{t-1}) =$$

$$\begin{cases} -|d_{t-1}|c + EV_{t+1}(\mathbf{x}_t, 0), & b^T A \mathbf{x}_{t-1} + \mu + (2d_{t-1} - 1)c + Es_{t+1}(\mathbf{x}_t) \le 0 \\ b^T A \mathbf{x}_{t-1} + \mu - |1 - d_{t-1}|c + EV_{t+1}(\mathbf{x}_t, 1), & \text{otherwise} \end{cases}$$

and the optimal decision is:

$$d_t = \begin{cases} 0 & b^T A \mathbf{x}_{t-1} + \mu + (2d_{t-1} - 1)c + Es_{t+1}(\mathbf{x}_t) \le 0 \\ 1 & \text{otherwise} \end{cases}$$

To sum up, we have the following lemma which expresses the optimal decision in terms of the function $h_{t+1}(\mathbf{x}_{t-1})$.

Lemma 1. For $t = T, T - 1, \ldots$, the optimal decision d_t at the end of day $t - 1$ is:

$$d_t = d_t(\mathbf{x}_{t-1}, d_{t-1}) = \chi((2d_{t-1} - 1)c + h_{t+1}(\mathbf{x}_{t-1}))$$

where

$$\chi(z) = \begin{cases} 0 & z \le 0 \\ 1 & z > 0, \end{cases}$$

and

$$h_{t+1}(\mathbf{x}_{t-1}) = b^T A \mathbf{x}_{t-1} + \mu + Es_{t+1}(\mathbf{x}_t)$$

The next lemma claims that $h_{t+1}(\bullet)$ is a function of $\mathbf{x}_{t-1}$ through the pivotal quantity $x_t = b^T A \mathbf{x}_{t-1}$. Note that $x_t = \phi(r_{t-1} - \mu) + \theta \varepsilon_{t-1}$ is the predicted value of $r_t - \mu$ (Hamilton, 1994).

Lemma 2. $h_{t+1}(\mathbf{x}_{t-1})$ is a function of $b^T A \mathbf{x}_{t-1}$ for $t = T, T - 1 \cdots$

Proof: We prove the lemma by mathematical induction. Since $s_{T+1}(\mathbf{x}_T) = 0$, $h_{T+1}(\mathbf{x}_{T-1}) = b^T A \mathbf{x}_{T-1} + \mu$, so it is true for $t = T$. Suppose it is true for $t = k + 1$, we will prove that it is true for $t = k$. Since $h_{k+1}(\mathbf{x}_{k-1}) = b^T A \mathbf{x}_{k-1} + \mu + Es_{k+1}(A \mathbf{x}_{k-1} + \xi_k)$, and:

$$s_{k+1}(A\mathbf{x}_{k-1} + \xi_k) = \begin{cases} c & h_{k+2}(A\mathbf{x}_{k-1} + \xi_k) \geq c \\ h_{k+2}(A\mathbf{x}_{k-1} + \xi_k) & \text{otherwise} \\ -c & h_{k+2}(A\mathbf{x}_{k-1} + \xi_k) \leq -c \end{cases}$$

From the assumption, $h_{k+2}(A\mathbf{x}_{k-1} + \xi_k)$ is a function of $b^T A(A\mathbf{x}_{k-1} + \xi_k) = b^T A^2 \mathbf{x}_{k-1} + b^T A \xi_k = \phi b^T A \mathbf{x}_{k-1} + (\phi + \theta)\varepsilon_k$. Therefore $h_{k+1}(\mathbf{x}_{k-1})$ is a function of $b^T A \mathbf{x}_{k-1}$. This completes the proof.

Because of Lemma 2, the vector function $h_{t+1}(\bullet)$ degenerates into a scalar function $u_{t+1}(\bullet)$ through the relationship $u_{t+1}(x_t) = h_{t+1}(\mathbf{x}_{t-1})$ for $x = b^T A \mathbf{x}_{t-1}$. The function $u_{t+1}(\bullet)$ has the following property.

Lemma 3.   For $t = T, T - 1, \cdots$, let

$$f_{t+1}(x) = \begin{cases} c & u_{t+2}(x) \geq c \\ u_{t+2}(x) & \text{otherwise} \\ -c & u_{t+2}(x) \leq -c. \end{cases}$$

Then $u_{t+1}(x) = x + \mu + E f_{t+1}(\phi x + \eta)$, where $\eta \sim N(0, (\phi + \theta)^2 \sigma^2)$

Proof: Since

$$s_{t+1}(\mathbf{x}_t)$$

$$= \begin{cases} c & h_{t+2}(\mathbf{x}_t) \geq c \\ h_{t+2}(\mathbf{x}_t) & \text{otherwise} \\ -c & h_{t+2}(\mathbf{x}_t) \leq -c \end{cases}$$

$$= \begin{cases} c & u_{t+2}(b^T A \mathbf{x}_t) \geq c \\ u_{t+2}(b^T A \mathbf{x}_t) & \text{otherwise} \\ -c & u_{t+2}(b^T A \mathbf{x}_t) \leq -c \end{cases}$$

$$= \begin{cases} c & u_{t+2}(\phi b^T A \mathbf{x}_{t-1} + b^T A \xi_t) \geq c \\ u_{t+2}(\phi b^T A \mathbf{x}_{t-1} + b^T A \xi_t) & \text{otherwise} \\ -c & u_{t+2}(\phi b^T A \mathbf{x}_{t-1} + b^T A \xi_t) \leq -c \end{cases}$$

We have $s_{t+1}(\mathbf{x}_t) = f_{t+1}(\phi b^T A \mathbf{x}_{t-1} + b^T A \xi_t)$, and

$$u_{t+1}(b^T A \mathbf{x}_{t-1}) = b^T A \mathbf{x}_{t-1} + \mu + E f_{t+1}(\phi b^T A \mathbf{x}_{t-1} + b^T A \xi_t)$$

Let $x = b^T A \mathbf{x}_{t-1}$, $\eta = b^T A \xi_t = (\phi + \theta)\varepsilon_t \sim N(0, (\phi + \theta)^2 \sigma^2)$, we have the result. This completes the proof.

Lemma 4. For every $t = T + 1, T, \cdots$, we have $u'_t(x) > 0$ for all x if $\phi > 0$, and $0 < u'_t(x) \leq 1$ for all x if $\phi < 0$.

Proof: We prove by induction. Since $u_{T+1}(x) = x + \mu$, the result is obvious for $t = T + 1$. Suppose that it is true for $t = k + 1$, we will prove that it is true for $t = k$. Since:

$$u_k(x) = x + \mu + Ef_k(\phi x + \eta)$$

$$\frac{\partial Ef_k(\phi x + \eta)}{\partial x} = \phi \int_{-c < u_{k+1}(\phi x + z) < c} u'_{k+1}(\phi x + z)\phi(z)dz$$

$$u'_k(x) = 1 + \phi \int_{-c < u'_{k+1}(\phi x + z) < c} u'_{k+1}(\phi x + z)\phi(z)dz$$

where $\phi(z)$ is the normal density function of $\eta \sim N(0, (\phi + \theta)^2\sigma^2)$. Therefore $u'_k(x) > 0$ if $\phi > 0$ and $0 < u'_k(x) \leq 1$ if $-1 < \phi < 0$. This completes the proof.

Lemma 5. For $t = T, T - 1, \cdots$,

(i). (a). If $\phi > 0 \ (< 0)$, $y = u_t(x)$ approaches the asymptote $y = x + \mu + c$, when $x \to \infty$, $(x \to -\infty)$. (b). If $\phi > 0 \ (< 0)$, $y = u_t(x)$ approaches the asymptote $y = x + \mu - c$ when $x \to -\infty \ (x \to \infty)$.

(ii). $x + \mu - c < u_t(x) < x + \mu + c$

Proof:

$$Ef_t(\phi x + \varepsilon) = c[1 - \Phi(a_{t+1} - \phi x) - \Phi(b_{t+1} - \phi x)]$$

$$+ \int_{b_{t+1} - \phi x}^{a_{t+1} - \phi x} u_{t+1}(\phi x + z)\phi(z)dz$$

where a_{t+1} and b_{t+1} satisfy $u_{t+1}(a_{t+1}) = c$ and $u_{t+1}(b_{t+1}) = -c$, $\Phi(x)$ is the cumulative density function of the normally distributed variable η. For $\phi > 0$, $\lim_{x \to \infty} Ef_t(\phi x + \eta) = c$, and $\lim_{x \to -\infty} Ef_t(\phi x + \eta) = -c$. For $\phi < 0$, $\lim_{x \to \infty} Ef_t(\phi x + \eta) = -c$, and $\lim_{x \to -\infty} Ef_t(\phi x + \eta) = c$. It then follows that $y = x + \mu + c$ and $y = x + \mu - c$ are the two asymptotas of the function $y = u_t(x)$. Since $Ef_t(\phi x + \eta)$ is strictly monotone increasing for $\phi > 0$ and decreasing for $\phi < 0$, we have (ii). This completes the proof.

C. The Optimal Trading Strategy

We now summarize the solution for the optimization problem into the following theorem.

Theorem 1.   For $t = T, T - 1, \ldots$, the optimal decisions are as follows:

$$d_t(x, 1) = \begin{cases} 0 & x \le b_{t+1} \\ 1 & x > b_{t+1} \end{cases}$$

$$d_t(x, 0) = \begin{cases} 0 & x \le a_{t+1} \\ 1 & x > a_{t+1} \end{cases}$$

where a_{t+1} and b_{t+1} satisfy $u_{t+1}(a_{t+1}) = c$, $u_{t+1}(b_{t+1}) = -c$, and $x = b^T A x_{t-1} = \phi(r_{t-1} - \mu) + \theta \varepsilon_{t-1}$, which is the forecast of $r_t - \mu$.

Proof: It is a direct result from Lemma 3, Lemma 4, and Lemma 5.

According to Theorem 1, the optimal trading strategy is given as follows:

1. When the investment position is "long" in day $t - 1$ ($0 \le t \le T - 1$), sell the risky asset at the close of day $t - 1$ to attain a "neutral" position in day t if $\phi(r_{t-1} - \mu) + \theta \varepsilon_{t-1} \le b_{t+1}$, otherwise do nothing to maintain the "long" position.
2. When the investment position is "neutral" in day $t - 1$ ($0 \le t \le T - 1$), buy the risky asset at the close of day $t - 1$ to attain a "long" position in day t if $\phi(r_{t-1} - \mu) + \theta \varepsilon_{t-1} \ge a_{t+1}$, otherwise do nothing to maintain the "neutral" position.

D. Effects of Transaction Costs

It is easy to see that the optimal strategy depends on the values a_t and b_t which are functionally dependent on the transaction costs c.

When there is no transaction cost, therefore, $c = 0$, we have from Lemmas 2 and 3, $f_t(x) = 0$. Hence $u_t(x) = x + \mu$, and therefore $a_t = b_t = -\mu$ for every $t = 1, 2, \cdots, T$. Thus the optimal decision in each step is:

$$d_t = \begin{cases} 0 & x + \mu \le 0 \\ 1 & x + \mu > 0 \end{cases}$$

Since $x + \mu$ is the forecast of next day's return, this means that if the predicted return next day is bigger than zero, then buy the risky asset, else hold the riskless asset. This is, of course, the simple market timing strategy commonly used in the literature.

In the presence of transaction costs, $a_t > -\mu$ and $b_t < -\mu$. This means that the market timer should switch from "neutral" to "long" if and only if the predicted return next day is bigger than $a_t + \mu$ or switch from "long" to "neutral" if and only if the predicted return next day is smaller than $b_t + \mu$. The constants a_t and b_t satisfy $b_t < a_t$. As shown in Section V, with the presence of a no-switching region, trading under transaction costs will become less frequent.

IV. LIMITING BEHAVIOR OF THE OPTIMAL STRATEGY

In this section, we first show the convergence of the optimal decisions given in Theorem 1, and then give the expected reward obtained per step by the limiting stationary strategy.

A. Convergence of $u_t(x)$

Lemma 6. $u_t(x)$ converges uniformly to a continuous function $u(x)$.

Proof: see Appendix 1.

Lemma 7.   (i). $\lim_{t \to \infty} a_t = a$,

(ii). $\lim_{t \to \infty} b_t = b$.

Proof: It is an obvious consequence of Lemma 6.

Lemma 8. $u(x)$, a, b satisfy the following integral equation

$$u(x) = x + \mu + c[1 - \Phi(a - \phi x) - \Phi(b - \phi x)] + \int_b^a u(z)\phi(z - \phi x)dz \qquad (4)$$

with boundary conditions $u(a) = c$ and $u(b) = -c$.

Proof: From Lemmas 2 and 6, $f_t(x)$ has a limit, denoted by $f(x)$. Since:

$$f(x) = \begin{cases} c & u(x) \geq c \\ u(x) & -c < u(x) < c \\ -c & u(x) \leq -c \end{cases}$$

and

$$u(x) = x + \mu + Ef(\phi x + \eta)$$

the result follows.

From the above lemmas, we have the following theorem:

Theorem 2.   When investment horizon tends to infinity, the optimal decision for the finite horizon problem converges to the following limiting stationary strategy:

$$d_t(x, 1) = \begin{cases} 0 & x \le b \\ 1 & x > b, \end{cases} \qquad d_t(x, 0) = \begin{cases} 0 & x \le a \\ 1 & x > a \end{cases} \tag{5}$$

where a and b satisfy Equation 4.

In Equation 4, only the last two terms in the right hand side are related to c. If $c = 0$, $a = b$ and $u(x) = x + \mu$.

B. Stationary Distribution and Average Return

From the above sections, we know that d_t is a function of $x_t = b^T A x_{t-1}$. Since:

$$x_{t-1} = A x_{t-2} + \xi_{t-1}$$

we have

$$x_t = b^T A^2 x_{t-2} + b^T A \xi_{t-1}$$

$$= \phi b^T A x_{t-2} + b^T A \xi_{t-1}$$

Let $\eta_t = b^T A \xi_{t-1} = (\phi + \theta)\varepsilon_{t-1} \sim N(0, (\phi + \theta)^2\sigma^2)$, it can be shown that x_t satisfies the following equation:

$$x_t = \phi x_{t-1} + \eta_t$$

According to Theorem 2, the optimal decision for the investment problem under a finite time horizon converges to a stationary policy. The following lemma gives the stationary distribution of (x_t, d_t).

Lemma 9.   Denote the stationary distribution of (x_t, d_t) by $f(x, y)$. If the joint distribution $f(x, y)$ has the following marginals: $p = P\{y = 1\}$, $1 - p = P\{y = 0\}$, $f_0(x) = f(x|y = 0)$, $f_1(x) = f(x|y = 1)$, then p, $f_0(x)$ and $f_1(x)$ satisfy the following three equations:

$$p = (1 - p) \int_a^\infty f_0(z)dz + p \int_b^\infty f_1(z)dz$$

$$pf_1(x) = (1 - p) \int_a^\infty \phi(x - \phi z)f_0(z)dz + p \int_b^\infty \phi(x - \phi z)f_1(z)dz$$

$$(1 - p)f_0(x) = (1 - p) \int_{-\infty}^a \phi(x - \phi z)f_0(z)dz + p \int_{-\infty}^b \phi(x - \phi z)f_1(z)dz$$

The proof is straight forward and is omitted.

Theorem 3. The expected return per step (= g) obtained by the stationary strategy in the long run is given as follows:

$$g = p \int_{-\infty}^{\infty} x f_1(x) dx - 2cp \int_{-\infty}^{b} f_1(x) dx + \mu p$$

Proof: see Appendix 2.

V. NUMERICAL RESULTS FOR THE LIMITING STRATEGY

A. Values of a and b

From Theorem 2, we know that the limiting trading strategy depends on a and b, which are determined by Equation 4. Given parameters μ, ϕ, θ, and σ, we can find a and b numerically from Equation 4. We only present the numerical results for the case $\mu = 0$ here. When $\mu = 0$, $h(x)$ is antisymmetric and hence $b = -a$. The first order autocorrelation coefficient of the ARMA(1,1) process (Equation 1) is given by:

$$\rho = \frac{(1 + \phi\theta)(\phi + \theta)}{1 + \theta^2 + 2\phi\theta} \tag{6}$$

(see Box et al., 1994, p. 81). In the financial literature where ARMA(1,1) is used as a model of the return series, parameters ϕ and θ vary a lot. For example, Amihud and Mendelson (1987) reported −0.4 as an average value of ϕ and 0.33 as an average of θ for the open-to-open return. Taylor (1986) estimates the two parameters for futures series, the range of the value of ϕ and θ is 0.5 to 0.975 and 0.453 to 0.967, respectively. In Poterba and Summers (1988), the parameter ϕ is about 0.985. In the following, we let ϕ vary from 0.4 to 0.9, and assume the first-order autocorrelation coefficient ρ to be equal to 0.1. The value of θ is determined by Equation 6. Let the standard deviation of the asset's return σ_r to be 0.02, which is quite typical in some futures markets. Then the variance σ^2 of the error term ε_t is given by (see Box et al., 1994, p. 80):

$$\sigma^2 = \frac{1 - \phi^2}{1 + \theta^2 + 2\phi\theta} \sigma_r^2$$

Table 1 shows the value of a for six pairs of values of ϕ and θ, and for four different values of c when $\mu = 0$. The first-order autocorrelation coefficient (ρ) is set to be 0.1 for all cases. For example, $a = 0.001543$ when $\phi = 0.4$, $\theta = -0.3033$ and $c = 0.2\%$, which means that a long position has to be neutralized whenever we predict the return to drop by 0.15% in a day. Table 1 also shows that a increases as c increases. This is reasonable because, if the transaction cost is high, investment position should be maintained unless there is more evidence of a turning point. The higher the transaction costs, the less frequent is the trading. Also a decreases as the

Table 1. Values for a when $\mu = 0$

(ϕ, θ)	Transaction Cost c			
	2.00e-03	6.00e-03	1.00e-02	1.40e-02
(0.4, −0.3033)	1.5430e-03	3.7781e-03	6.0596e-03	8.4208e-03
(0.5, −0.4048)	1.4524e-03	3.3387e-03	5.1567e-03	7.0815e-03
(0.6, −0.5068)	1.3677e-03	2.9634e-03	4.3612e-03	5.8234e-03
(0.7, −0.6096)	1.2860e-03	2.6404e-03	3.7062e-03	4.7418e-03
(0.8, −0.7143)	1.2004e-03	2.3448e-03	3.1620e-03	3.8842e-03
(0.9, −0.8242)	1.0897e-03	2.0208e-03	2.6337e-03	3.1339e-03

Table 2. Average Reward g for $\mu = 0$

(ϕ, θ)	Transaction Cost c			
	2.00e-03	6.00e-03	1.00e-02	1.40e-02
(0.4, −0.3033)	7.7335e-04	4.6235e-04	4.1441e-04	4.0205e-04
(0.5, −0.4048)	9.3533e-04	5.9996e-04	5.1051e-04	4.9270e-04
(0.6, −0.5068)	1.1603e-03	8.1761e-04	6.7891e-04	6.3142e-04
(0.7, −0.6096)	1.5021e-03	1.1734e-03	9.9755e-04	9.0166e-04
(0.8, −0.7143)	2.1089e-03	1.8215e-03	1.6371e-03	1.5072e-03
(0.9, −0.8242)	3.6578e-03	3.4724e-03	3.3209e-03	3.1991e-03

absolute values of ϕ and θ increase (although the first order autocorrelation coefficient remains the same).

B. Expected Reward of the Strategy

Table 2 provides the expected daily return derived under the stationary trading strategy when $\mu = 0$. For example, the average daily return is $7.73e - 04$ per day when $\phi = 0.4$, $\theta = -0.3033$ and $c = 0.2\%$, which is bigger than 0 for the buy-and-hold strategy.

From Table 2, we can see that g increases when the absolute values of ϕ and θ increase, although the first-order autocorrelation remains constant. This is probably due to the increase in autocorrelation of order higher than 1. For example, the second order autocorrelation coefficient $\rho_2 = \phi\rho$ increases when ϕ increases. Also, g decreases when the transaction cost c increases. It is also easy to see that g is greater than zero, which means that the limiting trading strategy can earn more profit than the buy-and-hold strategy.

VI. EMPIRICAL RESULTS

In this section, we report the performance of the simulated trading of the limiting stationary strategy in the Hang Seng Index Futures market in Hong Kong. Closing prices for Hang Seng Index Futures from July 1, 1986 to December 31, 1997 are used in the simulation. We divide each calendar year into two periods: the first half-year period and the second half-year period. For each period, we estimate the ARMA(1,1) parameters and use the fitted model to forecast the daily return in the following period. We compute the critical values (*b* and *a*) for the limiting trading strategy assuming that the same ARMA model works in the next period. The performance of the trading strategy will be compared of the performance with the simple strategy and the buy-and-hold strategy under different transaction costs.

A. Data Description

The Hang Seng Index is the most popular market index for the Hong Kong stock market. It has a very actively traded futures contract, therefore, the Hang Seng Index Futures contract (HSIF), which was launched on May, 6 1986 and is the most actively traded index futures contract in non-Japan Asia. Although Singapore (SIMEX) launched a futures contract on the Morgan Stanley Hong Kong Index on November 23, 1998, we have not seen any great influence on the trading volume of the HSIF contract in Hong Kong until now. Before November 20, 1998, the Hong Kong HSIF market opened at 10:00 A.M., closed for lunch at 12:30 A.M., reopened at 14:30 P.M. and ran until 16:00 P.M. The trading hour has been lengthened by half an hour per day, opening at 9:45 A.M. and closing at 16:15 P.M. since November 20, 1998.

The data used in this study are the daily settlements price of the spot month Hong Kong HSIF contract covering the period from July 1, 1986 to December 31, 1997. The settlement prices in the last two trading days in each month are substituted by the closing prices of the next month's HSIF contract, since most of the traders roll the contract over to another month in the last two trading days and the spot month contract is not actively traded during that period.

B. Parameter Estimation of ARMA(1,1) Model

To simulate trading by the proposed strategy, we divide each calendar year into two periods, the first half-year and the second half-year. By doing this, we have a total of 23 time periods with each time period having a 6-month span. We ignore the data before July 1, 1986 to make sure that every period has 6 months in length. We then estimate the ARMA(1,1) parameters for each time period. The results are summarized in Table 3. The last row in the table gives the average values over all periods.

The first column in Table 3 shows the time period in which parameters are estimated. For example, "87-1" denotes the first half of the year 1987, therefore, from January 1 to June 30, and "87-2" denotes the second half of the year 1987,

Table 3. ARMA(1,1) Model Estimation

Period	θ	φ	μ	σ	Portmanteau Test	ARMA(1,1) r
86-2	1.66e-01	−4.88e-02	3.15e-03	1.12e-02	0.754(12)*	
	(−0.21)	(−0.06)	(2.81)		0.178(24)*	
87-1	7.42e-01	−5.06e-01	1.79e-03	1.31e-02	0.077(12)	1.51e-01
	(−4.50)*	(−2.39)*	(1.32)		0.176(24)*	
87-2	−8.44e-02	1.00e-02	−2.57e-03	5.94e-02	0.33(12)*	−7.30e-02
	(0.07)	(0.01)	(−0.51)		0.843(24)*	
88-1	−1.20e-01	1.82e-01	1.46e-03	1.59e-02	0.013(12)	−2.07e-02
	(0.08)	(0.13)	(0.93)		0.020(24)	
88-2	3.63e-01	−2.54e-01	4.08e-05	9.12e-03	0.434(12)*	1.06e-01
	(−0.51)	(−0.34)	(0.05)		0.490(24)*	
89-1	−5.40e-01	4.09e-01	−1.62e-03	3.63e-02	0.002(12)	−1.04e-02
	(1.17)	(0.82)	(−0.62)		0.082(24)	
89-2	9.66e-03	−1.54e-01	2.02e-03	1.34e-02	0.247(12)*	1.02e-01
	(−0.02)	(−0.25)	(1.91)		0.678(24)*	
90-1	−6.79e-02	−7.27e-02	1.06e-03	9.06e-03	0.251(12)*	1.39e-01
	(0.10)	(−0.11)	(1.47)		0.218(24)*	
90-2	8.84e-01	−6.07e-01	−9.39e-04	1.61e-02	0.729(12)*	−1.69e-01
	(−12.34)*	(−5.01)*	(−0.58)		0.834(24)*	
91-1	7.35e-02	−9.31e-04	1.83e-03	1.11e-02	0.742(12)*	−1.46e-02
	(−0.06)	(−0.00)	(1.68)		0.592(24)*	
91-2	6.49e-01	−7.88e-01	9.56e-04	1.13e-02	0.196(12)*	−1.34e-01
	(−2.71)*	(−4.07)*	(1.04)		0.672(24)*	
92-1	9.94e-01	−9.45e-01	2.91e-03	1.08e-02	0.463(12)*	−2.06e-02
	(−26.84)*	(−15.37)*	(2.93)		0.510(24)*	
92-2	−3.96e-01	5.10e-01	−9.10e-04	1.67e-02	0.253(12)*	1.08e-01
	(0.68)	(0.93)	(−0.50)		0.249(24)*	
93-1	9.23e-01	−8.31e-01	2.24e-03	1.56e-02	0.517(12)*	2.30e-01
	(−9.02)*	(−5.84)*	(1.50)		0.493(24)*	
93-2	7.50e-01	−6.63e-01	3.93e-03	1.81e-02	0.403(12)*	9.52e-02
	(−2.12)*	(1.66)*	(2.31)		0.216(24)*	
94-1	−3.72e-01	1.64e-01	−2.86e-03	2.74e-02	0.709(12)*	3.09e-02
	(0.97)	(0.40)	(−1.54)		0.206(24)*	
94-2	−1.29e-01	2.54e-01	−4.74e-04	1.53e-02	0.013(12)	−1.21e-01
	(0.18)	(0.37)	(−0.30)		0.001(24)	
95-1	7.91e-01	−8.78e-01	1.46e-03	1.79e-02	0.681(12)*	−5.69e-02
	(−3.95)*	(−5.60)*	(0.95)		0.859(24)*	
95-2	4.31e-01	−5.12e-01	8.21e-04	1.06e-02	0.421(12)*	7.32e-02
	(−0.55)	(−0.69)	(0.91)		0.240(24)*	
96-1	4.17e-01	−6.04e-01	5.41e-04	1.33e-02	0.080(12)	2.16e-01
	(−1.24)*	(2.04)*	(0.51)		0.268(24)*	
96-2	9.26e-02	−1.89e-01	1.58e-03	1.04e-02	0.638(12)*	9.32e-02
	(−0.10)	(−0.21)	(1.85)		0.677(24)*	
97-1	8.44e-01	−7.33e-01	1.22e-03	1.35e-02	0.894(12)*	−4.66e-02
	(−4.79)*	(−3.31)*	(0.94)		0.937(24)*	
97-2	−1.79e-01	−3.88e-02	−2.69e-03	3.94e-02	0.017(12)	1.55e-01
	(0.43)	(−0.09)	(−0.96)		0.168(24)*	
mean	2.71e-01	−2.74e-01	6.51e-04	1.80e-02		2.50e-02

Note: *Portmanteau test *p* values are not significant.

therefore, from July 1 to December 31. The second, third, and fourth columns give the estimates of the parameters θ, φ, and μ in the ARMA(1,1) model; the figures in parentheses correspond to the t values of the estimates. The fifth column is the standard deviation of the return series within the period. The sixth column gives the p values of the Portmanteau test for time lag up to 12 and 24 (shown in parentheses), which tests the adequacy of the model (see Box et al., 1994, for details). Column seven is the correlation coefficient (r) of the actual return and the forecasted return by the use of the ARMA(1,1) model in the previous period. Thus, we act as if the model fitted in period "86-2" is also true in the next period, therefore, "87-1" use the fitted model in "86-2"to predict the return in "87-1".

From Table 3, it is easy to see that the p values for the Portmanteau test for most of the periods are not significant (17 out of 23), which means that an ARMA(1,1) model is appropriate for most of the periods. Also, the t values for the parameters θ and φ show that the parameters are significantly different from zero in more than one-third of the periods (9 out of 23). The average μ for the whole sample period is 0.0651% and the average volatility (σ) is 1.80%. From the last two columns, there are 12 periods (out of 22 periods) in which the correlation coefficients for the limiting strategy are positive. The average correlation coefficient over all periods is positive (0.025). This shows that the ARMA(1,1) models based on historical data do have predictive power in the subsequent time period that follows.

C. Limiting Trading Strategy under an ARMA(1,1) Model

After fitting an ARMA(1,1) model for each period, we compute the critical values (b, a) in the limiting trading strategy by solving the integral Equation 4. We adopt a round-trip transaction cost of 0.15%, a figure which was suggested in a presentation by Christoper Eoyand of Golman Sachs in an ISI Cutting Edge Conference held in Hong Kong on April 22, 1997. This corresponds to a value of $c = 0.075\%$. The values of b and a for each period are summarized in Table 4.

Take the time period "86-2" as an example. Since b equals −0.45% and a equals −0.3%, the corresponding strategy in "87-1" is: if we are taking a long position in the market and predict that tomorrow's return (minus its μ) will drop by more than 0.45%, then we should close our position at today's end. On the other hand, if we are holding no position today and predict that tomorrow's return (minus its μ) will drop by less than 0.30%, then we should enter into a long position at today's end. Otherwise, we should do nothing—just wait and see.

In this example, both b and a are negative. Therefore, even if the ARMA model predicts a drop tomorrow (but not very big), we still maintain a long position tomorrow. This is not surprising because we expect a positive μ within this period and the ARMA model only predicts the return after discounting the positive μ. On the other hand, if we expect a negative μ with large absolute value, then both b and a may be positive. In this case, even if the ARMA model predicts an increase today,

Table 4. Critical Values of the Limiting Strategies:
b and *a*

Period	b	a
86-2	–4.50e-03	–3.00e-03
87-1	–2.43e-03	–8.13e-04
87-2	2.21e-03	3.71e-03
88-1	–3.23e-03	–1.76e-03
88-2	–9.64e-04	7.69e-04
89-1	2.24e-03	3.67e-03
89-2	–3.14e-03	–1.61e-03
90-1	–2.35e-03	–8.24e-04
90-2	–6.52e-05	1.57e-03
91-1	–3.33e-03	–1.83e-03
91-2	–1.96e-03	–2.14e-04
92-1	–2.99e-03	–1.49e-03
92-2	1.51e-03	2.83e-03
93-1	–2.72e-03	–1.19e-03
93-2	–3.86e-03	–2.36e-03
94-1	3.00e-03	4.48e-03
94-2	1.22e-04	1.52e-03
95-1	–2.26e-03	–6.19e-04
95-2	–2.03e-03	–4.48e-04
96-1	–1.41e-03	3.29e-04
96-2	–2.82e-03	–1.30e-03
97-1	–2.16e-03	–5.06e-04
97-2	2.04e-03	3.54e-03

we may still leave the market. When μ is expected to be zero, the value of b should be exactly the same as the negative value of a.

D. Performance of the Limiting Trading Strategy

In this section, we compare the limiting trading strategy with the buy-and-hold and the simple strategy, which is the strategy most people used when testing for the predictability of a return model (e.g., Breen, Glosten, and Jagannathan, 1990; Leitch and Tanner, 1991; Pesaran and Timmermann, 1994, 1995; Knez and Ready, 1996; Lander, Orphanides, and Douvogiannis, 1997; and Lee, 1997). According to the simple strategy, we enter into the market whenever the return (excess return) is forecasted to be positive and leave the market whenever the return (excess return) is forecasted negative. The performance of the three strategies will be compared using transaction cost $c = 0.075\%$.

The results for $c = 0.075\%$ are reported in Table 5. Note that Table 5 starts with the period "87-1," while Tables 3 and 4 start with the period "86-2." This is because we use the model fitted in one period to forecast the future return. Hence, the limiting trading strategy can only be implemented starting from the period "87-1."

In Table 5, the first column shows the time period. Column 2 is the total number of trading days within each period, which is also the days for the buy-and-hold strategy to be in the market. Column 3 gives the total return of the buy-and-hold strategy. Column 4 is the number of days for the simple strategy to be in the market. Column 5 is the number of trades made by the simple strategy. Column 6 is the total return without transaction costs (w.o.c.) obtained by the simple strategy within the period. Column 7 is the total return net with transaction costs (w.c.) for the simple strategy. Column 8 is the number of days for the proposed strategy to be in the market. Column 9 is the number of trades of the proposed strategy. Column 10 is the total return (net of transaction costs) for the proposed strategy. The last two rows in the table give the mean and standard deviation over all periods.

In Table 5, only columns 7 to 10 are dependent on transaction costs. All other columns do not depend on transaction costs.

Take the period "87-1" in Table 5 as an example. The total number of days is 121. The return obtained by the buy-and-hold strategy in this period is 19.5% (an average daily return of 0.16%). The number of days for the simple strategy to be in the market is 113 and the total number of trades is 15. If there is no transaction cost, the total return for the simple strategy is 23.3%, which is better than that of the buy-and-hold strategy. After taking transaction costs into consideration, the total return becomes 22.2%, which is also higher than the return from the buy-and-hold strategy. For the proposed ARMA(1,1) strategy, the number of days in the market is 119, the total number of trades is 3; and the total return is 20.0%, which is higher than that of the buy-and-hold strategy but lower than the return from the simple strategy. We now compare the three strategies over all periods.

Let us first compare the simple strategy with the buy-and-hold strategy. If there is no transaction cost, there are 10 out of 22 periods that the simple strategy is better than the buy-and-hold strategy. With transaction costs, there are 8 periods in which the simple strategy can beat the buy-and-hold strategy. The average return per period obtained by the buy-and-hold strategy is 6.52%, a standard deviation of 22.2%, and a Sharpe ratio of 0.294. If there is no transaction cost, the average return per period for the simple strategy is 7.55%, which is better than the buy-and-hold strategy. However, with transaction costs, the average return reduces to 4.25% per period, which is lower than the buy-and-hold strategy. On the other hand, its standard deviation is only 14.6% and its Sharpe ratio is 0.291, which is almost the same as that of the buy-and-hold strategy.

Next, let us compare the buy-and-hold strategy with the proposed strategy. There are 8 out of 22 periods in which the proposed strategy can beat the buy-and-hold strategy. The proposed strategy performs well especially when the buy-and-hold strategy has negative total return, which means that the proposed strategy will not

Table 5. Performance of the Trading Strategies for c = 0.075%

Period	Buy-and-Hold		Simple Strategy				Limiting Strategy		
	# Days	Profits	# 'In' Days	# Trades	Profits w.o.c.	Profits w.c.	# 'In' Days	# Trades	Profits
87-1	121	1.95e-01	113	15	2.33e-01	2.22e-01	119	3	2.00e-01
87-2	125	-3.17e-01	80	85	1.18e-02	-5.19e-02	81	79	-4.05e-02*
88-1	122	1.55e-01	2	4	-1.35e-02	-1.65e-02	0	0	0*
88-2	126	5.90e-03	123	5	9.07e-03	5.32e-03	125	1	4.04e-03
89-1	121	-1.87e-01	65	74	2.13e-01	1.58e-01	65	46	1.90e-01*
89-2	125	2.48e-01	7	11	4.70e-02	3.87e-02	2	5	5.05e-02*
90-1	122	1.31e-01	116	11	1.34e-01	1.26e-01	120	3	1.25e-01
90-2	126	-1.06e-01	100	34	-2.42e-01	-2.67e-01	108	26	-1.98e-01*
91-1	121	2.27e-01	57	108	3.76e-02	-4.34e-02	57	104	-4.44e-02
91-2	127	1.48e-01	125	4	9.25e-02	8.95e-02	125	4	8.95e-02*
92-1	122	3.51e-01	88	63	2.64e-01	2.17e-01	104	34	2.79e-01*
92-2	128	-1.11e-01	102	50	-8.51e-03	-4.60e-02	103	49	-8.80e-02
93-1	121	2.61e-01	46	52	2.63e-02	-1.27e-02	16	18	1.96e-02*
93-2	128	5.20e-01	93	69	3.79e-01	3.27e-01	98	59	3.73e-01*
94-1	122	-3.19e-01	104	36	-2.10e-01	-2.37e-01	104	36	-2.37e-01*
94-2	126	-6.42e-02	13	21	-2.45e-02	-4.02e-02	7	9	-4.11e-02
95-1	121	1.27e-01	50	55	9.54e-02	5.42e-02	37	36	5.20e-02
95-2	126	9.19e-02	101	49	1.48e-01	1.11e-01	117	16	1.16e-01*
96-1	121	8.44e-02	93	53	5.97e-02	2.00e-02	115	7	4.55e-02*
96-2	128	1.99e-01	71	86	1.67e-01	1.02e-01	80	68	1.12e-01*
97-1	122	1.25e-01	108	26	9.66e-02	7.71e-02	118	8	1.60e-01*
97-2	123	-3.53e-01	74	83	2.78e-01	2.16e-01	82	68	2.14e-01
mean	124	6.52e-02	79	45	7.55e-02	4.25e-02	81	31	5.70e-02*
s.d.		2.20e-01			1.46e-01	1.40e-01			1.45e-01

lose as much as the buy-and-hold strategy in bad years. For example, in the last period "97-2," when the Asian financial turmoil was taking place, if one uses the proposed ARMA(1,1) strategy in that period, one can even make money and have a return of 21.4%, while, if one just buys and holds, one will encounter a loss of 35.3%. For the proposed strategy, the average return is 5.70%, the standard deviation is 14.5%, and the Sharpe ratio is 0.393, which is much higher than that for the buy-and-hold strategy. Also, even though the average return is slightly lower than that of the buy-and-hold strategy (6.52%), if we take into consideration the days for the strategy to be out of the market, the proposed strategy is comparable to, or even better than, the buy-and-hold strategy. For the proposed strategy, there are only 81 days in the market on average, and there are 43 (124–81) days when we are holding cash. If our money is deposited in the bank for these 43 days and has a daily return of 0.02%, a total of 0.86% (43*0.03%) should be added into the return from the proposed strategy. With this adjustment, we will get a total return of 6.56%, which is the same as the buy-and-hold strategy.

Finally, let us compare the proposed strategy with the simple strategy. This comparison is important because the proposed strategy is based on saving transaction costs over the simple strategy. Under transaction costs, there are 15 out of 22 periods (denoted by *) that the proposed strategy is better than the simple strategy. The average number of days in the market per period for the simple strategy is 79 and the average number of trades per period is 45. For the proposed ARMA(1,1) strategy, the average number of days in the market is 81, which is almost the same as the simple strategy, but the average number of trades is 31, which is much less than the simple strategy, consistent with our claim that transaction costs lead to less frequent trading. Because of this, the proposed strategy can significantly save transaction costs and has a greater total return. Generally speaking, the simple strategy does not give the best results for the model. If we use the proposed strategy, the results can be improved greatly.

From the empirical results in this section, we can conclude that the proposed trading strategy based on an ARMA(1,1) model is a reasonable trading strategy for the Hong Kong HSIF market. It is much better than the simple strategy. The greater the transaction costs, the better is the performance of the proposed strategy in comparison with the simple strategy. When a transaction cost is $c = 0.075\%$, and, if we include the investment return in the riskless asset, the proposed strategy is found to have a return comparable to that of the buy-and-hold strategy.

VII. CONCLUSIONS

In this paper, we assume that the risky asset's return follows an ARMA(1,1) model and construct the optimal market timing strategy under transaction costs. By the use of stochastic dynamic programming techniques, we derive the optimal trading strategy for finite investment horizon and analyze the limiting behavior of the strategy. The limiting stationary strategy is simulated using data in the Hang Seng

Index Futures Market in Hong Kong. The out-of-sample performance of the limiting stationary strategy is found to be comparable to that of a buy-and-hold strategy.

APPENDIX 1: PROOF OF LEMMA 6

Proof: For any $m > n$

$$|u_m(x) - u_n(x)|$$

$$= |x + \mu + Ef_m(\phi x + \eta) - (x + \mu + Ef_n(\phi x + \eta))|$$

$$= |Ef_m(\phi x + \eta) - Ef_n(\phi x + \eta)|$$

$$= |\int [f_m(\phi x + z) - f_n(\phi x + z)]\phi(z)dz|$$

$$\leq \int_{-\beta}^{\beta} |u_{m+1}(\phi x + z_1) - u_{n+1}(\phi x + z_1)|\phi(z_1)dz_1$$

$$(\text{where } \beta = 2c + \mu)$$

$$\leq \int_{-\beta}^{\beta}\int_{-\beta}^{\beta} |u_{m+2}(\phi(\phi x + z_2) + z_1) -$$

$$u_{n+2}(\phi(\phi x + z_2) + z_1)|\phi(z_2)\phi(z_1)dz_2 dz_1$$

$$\cdots$$

$$\leq \int_{-\beta}^{\beta} \cdots \int_{-\beta}^{\beta} |u_T(\phi^{T-m}x + z_1 + \phi z_2 + \ldots + \phi^{T-m-1}z_{T-m})$$

$$-u_{n-m+T}(\phi^{T-m}x + z_1 + \phi z_2 + \ldots + \phi^{T-m-1}z_{T-m})|$$

$$\phi(z_{T-m}) \cdots \phi(z_1)dz_{T-m} \cdots dz_1$$

$$= \int_{-\beta}^{\beta} \cdots \int_{-\beta}^{\beta} |Ef_{n-m+T}(\phi^{T-m}x + z_1 + \phi z_2 + \ldots + \phi^{T-m-1}z_{T-m})|$$

$$\phi(z_{T-m}) \cdots \phi(z_1)dz_{T-m} \cdots dz_1$$

$$\leq c \int_{-\beta}^{\beta} \cdots \int_{-\beta}^{\beta} \phi(z_{T-m}) \cdots \phi(z_1) dz_{T-m} \cdots dz_1$$

$$= c\hat{p}^{T-m}$$

where $\hat{p} = \int_{-\beta}^{\beta} \phi(z_{T-m}) dz_{T-m} = \cdots = \int_{-\beta}^{\beta} \phi(z_1) dz_1 < 1$.

This implies that $u_t(x)$ converges uniformly to a continuous function $u(x)$ as $T \to \infty$.

APPENDIX 2: PROOF OF THEOREM 3

In the long run, the expected reward per step is $ER(r_{t+1}, d_{t+1})$, where $R(r_{t+1}, d_{t+1}) = r_{t+1}d_{t+1} - |d_{t+1} - d_t|c$ is the return in time $t + 1$. From the state space representation of an ARMA(1,1) model (Section 3.1), $r_{t+1} = \mu + b^T\mathbf{x}_{t+1} = \mu + b^TA\mathbf{x}_t + b^T\xi_{t+1} = \mu + x_{t+1} + \varepsilon_{t+1}$.

By Lemma 9, we have

$$g = ER(r_{t+1}, d_{t+1})$$

$$= E(r_{t+1}d_{t+1} - |d_{t+1} - d_t|c)$$

$$= E(r_{t+1}d_{t+1}) - cE(|d_{t+1} - d_t|).$$

$$E(r_{t+1}d_{t+1})$$

$$= E((\mu + x_{t+1} + \varepsilon_{t+1})d_{t+1})$$

$$= E(x_{t+1}d_{t+1}) + \mu p$$

$$= p \int_{-\infty}^{\infty} xf_1(x)dx + \mu p$$

$$E(|d_{t+1} - d_t|)$$

$$= 1 \times P(d_t = 1, d_{t+1} = 0) + 0 \times P(d_t = 1, d_{t+1} = 1)$$

$$+ 0 \times P(d_t = 1, d_{t+1} = 0) + 1 \times P(d_t, d_{t+1} = 1)$$

$$= P(d_t = 1, d_{t+1} = 0) + P(d_t, d_{t+1} = 1)$$

$$= P(d_{t+1} = 0|d_t = 1)P(d_t = 1) + P(d_{t+1} = 1|d_t = 0)P(d_t = 0)$$

$$= p \int_{-\infty}^{b} f_1(x)dx + (1-p) \int_{a}^{\infty} f_0(x)dx$$

$$= p \int_{-\infty}^{b} f_1(x)dx + (p - p \int_{b}^{-\infty} f_1(x)dx)$$

(the first equation of Lemma 9 is used here)

$$= 2p \int_{-\infty}^{b} f_1(x)dx.$$

This completes the proof.

NOTE

1. The term 'market timer' refers to '0–1' timer in most literature. Of course, a market timer can shift only part of his funds between risky and riskless assets, but we only consider the 0–1 market timers in this study, i.e., the investor put either nothing or 100% of his funds in the risky asset.

REFERENCES

Admati, A.R., Bhattacharya, S., Pfleiderer, P., & Ross, S.A. (1986). On timing and selectivity. *Journal of Finance, 41(3)* 715–732.

Amihud, Y., & Mendelson, H. (1987). Trading mechanisms and stock returns: An empirical investigation. *Journal of Finance, 3*, 533–553.

Box, G.E.P., Jenkins, G.M., & Reinsel, G.C. (1994). *Time series analysis*. Prentice-Hall.

Breen, W., Glosten, L.R., & Jagannathan, R. (1990). Economic significance of predictable variations in stock index returns. *Journal of Finance, 44*, 1177–1189.

Brown, S.J., Goetzmann, W.N., & Kumar, A. (1998). The Dow theory: William Peter Hamilton's track record reconsidered. *Journal of Finance, 53(4)* 1311–1333.

Chang, E.C., & Lewellen, W.G. (1984). Market timing and mutual fund investment performance. *Journal of Business, 57*, 57–72.

Chopra, N., Lakonishok, J., & Riter, J.R. (1992). Performance measurement methodology and the question of whether stocks overreact. *Journal of Financial Economics, 31*, 235–268.

Conrad, J., & Kaul, G. (1989). Mean reversion in short-horizon expected returns. *The Reviews of Financial Studies, 2*, 225–240.

Constantinides, G. (1979). Multiperiod consumption and investment behavior with convex transaction costs. *Management Science, 25(11)* 1127–1137.

Constantinides, G. (1986). Capital market equilibrium with transactions costs. *Journal of Political Economy, 94(4)* 842–862.

Cox, J.C., & Huang, C. (1989). Optimum consumption and portfolio policies when asset prices follow a diffusion process. *Journal of Economic Theory, 49*, 33–83.

Cumby, E.R., & Modest, D. (1987). Testing for market timing ability: A unified framework for evaluation. *Journal of Financial Economics, 19*, 169–189.

Davis, M., & Norman, A. (1990). Portfolio selection with transaction costs. *Mathematics of Operations Research, 15(4)* 676–713.

De Bondt, W.F.M., & Thaler, R.H. (1985). Does the stock market overreact? *Journal of Finance, 40,* 793–805.

Dumas, B., & Luciano, E. (1991). An exact solution to the portfolio choice problem under transactions costs. *Journal of Finance, 46,* 577–594.

Fama, E.F., & French, K.R. (1988). Permanent and temporary components of stock prices. *Journal of Political Economy, 98,* 246–274.

Ferson, W.E., & Schadt, R.W. (1996). Measuring fund strategy and performance in changing economic conditions. *Journal of Finance, 51(2)* 425–461.

Hakansson, N., & Ziemba, W.T. (1995). Capital growth theory. In R.A. Jarrow, V. Maksimovic, & W.T. Ziemba (Eds.), *Handbooks in Operations Research and Management Science* (Vol. 9, pp. 65–86, "Finance"). Elsevier.

Hamilton, J.D. (1994). *Time Series Analysis.* Princeton, NJ: Princeton University Press.

Henriksson, R.D. (1984). Market timing and mutual fund performance: An empirical investigation. *Journal of Business, 57,* 73–96.

Hodrick, R.J., & Srivastava, S. (1987). Foreign currency futures. *Journal of International Economics, 22,* 1–24.

Hulbert, M. (1993). It's a matter of time. *Hulbert Financial Digest, August.*

Jagannathan, R., & Korajczyk, R.A. (1986). Assessing the market timing performance of managed portfolios. *Journal of Business, 59(2)* 217–235.

Knez, P.J., & Ready, M.J. (1996). Estimating the profits from trading strategy. *The Review of Financial Studies, 9(4)* 1121–1162.

Kon, S.J. (1983). The market-timing performance of mutual fund managers. *Journal of Business, 56,* 323–347.

Lam, K. (1990). Working's effect revisited-fitting univariate time series to stock price data. *OMEGA Int. J. of Mgmt. Sci., 18(3)* 337–338.

Lander, J., Orphanides, A., & Douvogiannis, M. (1997). Earnings forecasts and the predictability of stock returns: Evidence from trading the S&P. *The Journal of Portfolio Management, Summer,* 24–35.

Larsen, G.A., & Wozniak, G.D. (1995). Market timing can work in the real world. *The Journal of Portfolio Management, Spring,* 74–81.

Lee, W. (1997). Market timing and short-term interest rates. *The Journal of Portfolio Management, Spring,* 35–46.

Leitch, G., & Tanner, J.E. (1991). Economic forecast evaluation: Profits versus the conventional error measures. *The American Economic Review, 81(3)* 580–590.

Levich, R.M., & Thomas, L.R. (1993). The merits of active currency risk management: Evidence from international bond portfolios. *Financial Analysts Journal, 49(5)* 63–70.

Mark, N.C. (1988). Time-varying betas and risk premia in the pricing of forward foreign exchange contracts. *Journal of Financial Economics, 22,* 335–354.

Merton, R. (1969). Lifetime portfolio selection under uncertainty: The continuous-time case. *Review of Economics and Statistics, 51,* 247–257.

Merton, R. (1971). Optimum consumption and portfolio rules in a continuous-time model. *Journal of Economic Theory, 3,* 373–413.

Merton, R.C. (1981). On market timing and investment performance I: An equilibrium theory of value for market forecasts. *Journal of Business, 54,* 363–403.

Merton, R.C., & Henriksson, R.D. (1981). On market timing and investment performance II: Statistical procedures for evaluating forecasting skills. *Journal of Business, 54,* 513–534.

Pesaran, M.H., & Timmermann, A. (1994). Forecasting stock returns: Examination of stock market trading in the presence of transaction costs. *Journal of Forecasting, 3,* 335–367.

Pesaran, M.H., & Timmermann, A. (1995). Predictability of stock returns: Robustness and economic significance. *Journal of Finance, 50(4)* 1201–1228.

Poterba, J.M., & Summers, L.H. (1988). Mean reversion in stock prices: Evidence and implications. *Journal of Financial Economics, 22*, 27–59.

Samuelson, P. (1969). Lifetime portfolio selection by dynamic stochastic programming. *Review of Economics and Statistics, 51*, 239–246.

Shilling, A.G. (1992). Market timing: Better than a buy-and-hold strategy. *Financial Analysts Journal, Mar.-Apr.*, 46–50.

Summers, L.H. (1986). Does the stock market rationally reflect fundamental values? *Journal of Finance, 41*, 591–600.

Taylor, S.J. (1986). *Modelling financial time series*. Chichester: Wiley.

Taylor, S.J. (1988). How efficient are the most liquid futures contracts? A study of treasury bond futures. *The Review of Futures Markets, 7*, 574–592.

Taylor, S.J. (1992). Rewards available to currency futures speculators: Compensation for risk or evidence of inefficient pricing? *Economic Record, 68(supplement)*, 105–116.

Virtanen, I., & Yli-Olli, P. (1987). Forecasting stock market series in a thin security market. *OMEGA, 15(2)*, 145–155.

Wagner, J., Shellans, S., & Paul, R. (1992). Market timing works where it matters most . . . in the real world. *Journal of Portfolio Management, Summer*, 86–90.

Wagner, J.C. (1997). Why market timing works. *Journal of Investing, Summer*, 78–81.

PRICING INTEREST RATE SWAPS WITH STOCHASTIC VOLATILITY

William T. Lin

ABSTRACT

We compare the interest rate swap and the bond pricing behaviors between two general equilibrium models. The results demonstrate that the stochastic volatility model is superior to its constant volatility counterpart. This finding implies that shifts in yield curve are not parallel, and the volatility risk of the swap rate and of the bond price can be an important component of their total risks. There is a tendency for the stochastic volatility model to produce slightly higher swap rates and lower bond prices than its counterpart. This tendency suggests that the implied volatility derived from the constant volatility model exceed that from the stochastic volatility model.

I. INTRODUCTION

This paper aims to provide an empirical study on the use of the two-factor Longstaff and Schwartz (LS: 1992) model in the valuation of interest rate swaps, examining its superiority relative to the one-factor Cox, Ingersoll, and Ross (CIR: 1985) model. The LS model is a two-factor extension of the CIR model, taking short rate and its

Advances in Investment Analysis and Portfolio Management, Volume 7, pages 191–207.
Copyright © 2000 by JAI Press Inc.
All rights of reproduction in any form reserved.
ISBN: 0-7623-0658-0

volatility as the factors. LS and CIR can provide closed-form solutions for interest rate swaps with their proposed general equilibrium models.

CIR, using short rate as the single factor, implies that we can derive the whole yield curve from the short rate. As a result, the shift in the yield curve is parallel. Analyzing the principal components of the covariance matrix, Dybvig (1989) suggests that the volatility should be given priority attention if a new state variable is to be incorporated into one-factor interest rate models.

Longstaff and Schwartz show that their two-factor (LS) model outperforms the one-factor CIR model in describing changes in interest rates. They also verify that the volatility is an important component of the total price risk of a bond, especially for those with intermediate maturities. So do the findings of other multifactor versions of the CIR model, such as Chen and Scott (1993) and Balduzzi et al. (1996).

Chen and Scott (1993) present a maximum likelihood method for a class of multifactor models of yield curves, and argue that model selection is a trade-off between state variables and measurement errors. Using weekly and monthly Treasury data sets, they show that the volatility is an interaction of the second and third factors in the three-factor model.

Balduzzi et al. (1996) specify short rate, mean rate, and volatility directly as the state variables in their three-factor model. They offer an alternative maximum likelihood method to Chen and Scott (1993), and use a quasi-GARCH-M formulation to obtain the volatility of 1-month T-bill rates. They demonstrate that the multifactor models outperform the one-factor models in describing the movement of yield curve. In particular, they find that changes in the volatility are inversely related to changes in the interest rates of different terms.

When exploring the difference between the constant volatility and the stochastic volatility models in illustrating interest rate volatility and bond option pricing, Vetzal (1997) points out that the estimated prices of bond options under stochastic volatility models are lower than those under constant volatility models. This result suggests that the volatility implied by the stochastic volatility models must also be lower than by their corresponding constant volatility ones.

The LS and CIR comparisons made in this paper are mainly covered by investigating the impact of stochastic volatility on the pricing of interest rate swaps. However, parameter estimation is given primary weight in the application of the LS and the CIR models. Being indebted to LS for parameter estimation, this paper shows that changes in London Interbank Offered Rate (LIBOR) have a significant GARCH effect by using a simple Lagrange multipliers test. Time series estimates of volatility are calculated by using the GARCH(1,1)-M method developed by Bollerslev (1986).

The result of this research echoes findings by Longstaff and Schwartz that the interest rate model under stochastic volatility enjoys obvious advantages over the model under constant volatility in tracking interest rate changes. Furthermore, the empirical evidence argues that the CIR model estimates lower swap rates than the LS model for interest rate swaps of all terms. This suggests that the CIR implied volatility exceeds the LS implied volatility. Such a result is consistent with the findings of Balduzzi et al. (1996) and Vetzal (1997).

This research is as follows: Section II; the models and implementation procedures. Section III deals with the data and parameter estimation. Empirical results and analysis is discussed in Section IV. Section V provides a conclusion.

II. THE MODELS AND IMPLEMENTATION PROCEDURES

The swap rate of an interest rate swap is expressed in fixed rate. When calculating the swap rate, the following assumptions are made:

1. Payment day falls on the same day as floating interest rate reset date.
2. The market is the complete market with zero trading cost and zero tax.
3. The two payment days are apart from each other by a distance of six months.

The calculation of interest rate swap price is shown as follows:

$$\text{swap rate} = \frac{2^*(1 - P_T)}{\sum P_t} \tag{1}$$

where Pi is the price of the riskless discount bond with time to maturity, $T - t$.

From Equation 1, we need to obtain the unit discount bond prices before the swap rate is computed. Both the CIR and the LS models supply closed-form solution for the discount bond. There are a number of issues related to practical implementation of the two models.

A. The CIR Model and Its Implementation Procedure

CIR assumes that the dynamics of the short rate of interest r follows the square root process:

$$dr = \kappa(\theta - r)dt + \sigma \sqrt{r}dz \tag{2}$$

where κ is the speed of adjustment of short rate toward long-run mean rate θ; σ is the volatility of short rates and is assumed as a constant.

According to the above dynamics, CIR leads to the following basic pricing model for interest rate derivatives:

$$\lambda r P_r = \kappa(\theta - r)P_r + P_t + \frac{1}{2}\sigma^2 r P_{rr} - rP \tag{3}$$

where λ is the market price of risk.

When the boundary condition, $P(r, T, T) = 1$, of a unit discount bond is included, Equation 3 can be used to arrive at the closed-form solution of the discount bond:

$$P(r, t, T) = A(t, T) \times e^{-B(t,T)r}$$

$$A(\tau) = \left[\frac{2\gamma^* e^{\left[(\kappa+\lambda+\gamma)^* \frac{\tau}{2} \right]}}{(\gamma + \kappa + \lambda)(e^{\gamma\tau} - 1) + 2\gamma} \right]^{\frac{2\kappa\theta}{\sigma^2}}$$

$$B(\tau) = \left[\frac{2(e^{\gamma\tau} - 1)}{(\gamma + \kappa + \lambda)(e^{\gamma\tau} - 1) + 2\gamma} \right]$$

where $\tau = T - t$, $\gamma = [(\kappa + \lambda)^2 + 2\sigma^2]^{1/2}$.

A regressive equation of empirical research can be derived from the CIR model of Equation 4, which can conclude first-order autoregressive [AR(1)] process of Equation 5:

$$dr = \kappa(\theta - r)dt + \sigma \sqrt{r}dz \qquad (4)$$

$$r_{t+\Delta t} = e^{-\kappa\Delta t}r_t + \theta(1 - e^{-\kappa\Delta t}) + \xi_{t+\Delta t} \qquad (5)$$

The CIR model's conditional expectation value and conditional variance are shown in Equations 6 and 7:

$$E[r(s)|r(t)] = r(t)e^{-\kappa(s-t)} + \theta(1 - e^{-\kappa(s-t)}) \qquad (6)$$

$$V[r(s)|r(t)] = r(t)\left(\frac{\sigma^2}{\kappa} \right)\left(e^{-\kappa(s-t)} - e^{-2\kappa(s-t)} \right) + \theta\left(\frac{\sigma^2}{2\kappa} \right)\left(1 - e^{-2\kappa(s-t)} \right)^2 \qquad (7)$$

where $\Delta t = s - t$.

For parameter estimation, the above equation can be simplified as the following regression equation:

$$\bullet \ r_{t+\Delta t} = a + br_t + E(\xi_{t+\Delta t}) \qquad (8)$$

where $a = \theta(1 - e^{-\kappa\Delta t})$; $b = e^{-\kappa\Delta t}$; $E(\xi_{t+\Delta t}^2) = c + dr_t$.

But the residual item of Equation 8 is no longer independent. It can be inferred from the conditional variance of Equation 7 that Equation 8 can be viewed as the regressive process with heteroskedasticity in its variance. Thus the generalized least-square (GLS) method can be used for parameter estimation.

$E(\xi_{t+\Delta t}^2)$ of Equation 8 derived from the residual item must satisfy the conditional variance of Equation 7, shown below:

$$E(\xi_{t+\Delta t}^2) = r(t)\left(\frac{\sigma^2}{\kappa} \right)\left(e^{-\kappa(s-t)} - e^{-2\kappa(s-t)} \right) + \theta\left(\frac{\sigma^2}{2\kappa} \right)\left(1 - e^{-2\kappa(s-t)} \right)^2 \qquad (9)$$

$$c = \theta \left(\frac{\sigma^2}{2\kappa}\right)\left(1 - e^{-2\kappa(s-t)}\right)^2$$

$$d = \left(\frac{\sigma^2}{\kappa}\right)\left(e^{-\kappa(s-t)} - e^{-2\kappa(s-t)}\right)$$

Use the intersection and slope parameters of Equation 8 and the identity for c and d in Equation 9 to seek the solution of the CIR model parameters: κ, θ, and σ^2. This is shown below:

$$a = \theta(1 - e^{-\kappa\Delta t}) = \theta(1 - b)$$

$$b = e^{-\kappa\Delta t}$$

$$c = \theta \left(\frac{\sigma^2}{2\kappa}\right)\left(1 - e^{-2\kappa(s-t)}\right)^2 = \theta \left(\frac{\sigma^2}{2\kappa}\right)(1 - b^2)^2 \tag{10}$$

$$d = \left(\frac{\sigma^2}{\kappa}\right)\left(e^{-\kappa(s-t)} - e^{-2\kappa(s-t)}\right) = \left(\frac{\sigma^2}{\kappa}\right)(b - b^2)$$

Thus, we can derive that:

$$\theta = \frac{a}{1 - b}$$

$$\kappa = -\frac{1}{\Delta t} \ln b$$

$$\sigma^2 = \frac{2\kappa}{(1 - b^2)^2 \theta} * c \tag{10a}$$

$$\sigma^2 = \frac{\kappa}{b - b^2} * d$$

Both c and d can offer the solution of σ^2, out of which a suitable number, satisfying the non-negative condition of σ^2, can be chosen as parameter. The market price of risk is then obtained based on the above parameters estimates. We apply the market prices of U.S. Treasury Separate Trading of Registered Interest and Principal Securities (Strips), and arrive at λ, using the nonlinear programming solution, which results from minimizing the square sum of error between Strips market prices and theoretical discount bond prices.

B. The LS Model and Its Implementation

Suppose Q, real returns from real investment, can be shown with X and Y, two state variables:

$$\frac{dQ}{Q} = (\mu X + \theta Y)dt + \sigma \sqrt{Y}\,dZ_1$$

X is unrelated to uncertainty in production, while Y incorporates both uncertainty and certainty in production. The changes of the two are shown as follows.

$$dX = (a - bX)dt + c\sqrt{X}\,dZ_2$$

$$dY = (d - eY)dt + f\sqrt{Y}\,dZ_3$$

After a simple transformation of variables, the above equation can be shown with directly estimable economic variables. It gives these two variables as instantaneous short rate of interest and its volatility, with the instantaneous short rate of interest as the variable arrived at by offsetting expected production returns with production returns.

$$r = \alpha X + \beta Y$$

The above equation, calculated with Ito's lemma, leads to:

$$V = \alpha^2 X + \beta^2 Y$$

X and Y can be derived from the above two equations:

$$X = \frac{\beta r - V}{\alpha(\beta - \alpha)}$$

$$Y = \frac{V - \alpha r}{\beta(\beta - \alpha)}$$

Suppose α does not equal β. The dynamics of changes in r and V can be derived with Ito's lemma:

$$dr = \left(\alpha\gamma + \beta\eta - \frac{\beta\delta - \alpha\xi}{\beta - \alpha}r - \frac{\xi - \delta}{\beta - \alpha}V\right)dt + \alpha\sqrt{\frac{\beta r - V}{\alpha(\beta - \alpha)}}\,dZ_2 + \beta\sqrt{\frac{V - \alpha r}{\beta(\beta - \alpha)}}\,dZ_3$$

$$dV = \left(\alpha^2\gamma + \beta^2\eta - \frac{\alpha\beta(\delta - \xi)}{\beta - \alpha}r - \frac{\beta\xi - \alpha\delta}{\beta - \alpha}V\right)dt$$
$$+ \alpha^2\sqrt{\frac{\beta r - V}{\alpha(\beta - \alpha)}}\,dZ_2 + \beta^2\sqrt{\frac{V - \alpha r}{\beta(\beta - \alpha)}}\,dZ_3$$

The closed-form solutions of the price of a unit discount bond and its yield to maturity can be arrived at in the following equation:

$$P(v) = P(r, V, \tau) = A^{2\gamma}(\tau)B^{2\eta}(\tau)\exp(\kappa\tau + C(\tau)r + D(\tau)V)$$

$$Y(r, V, \tau) = -\frac{1}{\tau}[\kappa\tau + 2r \ln A(\tau) + 2\eta \ln B(\tau) + C(\tau)r + D(\tau)V] \qquad (11)$$

$$A(\tau) = \frac{2\phi}{(\delta + \phi)(\exp(\phi\tau) - 1) + 2\phi}$$

$$B(\tau) = \frac{2\varphi}{(v + \varphi)(\exp(\varphi\tau) - 1) + 2\varphi}$$

$$C(\tau) = \frac{\alpha\phi(\exp(\varphi\tau) - 1)B(\tau) - \beta\varphi(\exp(\phi\tau) - 1)A(\tau)}{\phi\varphi(\beta - \alpha)}$$

$$D(\tau) = \frac{\varphi(\exp(\phi\tau) - 1)A(\tau) - \phi(\exp(\varphi\tau) - 1)B(\tau)}{\phi\varphi(\beta - \alpha)}$$

$$v = \xi + \lambda$$

$$\phi = \sqrt{2\alpha + \delta^2}$$

$$\varphi = \sqrt{2\beta + v^2}$$

$$\kappa = \gamma(\delta + \phi) + \eta(v + \varphi)$$

The weekly changes in one-month LIBOR rates tend to cluster and are also shown to be a significant GARCH effect by using a simple Lagrange multipliers (LM) test [LM(5) = 144.134, p value = 0.01]. Thus the parameter estimation method of Longstaff and Schwartz (1993a), a historical/cross-sectional approach, is referred to here as follows:

1. Use the GARCH method to provide the time series estimates for the volatility.
2. Use the interest rate data and the time-series estimates of volatility to calculate the model's parameters.

The GARCH(1,1)-M model, describing the relationship between short-term interest rate and its volatility, is used in this research and is shown as follows:

$$r_{t+1} - r_t = a_0 + a_1 r_t + a_2 V_t + \varepsilon_{t+1}$$

$$\varepsilon_{t+1} \sim N(0, V_t) \qquad (12)$$

$$V_t = b_0 + b_1 r_t + b_2 V_{t-1} + b_3 \varepsilon_t^2$$

where a_i, $i = 0, 1, 2$ and b_j, $j = 0, 1, 2, 3$ are the coefficients of the GARCH model. The GARCH model for the short-term interest rate is estimated through the maximum likelihood (ML) method. After assigning the initial values of the said coefficients and applying the time series data of the short-term interest rate, the maximum likelihood coefficients shown in Equation 12 can be inferred by using a numerical algorithm. Time series estimates of interest rate volatility can be calculated by using the estimated ML coefficients through Equation 12. The calculated short rates and their volatilities at each period are then used to provide the model's six parameters: α, β, γ, δ, η, and ξ, as shown in Equation 13.

$$\alpha = \min\left(\frac{V_t}{r_t}\right)$$

$$\beta = \max\left(\frac{V_t}{r_t}\right)$$

$$\delta = \frac{\alpha(\alpha + \beta)[\beta E(r) - E(V)]}{2[\beta^2 Var(r) - Var(V)]}$$

$$\gamma = \frac{\delta[\beta E(r) - E(V)]}{\alpha(\beta - \alpha)} \tag{13}$$

$$\xi = \frac{\beta(\alpha + \beta)[E(V) - \alpha E(r)]}{2[Var(V) - \alpha^2 Var(r)]}$$

$$\eta = \frac{\xi[E(V) - \alpha E(r)]}{\beta(\beta - \alpha)}$$

In addition to α, β, γ, δ, η, and ξ, we need one more parameter ν (i.e., the term structure parameter) to calculate the discount bond price. ν is the sum of parameter ξ and market price of risk λ. Using grid search algorithm that minimizing the sum of squared error between the market and the theoretical bond prices, the term structure parameter ν is estimated.

III. THE DATA AND PARAMETER ESTIMATION

A.   The Data

This section briefly summarizes the data used in this paper. The interest rate used in this research to estimate the model's parameters is based on the weekly average of 1-month LIBOR rates for 5,100 daily observations in the period January 1977 through December 1996. LIBOR is obtained from the AREMOS Data Base of the

Ministry of Education of Taiwan. Strips is the pricing data provided by Bear Stearns via Street Software Technology Inc. and published on *The Asian Wall Street Journal*. The weekly average quotation price (the average of bid price and ask price) of Strips of, respectively, 1-, 2-, 3-, 5-, 7-, and 10-year terms, is used for empirical analysis so as to estimate the model's parameters. Swap rates data are offered by Data Analysis Risk Technology Ltd. This review uses the weekly average interest rate swap rate (the average of bid rate and offer rate) of, respectively, 2-, 3-, 4-, and 5-year terms for empirical analysis.

The above data are used to estimate the model's parameters, and to forecast Strips prices of different times to maturity as well as the swap rates, so as to compare with market price data, examine the pricing capability of the CIR and LS models, and finally explore the reasons for the differences.

Besides, the sample period is divided into two subperiods to examine the robustness of the results. The research covers data from the first period (from January 1977 to December 1995) used for parameter estimation, and those from the second period (from January 1996 to December 1996) for the calculation of theoretical prices, based on the estimated parameters from the former data.

B. The Parameter Estimation for the CIR Model

By employing the GLS method discussed in Section II.A, we can now arrive at the estimated GLS coefficients a, b, c, and d of Equation 10. With the calculated a, b, c, and d in Table 1, the CIR model's parameters κ, θ, σ^2, and λ can be obtained with the identity of Equation 10a.

$$\theta = \frac{a}{1-b}$$

$$\kappa = -\frac{1}{\Delta t}\ln b$$

$$\sigma^2 = \frac{2\kappa}{(1-b^2)^2\theta} * c \tag{10a}$$

Table 1. The Estimated GLS Coefficients of Equation 8

Parameters	Estimates	(t-Value)
a	0.0004516663	(1.53151)
b	0.9947420178	(310.70299)
c	–3.4614E-005	(–7.48745)
d	5.7347E-004	(11.42678)

Table 2. The CIR Model's Parameters

Parameters	Estimates
κ	0.063264
θ	0.085901
σ²	0.006937
λ	0.092948

$$\sigma^2 = \frac{\kappa}{b - b^2} * d$$

Table 2 shows that the estimated value of parameter κ, which stands for the adjustment speed of interest rate volatility in the CIR model, is 0.063264; that of parameter θ, which stands for long-term average level of interest rate, is 0.085901; that of interest rate unconditional variance is 0.006937, and the estimated parameter λ, which stands for market price of risk, is the positive value of 0.092948.

C.   The Parameter Estimation for the LS Model

The GARCH(1,1)-M model is used to estimate interest rate volatility of the two-factor LS model. Figure 1 shows the evolution in LIBOR rates, and Figure 2 illustrates the weekly changes in LIBOR rates. The important conclusion from the two figures is that volatility tends to cluster in nature through time. Periods of

Figure 1.   1-Month LIBOR

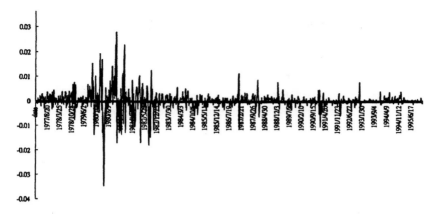

Figure 2. Changes of Weekly LIBOR Rates

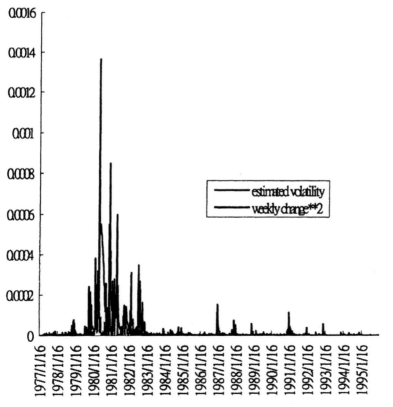

Figure 3. Estimated Volatility of Changes in 1-Month LIBOR

greater market fluctuation tend to follow other greater fluctuation periods, while periods of tranquility tend to follow other periods of tranquility.

To verify that GARCH model is a suitable volatility model in describing the volatility of interest rate, a LM test of Engle (1982) is performed. The simple Lagrange multipliers test statistics of LM(5) is 144.134. Hence, the result supports that there is a significant GARCH effect in the changes of LIBOR rates.

Figure 3 places estimated interest rate volatility alongside the square change in weekly LIBOR rate, served as an *ex post* measure of volatility. The result suggests that the evolution of estimated volatility is obviously linked with that of the square change in the weekly market interest rate, and that the GARCH(1,1)-M model used for volatility forecast appears to fit well the patterns of the *ex post* measure of interest rate volatility.

When calculating time series estimates of volatility, we apply the following GARCH(1,1)-M model of Equation 12 shown in Section II.B.

$$r_{t+1} - r_t = a_0 + a_1 r_t + a_2 V_t + \varepsilon_{t+1}$$

$$\varepsilon_{t+1} \sim N(0, V_t) \tag{12}$$

$$V_t = b_0 + b_1 r_t + b_2 V_{t-1} + b_3 \varepsilon_t^2$$

The coefficient's maximum likelihood estimates by using the GARCH(1,1)-M procedure is shown in Table 3. Of the coefficients estimated, $a_0 > 0$, $a_1 < 0$, suggests that short-term interest rate satisfies the phenomenon of mean reversion. Although the result shows $b_0 < 0$, when $b_0 + b_1 r > 0$, however, all the interest rates must accord that $r > 1.825\%$, and this research also satisfies the condition required by a stationary GARCH process: $b_2 + b_3 < 1$.

Substituting the estimated short rates and their volatilities of Equation 12 into Equation 13, we can solve the LS model's six parameters, α, β, γ, δ, η, and ξ (Table 4). Then, the theoretical discount bond price can be calculated. Together with

Table 3. GARCH(1,1)-M Coefficients of Equation 12

Coefficients	Estimates[a]	(t-Value)
a_0	3.1279E-04	(9.26142)
a_1	−6.37E-03	(−10.95864)
a_2	49.5133	(67.11918)
b_0	−8.9921E-08	(−3.09041)
b_1	4.926E-06	(36.63232)
b_2	0.7708	(233.09835)
b_3	0.1589	(76.16662)

Note: [a]Significant, *p*-value = 5%. Likelihood function value = 5560.07; total number of observations is 991, and usable observations 989.

Table 4. The LS Model's Parameters

Mean Value of r	0.08438
Variance of r	0.00136
Mean Value of V	1.73826E-05
Variance of V	3.19017E-09
Minimum Ratio of V/r	3.13831E-06
Maximum Ration of V/r	0.00578
α	3.13831 E-06
β	0.00578
γ	2.61595
δ	1.00839E-04
η	0.08979
ξ	0.04598
ν	−0.44881

market data of Strips, we use a grid search method to solve the term structure parameter ν.

$$\alpha = \min\left(\frac{V_t}{r_t}\right)$$

$$\beta = \max\left(\frac{V_t}{r_t}\right)$$

$$\delta = \frac{\alpha(\alpha + \beta)(\beta E(r) - E(V))}{2(\beta^2 Var(r) - Var(V))} \tag{13}$$

$$\gamma = \frac{\delta(\beta E(r) - E(V))}{\alpha(\beta - \alpha)}$$

$$\xi = \frac{\beta(\alpha + \beta)(E(V) - \alpha E(r))}{2(Var(V) - \alpha^2 Var(r))}$$

$$\eta = \frac{\xi(E(V) - \alpha E(r))}{\beta(\beta - \alpha)}$$

IV. EMPIRICAL RESULTS AND ANALYSIS

Using the estimated parameters for the CIR and the LS models in the previous section, we can compute discount bond prices, and then the swap rates for the two models, respectively.

Table 5. Comparison between the CIR and the LS Bond Prices

TTM	1 year		2 years		3 years		5 years		7 years		10 years	
	Average	Error	Average	Error	Average	Error	Average	Error	Average	Error	Average	Error
Strips price	94.378		88.833		83.516		73.508		64.225		51.97	
CIR price	94.78	0.0005	90.1	0.014	85.891	0.03	78.617	0.07	72.518	0.13	64.901	0.2599
LS price	94.611	0.0005	89.252	0.0009	83.827	0.101	72.321	0.02	59.406	0.074	39.486	0.23913

Note: [a]Let the face value of the Strips = $100. Error = average absolute value of (Strips price – model price)/Strips price.

A. Comparison between Theoretical and Market Discount Bond Prices

Using Strips prices, serving as the criterion to measure the pricing errors, Table 5 compares the pricing errors of discount bonds for the two models, respectively. In general, the results show that the LS model leads to a smaller error than the CIR model in pricing the bonds, which suggests that when interest rate volatility is considered as a state variable, the model's pricing capability is enhanced. This implies that shifts in the yield curve are quite different from parallel shifts, and changes in volatility would be useful in explaining yield movements.

In terms of discount bond pricing, with the increase in time to maturity, both models lead to reduction in the bond price and increase in pricing error, whereas the LS model accounts for a sharper price reduction than the CIR model.

Based on Table 5, Figure 4 demonstrates that the CIR model bond price is higher than the LS model one. In terms of discount bonds of all terms, the CIR model price is higher than the Strips market price, while the LS model overestimates the short- and medium-term bond prices, and the underestimates long-term prices.

B. Comparison between Theoretical and Market Swap Rates

Table 6 shows that the result of interest rate swap pricing is consistent to that of discount bond pricing with the LS and CIR models.[1] With the increase in time to maturity, the CIR model leads to an increase in pricing error and a reduction in swap

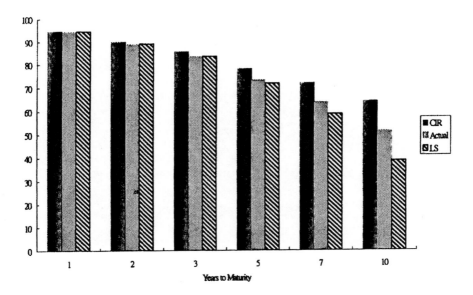

Figure 4. U.S. Strips Prices

Table 6. Comparison between the CIR and the LS Swap Rates (in percent)[a]

TTM	2 Years		3 Years		4 Years		5 Years	
	Average	Error	Average	Error	Average	Error	Average	Error
Market rate	6.032		6.218		6.361		6.48	
CIR rate	5.286	0.1205	5.1455	0.20879	5.016	0.20879	4.8967	0.24189
LS rate	5.755	0.07976	5.943	0.07821	6.188	0.06766	6.497	0.05537

Note: [a] Error = average absolute value of (market rate – model rate)/market rate.

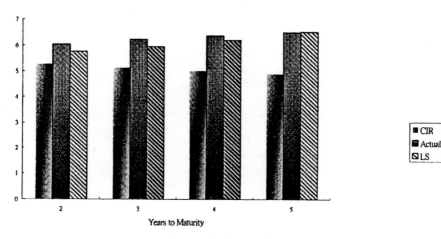

Figure 5. Swap Rates

rates. In terms of swaps of all terms, the CIR model rate is lower than the market rate.

Based on Table 6, Figure 5 shows that the LS model swap rate is higher than the CIR model one. The swap rate estimated by the LS model increases along with the increase in time to maturity, and the short and medium term LS swap rate is lower than the market rate while its long-term swap rate is higher than the market rate.

VII. CONCLUSION

We mainly aim to compare the general equilibrium models of the one-factor CIR model and the two-factor LS model. U.S. interest rate swaps data and Strips data are used for empirical analysis.

We find that the LS model leads to a smaller pricing error than the CIR model in terms of discount bond prices and interest rate swap rates. This evidence shows that term structure shifts are not parallel, and changes in volatility would be useful in explaining yield movements. This suggests that the volatility risk of Strips and interest rate swaps can be an important component of their total risks.

Of greater importance is that the results echoes the finding of Balduzzi et al. (1996) and Vetzal (1997). This result suggests that the implied volatility derived from the LS stochastic volatility model is lower than that from the CIR constant volatility model.

NOTE

1. Discount bond price moves in a reverse direction from its yield.

REFERENCES

Balduzzi, E., Das, S., Foresi, S., & Sundaram, A. (1996). Simple approach to three-factor affine term structure models. *Journal of Fixed Income, December*, 43–53.

Brown, S.J., & Dybvig, P.H. (1986). The empirical implications of the Cox, Ingersoll, Ross theory of the term structure of interest rates. *Journal of Finance, 41*, 617–630.

Bollerslev, T. (1986). Generalized autoregressive conditional heteroskedasticity. *Journal of Econometrics, 31*, 307–327.

Chen, R., & Scott, L. (1993). Maximum likelihood estimation for a multifactor equilibrium model of the term structure of interest rates. *Journal of Fixed Income, December*, 14–31.

Cox, J., Ingersoll, J., & Ross, S. (1985a). An intertemporal general equilibrium model of asset price. *Econometrica, 53*, 363–384.

Cox, J., Ingersoll, J., & Ross, S. (1985b). A theory of the term structure of interest rates. *Econometrica, 53*, 385–407.

Dybvig, P.H. (1989). Bond and bond option pricing based on the current term structure. Working paper (Washington University, St. Louis, MO).

Engle, R.F. (1982). Autoregressive conditional heteroscedasticity with estimates of the variance of United Kingdom inflation. *Econometrica, 50*, 987–1007.

Longstaff, F.A., & Schwartz, E.S. (1992). Interest rate volatility and the term structure: A two factor general equilibrium model. *Journal of Finance, 47*, 1259–1282.

Longstaff, F., & Schwartz, E. (1993a). Implementation of the Longstaff and Schwartz interest rate model. *Journal of Fixed Income*, 7–14.

Vetzal, K. (1997). Stochastic volatility, movements in short-term interest rate and bond option values. *Journal of Banking & Finance, 21*, 169–196.